Palgrave Studies in the History of Economic Thought

Palgrave Studies in the History of Economic Thought publishes contributions by leading scholars, illuminating key events, theories and individuals that have had a lasting impact on the development of modern-day economics. The topics covered include the development of economies, institutions and theories.

The series aims to highlight the academic importance of the history of economic thought, linking it with wider discussions within economics and society more generally. It contains a broad range of titles that illustrate the breath of discussions – from influential economists and schools of thought, through to historical and modern social trends and challenges – within the discipline.

All books in the series undergo a single-blind peer review at both the proposal and manuscript submission stages.

For further information on the series and to submit a proposal for consideration, please contact Wyndham Hacket Pain (Economics Editor) wyndham.hacketpain@palgrave.com.

Andreas Ortmann · Benoît Walraevens

Adam Smith's System

A Re-Interpretation Inspired by Smith's Lectures on Rhetoric, Game Theory, and Conjectural History

palgrave
macmillan

Andreas Ortmann
UNSW Business School
University of New South Wales
Sydney, NSW, Australia

Benoît Walraevens
Center for Research in Economics
and Management
Cherbourg Institute of Technology
University of Caen Normandy
Cherbourg en Cotentin, France

ISSN 2662-6578 ISSN 2662-6586 (electronic)
Palgrave Studies in the History of Economic Thought
ISBN 978-3-030-99703-8 ISBN 978-3-030-99704-5 (eBook)
https://doi.org/10.1007/978-3-030-99704-5

Cover illustration: GRANGER—Historical Picture Archvie/Alamy Stock Photo

This Palgrave Macmillan imprint is published by the registered company Springer Nature Switzerland AG
The registered company address is: Gewerbestrasse 11, 6330 Cham, Switzerland

AO dedicates this book to the women in his life. BW dedicates it to his parents, Annie and Gérard.

Preface

Inspired by his lectures on rhetoric and by game theory, we provide a new interpretation of Smith's system of thought, showing its coherence through the identification, and conjectural history, of three reasoning routines and a meta-reasoning routine throughout his work on languages and rhetoric, moral sentiments, and self-command, and the nature and causes of the wealth of nations. The identification of these reasoning routines allows us to uncover a hitherto poorly understood deep structure of Smith's work, and to explain its main characteristics. We also trace, in the very Smithian tradition of conjectural history, how these routines emerged in Smith's early research on the principles of the human mind.

While our approach does not explain Smith's complete oeuvre, it does shed new light on the man and his work. Specifically, our analysis of Smith's reasoning routines highlights his sophisticated understanding of strategic interaction in all things rhetorical, moral, and economic. Game theory is a set of concepts, a language as it is, to capture this strategic interaction in precise terms and to then draw on its rich analytic arsenal.

For Smith, people are naturally sociable creatures, "commercial animals" (Walraevens 2010a, 2010b) that take pleasure in exchanging ideas, sentiments, and goods. They look after the approbation of their opinions, conduct, and valuation of goods by their fellow animals. The unity of Smith's conception of humans is not based on self-interest (although Smith overall left little doubt that self-interest is a major driver of people's motivations) but rather on sociability which is a social construct. Our languages, moral sentiments, and modes of commercial exchange evolve and are not God-given, a provocative idea when and where Smith lived and worked. We identify the Wonder–Surprise–Admiration mechanism as the precursor of the prediction error minimization mechanism now widely accepted in neuro-economics as the driver of these evolutionary processes.

While our work is addressed (and, we hope, should be of interest) to people with different academic backgrounds and interests (in economics, political science, philosophy, Enlightenment studies, history of ideas), it also suggests an alternative approach to history of economic thought, and the fruitfulness of different approaches in the field.

Lapidus (2019) has proposed a typology based on three alternative approaches, "distinguished on the basis of the way they conceive of the link between statements, old and contemporary," respectively called "extensive," "retrospective," and "intensive." The extensive approach "refers to any account of old statements in terms of other old statements, whatever their nature." The retrospective approach "accounts for old statements in terms of the present-day economic statements which they prefigure." Finally, the intensive approach "addresses old statements insofar as they can produce new statements, thus renewing our present knowledge." Our book is a mix of all three approaches. As to the extensive approach, we analyze the personal, intellectual, political, and economic context of Smith's writings and try to show how it influenced his economic ideas and way of writing (see in particular chapter 2) and more generally his ways of thinking about the natural and social world (see chapter 7). As to the retrospective approach, we show Smith's deep interest in, and understanding of, various forms of strategic interactions, by modeling game-theoretically different parts of *The Theory of Moral Sentiments* and *The Wealth of Nations* (*WN*) (see chapters 3 and 5 in particular). Last but not least, we think that there are lessons to be drawn for contemporary economics from Smith's complex view of man, reconstructed in our book, as a fundamentally moral (self-reflective) and speaking (persuasive) animal moved by his imagination and passions/emotions, and by his understanding of social rules and norms. Following Smith and Wilson (2019) and McCloskey (2021), we believe that Smith's works might help to create a better, more open, and human science of economics, a "Humanomics."

The beginnings of this book go back many years. AO and Steve Meardon sketched out some basic ideas when they were both at Bowdoin

College, Maine, USA in the last decade of the previous century. Life's circumstances, and the pressures of academic hiring and promotion processes (which rarely look kindly on HoT contributions), had the project simmer on the back-burner for a number of years. Meanwhile, in Paris, BW was independently developing his project which resulted, among other outputs, in a 2010 publication on the language of exchange. AO chanced upon it a couple of years later and proposed a collaboration. Alas, here we are. And here you are!

Over the years we have received, at various stages, generous feedback by people we know and that we do not know (e.g., anonymous referees). We are indebted for insightful comments on various bits and pieces to (in alphabetical order by last name) Tony Aspromourgos, Dave Baranowski, Ken Binmore, Laurie Bréban, David Colander, Dave Collings, Jean Dellemotte, Daniel Diatkine, Sheila Dow, Ryan Hanley, Geoff Harcourt, Gavin Kennedy, David Levy, Steve Meardon, Leonidas Montes, Ecem Okan, Spencer Pack, Nicholas Phillipson, Vernon L. Smith, and seminar participants. Given the time it has taken for this book to become a reality, there is a good chance our recollections are imperfect and we apologize to those who we forgot to mention here or in the acknowledgments to individual chapters.

Thank you to the publishers of *History of Economic Ideas (chapter 6)*, *History of Political Economy (chapter 4)*, and *Rationality & Society (chapter 3)* for permission to reprint selected chapters.

A very special thank you to Nicole Sung for excellent editing suggestions and for compiling the indices.

Thank you to various Palgrave editors who stuck to us over years of disruption.

Special thanks to Steve Meardon for allowing us to draw on pieces he co-authored (namely, chapters 3 and 5) and for which he helped lay the groundwork (chapters 5 and 7).

Sydney, Australia — Andreas Ortmann
Cherbourg en Cotentin, France — Benoît Walraevens

References

Lapidus A (2019) Bringing them alive. Eur J Hist Econ Thought 26(6):1084–1106

McCloskey DN (2021) Bettering Humanomics: A New, and Old, Approach to Economic Science. University of Chicago Press, Chicago

Smith VL, B Wilson (2019) Humanomics. Moral Sentiments and The Wealth of Nations for the Twenty-First Century. Cambridge University Press, Cambridge

Walraevens B (2010a) Croissance et progrès chez Adam Smith. These de doctorat en sciences economiques, Universite Paris 1 Panthéon Sorbonne

——— (2010b) Adam Smith's economics and the Lectures on Rhetoric and Belles Lettres: the language of commerce. Hist Econ Ideas 18(1):11–32

Contents

List of Tables

CHAPTER 1

Introduction

> To say anything new on Adam Smith is not easy; but to say anything of importance or profit, which has not been said before, is well-nigh impossible.
>
> (Price 1893, p. 293)

> Students in need of some grounding in these modern concepts (e.g., "the principal/agent problem, moral hazard, ..., the theories of screening and sorting, rent seeking, ..., the theories of public goods and externalities ...") may indeed find an introduction to them, through the eyes of Adam Smith, to be a good preparation for the current textbook treatment.
>
> (West 1990, p. 1)

> Had Smith had more confidence in his own thoughts on rhetoric, and his lectures published earlier, then perhaps his own use of rhetoric, and its connection with his moral philosophy, would have led to a different interpretation of his economics.
>
> (Dow 2009, p. 18)

> Many of the difficulties in Smith's views and arguments arise from the fact that he was dealing with questions that remain difficult for us today. ... We can learn from Adam Smith today, but to do so we need to distinguish carefully between his local and universal teachings.
>
> (Fleischacker 2004, pp. xvi, xvii)

A. Ortmann and B. Walraevens, *Adam Smith's System*, Palgrave Studies in the History of Economic Thought,
https://doi.org/10.1007/978-3-030-99704-5_1

Over the last couple of decades, there has been a considerable re-appreciation of Smith's work. It was fueled by the Glasgow edition of Smith's then known complete works and its popularization by the Liberty Fund at the end of the 1970s and early 1980s. These publications, because of the new attention paid to *The Theory of Moral Sentiments* (*TMS*) in particular—which is not even mentioned in Price (1893)—re-vitalized the old *Adam Smith problem*[1] many cognoscenti had long declared, and in our view correctly, a misunderstanding (e.g., Raphael & Macfie 1982; Bryce 1985; Tribe 1999, 2008; Montes 2003, 2014, 2016, 2019; McKenna 2006; Dow 2009; see earlier also Oncken 1897 and Eckstein 1926, 1927, also discussed in Tribe). Dow (2009), along similar lines to Tribe (2008), Montes (2019), and for that matter Walraevens (2010), note that *Das Adam Smith problem* results from an incomplete reading of Smith's whole oeuvre and traces this understanding of his major works to scholars now "taking seriously his system of rhetoric, and applying it to his own work" (p. 18). She gives Smith a failing grade though, arguing "Had Smith had more confidence in his own thoughts on rhetoric, and his lectures published earlier, then perhaps his own use of rhetoric, and its connection with his moral philosophy, would have led to a different interpretation of his economics" (ibid.).

Be that as it may, the publication of Smith's complete works did bring renewed attention to other parts of Smith's work such as the *Lectures on Rhetoric and Belles Lettres (LRBL* from here on), both among economists (e.g., prominently, Bryce 1985; Pack 1991, chap 6; Brown 1994, 2016; Tribe 1999; Dow 2009; Ortmann & Walraevens 2018 and references therein; Ortmann, Walraevens & Baranovski 2019; Montes 2019; see also Collings & Ortmann 1997 on Brown), other social scientists (e.g., importantly McKenna 2006), and also among political scientists (e.g., prominently, Kalyvas & Katznelson 2001; Kapust & Schwarze 2016; see Garsten 2011 for a review of the "rhetorical revival" in political science).

It is now well established that Adam Smith taught rhetoric from the very beginning of his career and throughout his life (West 1976; Stewart

[1] The Adam Smith problem is the claim that the author of *The Theory of Moral Sentiments* and *The Wealth of Nations* started from different basic assumptions about human nature. Tribe (2008) has summarized masterfully the relevant literature and makes a persuasive case why *the problem* is ultimately the result of a lack of acknowledgment of biographical details that happen to matter.

1982; Bryce 1985; Kennedy 2005, 2010 [2008], 2017; Ross 2010 [1995]; Phillipson 2010; Rasmussen 2017). Indeed, he was commissioned in 1748 to deliver public lectures for fee-paying attendees from the general public and universities on the topic. Smith's reputation grew with each lecture series and helped him secure professorships in Logic in 1751 and Moral Philosophy in 1752 at the University of Glasgow. Yet even after he was appointed professor of moral philosophy, he continued teaching rhetoric in private lectures for students of his university for years (Bryce 1985).

Four things are remarkable about these lectures:

Firstly, and in contrast to what was in favor then, Smith made the case for simplicity and clarity ("perspicuity") as important means of communication and persuasion. He criticized the excessive use of figures of speech which he saw as barriers to the free communication of ideas and thoughts, in a way foreshadowing his later and well-known critique of restrictions to the liberty of commerce.

Secondly, Smith understood that the relation between writer (speaker) and readers (listeners) might be afflicted by conflicting viewpoints and interests (prominently, but not only, in the political sphere), that communication and persuasion might take place in situations of what economists nowadays call asymmetric information, and that they were in any case highly contextual. This aspect—now often called principal–agent interaction—has been overlooked in the literature that discusses Smith's use of rhetoric (e.g., Otteson 2002a, 2002b, 2002c; Brown 2016; Kapust & Schwarze 2016; Garsten 2011).

Thirdly, Smith understood that languages, social norms, and prices are conventions which evolve over time as the result of repeated interactions of motivated agents. In fact, as others have noticed, there are strong and unmistakable parallels in his conceptualization of the evolution of languages and moral sentiments (prominently, Bryce 1985; see also Ortmann & Meardon 1995; Otteson 2002a, 2002b; 2002c). It was no coincidence, that—starting with the third edition—Smith added his essay on the origin and evolution of languages to the *TMS*.[2]

[2] Puzzlingly, in particular in light of Bryce's excellent introduction in which he stressed that (even) "Smith's students must have noted the multi-faceted relationship between the ethics and rhetoric" (Bryce 1985, p. 9), the editors of the Glasgow edition decided to remove it from the place that Smith had intended for it, for good reason: "Just as we act

Fourthly, and relatedly, Smith used his strategy of "theoretical or conjectural history" (Stewart 1795 in Smith 1982, pp. 292–293), or historical theorizing, to fill gaps where facts were not available in his analysis of the origin and evolution of language, and by extension of moral sentiments, of law, of price discovery in markets, and of government.

As to the second point, the fact that the relation between writer (speaker) and readers (listeners) might be afflicted by conflicting interests and that communication and persuasion might take place in a situation of asymmetric information suggests that this strategic interaction can be framed game-theoretically. In fact, it is a very natural thing to do.

The advantage of bringing game theory to Smith's work is twofold.

Firstly, it allows us to bring a well-established, precise language (e.g., players' actions, payoffs, information conditions, etc.) and an impressive conceptual apparatus (e.g., the distinction of the equilibrium outcomes of finitely and indefinitely repeated stage games, something that routinely confounds Smith scholars because they do not understand the observational equivalence of behavior resulting from indefinitely repeated actions such as the game of life, and pro-social preferences) to the subject matter. This turns out to be important when, to give just one of many possible examples, one wants to properly conceptualize the acquisition of self-command which is now recognized as a necessary step to recover the connection between Smith's political economy and moral philosophy (Montes 2016, p. 152, 2019), i.e., the connection between *The Wealth of Nations* (*WN*) and the *TMS*.

Game-theoretic framing, secondly, allows us—contra scholars such as Schumpeter (see also Ortmann, Walraevens, & Baranowski 2019)—to

under the eye of an impartial spectator within ourselves, the creation of an imaginative self-projection into an outsider whose standards and responses were constructed by sympathy or ability to feel as he does, so our language is enabled to communicate our thoughts and 'affections' (i.e., inclinations) by our ability to predict its effect on our hearer. This is meant by seeing the Rhetoric and *TMS* as two halves of one system, and not merely at occasional points of contact. The connection of 'sympathy' as a rhetorical instrument with the vision of speech and personality as an organic unity need not be labored. Again, it should be obvious how often Smith's concern is with the sharing of sentiments and attitudes rather than mere ideas or facts. The art of persuasion are close to his heart for this reason" (Bryce 1985, pp. 18–19). The main edition and translation of *TMS* in French by Biziou, Pradeau, & Gauthier also does not reproduce Smith's essay on the origin and evolution of language. A notable exception is Hanley's Penguin Classics edition of *TMS* which includes that essay.

show that Smith was a first-rate economic theorist and not merely a "synthesizer." When West wrote, rather astutely, that

> Students in need of some grounding in these modern concepts (e.g., "the principal/agent problem, moral hazard, ..., the theories of screening and sorting, rent seeking, ..., the theories of public goods and externalities ...") may indeed find an introduction to them, through the eyes of Adam Smith, to be a good preparation for the current textbook treatment. (West 1990, p. 1)

he identified, without ever using the language of game theory or being precise about the implications of its conceptual apparatus, why Smith was indeed a very modern economic theorist. As we shall see in chapter 7, our game-theoretic framing allows us to distill the deep structure of Smith's work that would otherwise be difficult to extract.

It also allows us to bring to light Smith's universal take-home messages and arguments of which many remain controversial (e.g., Tribe 1999; Fleischacker 2004, 2016, 2021; Otteson 2016; Kennedy 2010 [2008], 2016, 2017; Hill & Montag 2015). Using the language of game theory gives us the opportunity to strip away context ("the local teachings" in Fleischacker's words; see ibid, pp. xvi, xvii) and focus on the incentive structure that the interacting players face, to identify what one might want to call problem isomorphs, i.e., structurally identical incentive problems which otherwise may be read as different problems because of the context in which they are shrouded.

For example, in some of our work (see chapters 3 and 4), we have demonstrated that the very speaker–listener stage game is isomorph to the game that Man Today and Man Tomorrow play in the *TMS* and that the buyers and sellers of goods of adjustable quality play in the *WN*. This formalizes some of the intuition of previous writers (namely West 1990, chapter 6) and adds considerably to the analytical depth that we can provide, as well as to our understanding of the relation of the various moving parts that constitute Smith's oeuvre.

In other words, Smith, in our reading, offered a very perceptive and sophisticated analysis of strategic interactions, last but not least in Book V of his *WN*, a book which, in our view, is falsely neglected by many (Ortmann & Walraevens 2018 [2014]), and often misread even by outstanding connoisseurs such as West (1976; see Tribe 1999, fn. 30) as being inconsistent with Smith's analysis in Book I of the *WN*.

For us, Smith provided a thoroughly modern analysis of the incentive-compatible industrial organization of government and joint-stock companies, educational, and ecclesiastical institutions (Ortmann 1999, Ortmann & Walraevens 2018 [2014]; Ortmann, Walraevens, & Baranowski 2019; see chapters 4–7 in this book) but also of the very difficult problems of public good provision and externalities and what role the state should be playing in addressing them.

We note that the game-theoretic framing has been used on other prominent representatives of the Enlightenment (Hobbes, Hume, and Rousseau in particular) and we will discuss those instances below when we deal with the relation of our work to that of the extant literature.

1 A Summary of the Book

Before we contextualize our work, we provide a chapter-by-chapter summary of what the reader can expect.

In chapter 2, unpublished and titled "The Rhetorical Structure of Adam Smith's *Wealth of Nations* (And What Caused It)," we first review Smith's understanding and use of rhetoric. We stress that Smith was very much aware of the strategic nature of the interaction between speaker or writer and listener(s) or reader(s) and that in situations of divergent interests (these days known in the economic literature as asymmetric information and typically framed game-theoretically as principal–agent games), different strategies might have to be applied, compared to situations where the only purpose was to impart/instill knowledge. Contra Brown (1994; see also Collings & Ortmann 1997 and Ortmann, Walraevens, & Baranowski 2019), and providing more detailed evidence to the sketch provided in Ortmann & Meardon (1995), we argue that the strategic nature of interaction motivated the very specific sequencing of books in Smith's second major published work, *An Inquiry into The Nature and Causes of The Wealth of Nations*. Analyzing furthermore the political context of its publication, we make the case for the central importance of its Book V, "Of the Revenue of the Sovereign or Commonwealth," which tends to be neglected in most accounts of Smith's oeuvre (even, most recently, in the outstanding Phillipson 2010). In our reading, it is not only a general treatise on just and optimal taxation and spending, but also a book focused on the future of the British Empire being threatened by the Mercantilist system (see also Diatkine 2021 [2019] and references in the chapter). Aware that those he targeted (merchants and manufacturers and their political supports, i.e., the core of his readership), would not take kindly to the attack, Smith made his case against the Mercantilist system as well as its colonial policy by marshaling—confidently—his earlier insights into rhetorical theory and practice, slowly unfolding, step by step, his critique of that system and presenting, in the very last pages of the book, his view of the American Question as a well-informed, pragmatic (see Hill 2021), and impartial spectator in order to make the deepest impression on the minds of his readers.[3]

In chapter 3, previously published in *Rationality and Society* as "Self-Command in Adam Smith's Theory of Moral Sentiments. A Game-Theoretic Reinterpretation," Meardon & Ortmann—building on a detailed analysis of Adam Smith's enumeration of five classes of passions—formalized the idea of the acquisition of self-command, the central construct of Smith's first major book, his *TMS*, with a numeric example that ties the principal's (Man Tomorrow) and agent's (Man Today) actions to their respective payoffs. They show that this game can be framed game-theoretically as an interaction between the two protagonists battling it out within (wo)man. It turns out that the game between speaker(s) or writer(s) and listener(s) or reader(s) is essentially the same as that between the two inner selves that struggle with the passions, i.e., an internal reputation game. In chapter 3, we also briefly address the parallels between the emergence of languages and moral sentiments, a parallel that Smith clearly saw and wanted to underline. While acknowledging

[3] Tony Aspromourgos (personal communication) expressed his reservation about our claim as follows: "book V as the 'central chapter' and 'key Book' of WN. I'm very skeptical of that being AS's intention. If he really believed that, it's a strange rhetorical strategy to place it at the end of what is, altogether, a very big book. How many readers did he expect would actually read the whole book (which is more or less what would be required, in order for a reader to be exposed to the rhetorical strategy you subsequently propose)?" Fair enough. It bears remembering though that the book distilled, and expanded, on lectures that in total were as long (e.g., recall *LRBL*), and that when Smith wrote the book, it did compete with significantly fewer alternatives for interested readers' attention. Plus the issue of the American question was the topic of the day in British politics, so surely interested parties (including those that knew that Smith advised some important politicians) (see Hill 2021) were curious to hear what the famous author of the *TMS* had to say about it. The point is that our conjecture about his rhetorical strategy makes sense of observations by the likes of Pack (2010) and Sagar (2021) who stress that, discussing a topic like the conspiracy of merchants, one has to make sense of seemingly contradictory statements about them that are located in very different parts of the book. Our explanation provides a simple explanation that makes sense of this dispersion of observations.

Smith's views on the evolutive nature of the general rules of morality (as well as individuals' understanding of them; see Ortmann & Meardon 1995), Meardon & Ortmann took the general rules as given (Meardon & Ortmann 1996b), as all deductive game theory has to do to make it work. Their game-theoretic re-interpretation of *TMS* shed new light on the acquisition of self-command and cast Smith as a sophisticated early theorist who dealt with the issue of reputational enforcement, and wrestled with the same tension that has led to the eductive and evolutive approaches[4] to non-cooperative game theory (Binmore 1994, 1997). In his astute exposé of how self-command is acquired, Smith not only laid the foundation for his work on languages and moral sentiments, but he also anticipated Schelling's work on self-command (Ortmann & Weber 2007).[5] Meardon & Ortmann (1995) provided, in passing, evidence against claims that Smith's account of (the acquisition of) self-command cannot be assembled into a plausible model (see Otteson 2002c, p. 191, for a discussion of that claim).

In chapter 4, previously published in *History of Political Economy* as "The Nature and Causes of Corporate Negligence, Sham Lectures, and Ecclesiastical Indolence: Adam Smith on Joint-Stock Companies, Teachers, and Preachers," Ortmann frames Smith's discussion of joint-stock companies, educational, and ecclesiastical institutions, in terms of modern Industrial Organization theory and in particular the differences between search, experience, and credence goods, i.e., essentially principal-agent games that come with different quality verification options. The proper role for government, game-theoretically, for Smith again, the principal-agent interaction is at the heart of the argument, although other forms of strategic interactions and issues of proper incentivization (in particular of teachers) are discussed.

[4] Binmore uses these terms in his various writings to describe broadly two classes of game theory. One, the eductive one, is typically taught in standard social sciences classes, normal-form, extensive-form, and all. The other, the evolutive one, starts with normal-form formulations of, say, a principal-agent game and defines on it evolutionary processes involving repeated interactions of principals and agents under various conditions. One of the key insights from the resultant literature is that the fixed points of such constructed evolutionary processes, under reasonable restrictions on the dynamics, are the Nash equilibria of the underlying normal-form game that was used to define the evolutionary process. A classic paper demonstrating this result is Friedman (1991).

[5] For the record, Schelling was less than forthcoming in acknowledging what he—clearly—owed Smith.

In chapter 5, previously unpublished but building on Ortmann & Meardon (1995) and now titled "The proper role for government, game-theoretically, for Smith," we cast in game-theoretic terms in particular, but not exclusively, the numerous public-good provision and externalities problems in Book V of *WN* in particular as an additional illustration of our argument that Smith understood well the strategic nature of all things rhetorical, moral, and economic.

Our approach contributes to our identification of Smith as an early (and arguably the first) analyst of incentive-compatible state intervention. By showing how game theory can be fruitfully applied to Smith's oeuvre, we suggest a methodology—controlling for the different stages of societies' development (Kennedy 2010 [2008], Paganelli 2020)—that allows an answer to the question: "What would Smith say if he were alive today?" This is another way of describing the search for "universal (rather than local) teachings" that Fleischacker encouraged (Fleischacker 2004, pp. xvi, xvii). An answer to this question is important in determining Smith's stance regarding the proper role of government which is, as Smith himself never tried to emphasize, very different in the different states of society. The chapter is another example of the analytic value added when key parts of Smith's work are framed game-theoretically.

In chapter 6, previously published in *History of Economic Ideas* as "Adam Smith's economics and the Lectures on Rhetoric and Belles Lettres: the language of commerce," Walraevens argued that in Smith's work, there exists an analogy between the exchange of goods and services, the exchange of passions and sentiments, and the exchange of ideas and thoughts. Contra an ongoing—but in our view long decided—debate about *Das Adam Smith Problem*, Walraevens argued that Smith presented a unified vision of man as a "commercial animal" who loves that his opinions, ideas, sentiments, and valuations of goods be in agreement or "harmony" with that of others. The paper also underlines the ethical character of economic agents for Smith, highlighting the role of sympathy, self-command, and the desire of approbation and good reputation in economic exchanges.

This theme is expanded on in the previously unpublished chapter 7, a capstone chapter of sorts titled "Adam Smith's Reasoning Routines and the Deep Structure of His Oeuvre." In order to identify the "deep structure" of Smith's works, we identify a set of three "reasoning routines" that are triggered by Smith's Wonder–Surprise–Admiration meta-routine

(*WSA* routine from here on) that, at an early stage of his career, in juvenile works such as "History of Astronomy" (Smith 1982, *HA*) and early lectures such as those on languages and rhetoric (Smith 1985, *LRBL*), Smith developed and later put to good use as moral philosopher, in *The Theory of Moral Sentiments* (Smith 1982b), and as economist, in *An Inquiry into the Nature and Causes of the Wealth of Nations* (Smith 1981).[6]

We think of the three reasoning routines, and the *WSA* routine that triggers them, together as a conceptual lens (Allison 1969; Ortmann 2008), or a set of particular ways of thinking about the world or specific domains such as ethics or economics. In *HA*, Smith identified a basic way of thinking about the world—both the natural and the social world—that he conceptualized as a machine that followed certain invisible laws of motion (such as gravity) which the philosopher's mind was to discover and distill, preferably to as minimal a set of principles as possible.

Whenever observations were in conflict with established principles, they had the potential to cause wonder and surprise and admiration which triggered the search for new explanations and a revision of the few common principles explaining the natural and social world.

This first reasoning routine—Smith's conceptualization of the world as a machine that followed certain laws of motion—reflects Smith's well-documented infatuation with the Newtonian, or deductive, view of the world, and his attempt to do for moral philosophy what Newton had done for natural philosophy. "The History of the Astronomy" (Smith 1982) is exhibit A for this claim. The Newtonian perspective is widely perceived to be about the equilibrium or order of a system.

The second reasoning routine—really a set of reasoning sub-routines as we will see—is reflected in his understanding of the strategic nature of all things rhetorical, moral, political, and economic. The conceptualization

[6] Smith considered himself first and foremost a moral philosopher, as attested for example by his willingness to sign his *WN* as "Adam Smith, Formerly Professor of Moral Philosophy at the University of Glasgow" (Smith 1981, p. 1). And it bears repeating that Smith saw himself, maybe even more so, from the very beginning as a philosopher: As Stewart reported famously (after Smith had died), Smith thought that "[t]he best method of explaining and illustrating the various powers of the human mind, the most useful parts of metaphysics, arises from an examination of the several ways of communicating our thoughts by speech, and from an attention to the principles of those literary compositions which contribute to persuasion or entertainment" (Stewart 1795 in Smith 1982, p. 274).

of life as being beset with strategic interactions featured prominently first in Smith's papers on rhetoric and the emergence of languages and then, as discussed above, also in the *TMS*.

The third reasoning routine[7] reflects Smith's belief in the evolutionary, or inductive, nature of many systems, be they social or other. "The Considerations Concerning the First Formation of Languages" (Smith 1985, pp. 203–226) is exhibit A for this claim. The evolutionary view is essentially about the process toward equilibrium if it exists. Smith, who modelled the origin and the evolution of languages as a bottom-up process, realized *peu a peu* that some such program might be path-dependent and not necessarily, like the laws of motion of the natural world, be something that could essentially not be changed.

We argue that while moving from rhetoric to moral philosophy, Smith looked at the latter through the conceptual lenses of the former. While moving from moral philosophy to economics, he looked at the latter through the conceptual lens of the former. By the chain rule, he looked at economics through the conceptual lens of rhetoric. We argue, furthermore, that understanding how people reasoned and tried to make sense of the natural and social world around them was Smith's overriding initial interest, an interest that never waned. The examination of the ways our thoughts come about and how we communicate them, for entertainment, persuasion, and conviction, was in Smith's view the best method of explaining and illustrating the various powers of the human mind. His interest in various subject matters thus was a derived one, and as such he was, initially, an experimental philosopher[8] as well as a cognitive and social psychologist.

[7] To avoid misunderstandings, we note here and make clear in the chapter in detail that we see these three reasoning routines, in particular the first and the third, to be on the same level. The first is the discovery of the laws of motion of the machine called natural and/or social world. This discovery—for the social world in particular—requires evolutionary processes whose beginnings can only be reconstructed through historical theorizing. The second reasoning routine or, maybe better, set of reasoning routines, rides on the first and/or the third in that it highlights the interactive nature of the interactions that we consider. The numbering of the reasoning routines is therefore just a convention without deep meaning.

[8] See, as mentioned earlier, Smith's early use, reported by Stewart, of the method of "conjectural and theoretical history" in his analysis of the origin of languages and moral sentiments.

2 Relation of Our Book to Other Literature

Our project brings, through the facets expressed in the sub-title of our manuscript, analytic insights to Smith's studies as well as a general, "systemic" interpretation of Smith's oeuvre and its unity. It addresses issues such as the alleged inconsistencies within (Tribe 1999, fn 30) and across his works (e.g., Raphael & Macfie 1982; Bryce 1985; Tribe 1999, 2008; Montes 2003, 2016; Dow 2009; see earlier also Oncken 1897 and Eckstein 1926, 1927, also discussed in Tribe).

While Smith's work on rhetoric has, as noted, attracted considerable attention from economists and other social scientists, we add two facets that have received very little. The first facet is our emphasis on information asymmetries in situations of strategic interactions that tend to come with conflicting interests, i.e., the importance of persuasion. It is, for example, an aspect that is completely overlooked in Kapust & Schwarze 2016. The second facet is the investigation of the impact of rhetoric on Smith's oeuvre from a view that transcends what Smith had to say about tropes etc., in order to understand how his rhetorical strategies affected the structure of his work on a level beyond sentences, paragraphs, and chapters, ultimately affecting even the composition of the whole *WN* itself.

Because Smith's work is prominently about persuasion, i.e., strategic interactions, game theory is a natural candidate to frame his ideas. In its emphasis on the rhetorical organization and purpose of Smith's work and its game-theoretic framing, our work is a radical departure from traditional research on Smith's work.

While others have stressed the importance of rhetoric (see our review in chapter 2, or Ortmann & Walraevens 2018), very few have demonstrated that there is value in using game theory to frame Adam Smith's ideas (for the lone exception, see Weingast 2018b), and to the best of our knowledge, we are the first to explore Smith's work through the combined conceptual lenses of rhetoric and game theory.

Methodologically speaking, our work on Smith is also original in its combination of a contextual approach to his texts and ideas with a retrospective approach. As to the former, we explain (for example in chapter 2) that the *WN* is a product of its time and place, of its social, political, and economic context, and that it influenced the way Smith had to present his ideas on political economy to the public. More deeply, we show how his main ideas and the foundations of his whole work, his reasoning routines, are the product of his personal, social, and academic life (see chapter 7, especially Section 3). To take one example, a very young Adam Smith very likely observed the "higgling and bargaining" on the market he passed through while going to school in Kirkcaldy (Phillipson 2010, p. 17). He also had to negotiate his early leave from Oxford (Kennedy 2017 pp. 19–33). For us, these are not just anecdotes but situations that helped him sharpen his reasoning routines or understanding of how the world works. As did his first lectures on rhetoric matters. As to the retrospective approach, we use the language of game theory to formalize and extract Smith's universal take-home messages which would otherwise be difficult to extract. Doing so allows us to better capture the relations between the different parts of Smith's system and it is one way of demonstrating the unity in Smith's corpus.

That said, and taking into account that the present book goes back to many years of published and unpublished thinking, there are some important reference points.

Some of the editors of the Glasgow edition of Smith's works (notably Bryce 1985 but see also Raphael & Macfie 1982) had stressed the parallels in the constructs of the four distinct themes that Smith pursued, rhetoric—ethics—jurisprudence—economics, namely the parallels between the evolution of languages and moral sentiments (but they did not realize the principal-agent aspect that is really central to the theory of self-command).

We also acknowledge that game-theoretic framing has been used on the work of other prominent representatives of the Enlightenment. Binmore, for example, applied in the 1980s (see Binmore 1990, 1991, 1994, 1997) bargaining theory to John Rawls's original position. He famously "deKanted Rawls" (Binmore 1994; see also Ortmann 1996). Binmore argued that Kant's categorical imperative was conceptually and empirically flawed because it rests on a priori notions of standards of moral conduct or common will (i.e., on conventions) that are in conflict with notions of self-interested behavior, and in any case should be derived from models of self-interested actors in repeated games. For example, in a one-shot prisoners' dilemma game, one might be tempted to induce cooperative behavior by appealing to the categorical imperative. The empirical (including the experimental) literature, however, demonstrates convincingly that individual rationality (in the sense of payoff-maximization) often makes individuals ignore such ethical tenets. However, in a(n) (indefinitely) repeated prisoner's dilemma, cooperative behavior emerges, under well-defined conditions, as equilibrium behavior of individuals who are self-interested, albeit in an enlightened manner. As Binmore put it, "ethical principles are 'no more' than common understandings that have evolved to coordinate the behavior of those acting in their own enlightened self-interest" (ibid, p. 17). Instead of voluntary surrender by all, of their rights and liberties into the hands of a Hobbesian *Leviathan*, Binmore visualized the social contract as an "implicit self-policing agreement between the members of society to coordinate on a particular equilibrium in the game of life" (ibid, p. 35). This, it turns out, is very much the basic intuition underlying Smith's conceptualization of the origin and evolution of languages and moral sentiments. This distinction also maps onto the distinction that modern Industrial Organization scholars make of the firm as a nexus of contracts vs a nexus of reputations (e.g., Kreps 1990; Wiggins 1991 and references therein).

Indeed, the Scottish Enlightenment, and Hume and Smith among them in particular, tried to find an alternative to Hobbes's political theory (Sagar 2018) which grounded the origin of government and sovereignty of the state in a coercive social contract by which everyone renounced their natural rights to everything in return for the protection of the State, the *Leviathan*. The Scots, in contrast, offered an evolutionary view of the origin of society and government (and of institutions like languages and moral norms) with the "four-stages theory," which relied on proto-ethnographic descriptions of the life of the primitive people or "savages" to imagine the infancy of society (see Meek 1976) and on the method of "theoretical and conjectural history" to fill in gaps when data were missing in their reconstruction of the "natural history of mankind."[9]

Binmore's main theme throughout both his 1994 and 1997 publications (see Ortmann 1996, 1997) is the conditions that generate moral behavior. While much of his discussion focuses on the conceptual and

[9] "Questions of the origins of society led to imaginative debates throughout the seventeenth and eighteenth centuries. Two main camps were in evidence: (1) those who believed that humans formed societies because they were induced by 'social contracts' to do so (Locke) and (2) those who believed they were coerced or induced into societies by powerful sovereigns (Hobbes)" (Kennedy 2010 [2008] p. 18). Kennedy points out that these competing views of society's origin were supported by travelers' accounts of "savage" societies in America, Africa, and the Pacific Islands that left considerable room for historical historizing, or "theoretical or conjectural history" (Stewart 1795 in Smith 1982, pp. 292–293). Contra Kennedy, we believe that Scots such as Hume and Smith really constituted a third and indeed very consequential and rather revolutionary camp.

foundational problems such as the possibility of intra- and interpersonal utility comparisons, his main message is that the social fabric, and its underlying seemingly flimsy foundation of commonly understood conventions, can—and ought to—be conceptualized as "a bottom-up approach to ethical issues" (Binmore 1994, p. 139; see also Binmore's own theory of "the game of morals" in chapter 4 of Binmore 1997). In making his case, Binmore repeatedly reviews the arguments of earlier philosophers, including, prominently Hume who, like Smith, argued against the deontological theories that posit "the existence of natural rights, which is our duty to protect regardless of the consequences" (Binmore 1996, p. 139).[10]

Drawing on Binmore's work, last but not least his excellent textbook (Binmore 1992), Meardon and Ortmann (namely, Ortmann & Meardon 1995, Meardon & Ortmann 1996a, 1996b) sketched out the details of the game-theoretic argument as they extracted them from Smith's oeuvre. Vanderschraaf (1998) provided an account of the informal game theory in Hume's account of convention and of Hume's game-theoretic business ethics (Vanderschraaf 1999) arguing that "the problem Hume leaves unsolved is one of equilibrium selection, that is: Why do agents follow an equilibrium corresponding to just economic exchanges rather than some other equilibrium corresponding to unjust exchanges" (ibid p. 47). Because Smith increasingly realized that bottom-up processes do not inevitably converge to a pre-determined natural state, this is a concern for Smith's conceptualization of the origin and evolution of moral sentiments, too. Vanderschraaf also argues that "contemporary game theory still lacks a satisfactory theory of equilibrium selection" (ibid., p. 47) which was a fair assessment then but is not now (e.g., Devetag & Ortmann 2007; Riedl, Rohde, & Strobel 2015; Banerjee 2018; see also Liu & Weingast 2021).

For the sake of completeness, we mention here also Tullock's claim that Adam Smith's insights on "the discipline of continuous dealings" can be framed "in the terminology of game theory" and that Smith was right to

[10] Sagar (2017) argues that Smith rejected Hume's moral theory but for our purpose here—which focuses on the acquisition of self-command and the evolutionary process of learning socially acceptable behavior on which the acquisition of self-command surfs—this is not of consequence, as "Smith was in fact in broad agreement with Hume's theoretical position regarding sociability, even if he thought that technical aspects of Hume's argument needed alteration" (p. 691).

think that there are many cases in which people can behave cooperatively when reputation effects are at stake (Tullock 1985, p. 1073).

Along the lines of Tullock (1985), Bruni & Sugden (2000) argue that Smith's theory of trust can be characterized as what they call the "mainstream modern position": the rationality of trust is based on the idea of reputation (2000, p. 32). In order to show this, they also rely on Smith's passage of his *LJ* (Smith 1982a, pp. 538–539) explaining why "a dealer, afraid of losing his character ... is scrupulous in performing every engagement" out of self-interest because of the repetition of interactions. They conclude, though, that it is not very clear "whether Smith's concept of character is better translated into the modern game-theoretic concept of reputation or into Gauthier's concept of disposition" and it seems possible for them "to sharpen Smith's concept in either direction" (Bruni & Sugden 2000, p. 33).

Shearmur & Klein (1997) also underline the link between self-interest, repeated interactions, reputation, and good conduct in Smith's moral ***and*** economic thought. In line with the argument in Ortmann & Meardon (1995), they claim, rightly we believe, that "Smith identified problems similar to those identified by modern theorists" (Shearmur & Klein 1997, pp. 1–2), and that "[w]ithin the setting of commerce, he identified the essential logic of repeated-game thinking" (ibid., p. 4). Shearmur & Klein also stress that some such conceptualization is attractive because "it is couched in terms of self-interest" (p. 8) and hence a way towards a case for the unity of Smith's oeuvre.

West (1990) extracts (in our view, very well) the essence of Smith's *WN* when he identifies, for example in his tellingly titled chapter 5 ("Principal-Agent Problems, Moral Hazard and the Theory of the Firm"), issues of asymmetric information and organizational issues. In successive sections, he identifies agency problems in foreign trade, in donor non-profit organizations, and public companies. He discusses, in rather modern language, the need for special incentive structures, as articulated by Smith, and also the theory of the firm: "Smith's treatment is more comprehensive than that of the neoclassical writing that succeeded him. For even though it is of an embryonic kind, there *is* a theory of organization in *The Wealth of Nations*, and rudiments of the modern concepts of transaction costs, principal/agent problems and moral hazard can also be found in the same classic work" (West 1990, p. 63). In chapters 7 and 8, he shows that Smith's recommendations for government intervention were more systematic and principled than, for example, suggested by Viner (ibid., p. 83). In chapter 9, he argues (quite persuasively in our view) that "no writer in the history of economic thought has placed greater emphasis than Smith on the need to promote free market competition and to eradicate all forms of monopolies" (ibid., p. 131). It is important to remember that West's excellent book[11] was published in 1990, formally two years after Tirole published the English version of his path-breaking *Theory of Industrial Organisation* (Tirole 1988) which game-theoretically completely reframed industrial organization as it was known at that point (and competently captured by West). One important change was that, rather than starting to talk about the limit cases of perfect competition and monopoly that allow for static analysis, the game-theoretic reframing of industrial organization highlighted the importance of beliefs (also about the actions and belief of others) and issues such as entry, etc.

Sandmo (2016) argues, very much along the lines of West (1990), that Adam Smith created an agenda for economic theory whose outline can still be seen in the structure of modern economics (ibid., p. 231). He underlines that this is particularly true in the theory of price discovery, Smith's ideas about the market economy and the public interest, his reflections on the role of state, and his analysis of the sources of economic growth. Again, very much in line with West's exhortation to students in need of some grounding in modern concepts, the mastery of modern techniques "is not sufficient to make a good economist. He or she must also be able to develop a more intuitive grasp of the connection between abstract models and the real economy. In this respect, Adam Smith is still a good role model" (ibid., p. 244).

Sen (2016) likewise focuses on Smith's ideas about the market economy and the role of the state, distinguishing errors of commission and errors of omission that might lead to market failure and the need to address it. But he also points out that "despite all Smith did to explicate the contributions of the market mechanism, he was deeply

[11] This is the appropriate place to mention that West (1976) is equally excellent. We find it puzzling that many alleged Smith scholars either ignore, or really do not know, the book which provides a very good discussion of Smith last but not least because West traces—somewhat similar to what the equally outstanding Nicholson and Kennedy have done—some of Smith's ideas to specific phases in Smith's life (e.g., the Canal du Midi discussion; see West 1976, pp. 156–158).

concerned about the incidence of poverty, illiteracy, and relative deprivation that might remain despite an otherwise well-functioning market economy" (ibid., p. 289). Sen stresses in this context that "a market economy demands a variety of values for its success, including mutual trust and confidence, whether derived from the discipline of 'repeated games' (when that works) or from reasoning of other kinds that do not draw only in self-interest" (ibid., p. 297).

Along similar lines, Kennedy (2010, [2008]) submits that the notion of laissez-faire is wrongly associated with Adam Smith—in fact Smith never used that word—and that any such attempt to recruit Smith as apologist for unfettered "nineteenth-century 'Manchester School'" style capitalism (ibid., p. 180) mispresents Smith's overall policy program.[12] Smith, in Kennedy's view, "identified a fairly large legislative agenda for restoring and initializing natural forms of liberty, and he outlined what was wrong with the mercantile economy. ... smooth sought to persuade legislators and those who influenced them to terminate many existing legislative interventions, and he left 'to the wisdom for future statesmen and legislators to determine' what should replace them (*WN* 606)" (ibid., pp. 180–181). Kennedy repeats what cannot be disputed since Smith was quite clear about defence, justice, public works and institutions, as well as the "dignity of the sovereigns" but then goes on and enumerates no less than 27 instances where Smith saw a role for government (Kennedy 2010 [2008], pp. 182–183).

Otteson (2002a, 2002b, 2002c) argues that Smith applied the same "market model" to explain the formation and evolution of moral, economic, and linguistic customs, rules and norms, building upon the idea that these institutions are "spontaneous orders." He identifies on pages 286–287 [2002], 80 [2002a], and 206–207 [2002b] respectively, the motivating desire, rules developed, currency, and resulting "unintended system of order" across *TMS*, *WN*, and *Considerations*. This is very much in the spirit of, for example, Bryce (1985) and Ortmann & Meardon (1995) but as Berry (2003, p. 186) has also noted, there is

[12] This is not news to those who have followed the literature on Smith closely post-Glasgow/Liberty edition in the late seventies and early eighties but it remains a prominent point of view among those that have not and that, maybe for political reasons, claim Smith to be the father of their understanding of modern economics. It is the latter kind of people that people like Kennedy (2005, 2010 [2008], 2017) have taken on. See also Huehn & Dierksmeier (2016).

considerable handwaving here in the details of Otteson's "single-project" interpretation. In terms of the reasoning routines that we will propose in our chapter 7, Otteson's focus is on the third that we identify and he more or less ignores what we identify as the second one and there in particular situations of information asymmetry that in our view are extremely important for an understanding of persuasion and self-command. While Otteson's *Marketplace of Life* and the related spinoffs offer ideas that go in similar directions (e.g., the "equilibrating" feature of the impartial spectator), he misses the principal-agent aspect which differentiates the processes of the formation of languages and moral sentiments, for example, from the price discovery process.

Kennedy (2010 [2008], specifically chapter 3) has summarized Otteson's work insightfully and quite reasonably and more generally suggests that Smith's underlying model, more fundamentally, is one of exchange.

Another worthy contribution to the attempts to rationalize "the unity in Smith's corpus" is Liu & Weingast (2021), whose title—"Deriving 'General Principles' in Adam Smith: The Ubiquity of Equilibrium and Comparative Statics Analysis throughout his Works"—is programmatic. Specifically, they argue that Smith across his oeuvre relied on *equilibrium* arguments to explain why a given pattern of economic, political, or social interaction is stable; and *comparative statics* arguments to explain how a stable pattern changes. They illustrate this claim with Smith's discussion of wages in Book I, chapter x, of *WN*, Smith's analysis of the feudal equilibrium and the political-economic development of Europe, as well as—and of particular interest to us in light of our previous published work—a discussion of Smith theory of the acquisition of self-command (and development of moral sentiments) and Smith considerations concerning the first formations of languages. Smith's concept of the *impartial spectator* becomes the lynchpin in understanding how individuals equilibrate on certain moral norms but they do not unpack the process.

Recently, Schliesser (2017) provided another systemic reading of Smith. Like Phillipson (2010; see Ortmann & Walraevens 2012), Schliesser treats Smith as systematic philosopher and public thinker, but he strips away much of the biographic details so richly and persuasively provided in Phillipson (and so important to our reconstruction of the foundations of Smith's system of thought) for a focus on a systemic analysis, or "systematicity"[13] (ibid., p. 19) of what Smith has to offer. In this endeavor, Schliesser focuses on Smith's interest in contributing to "(i) the development of particular intra-scientific systems (note the plural), (ii) the creation of systematic science(s), (and) (iii) the development of a system of science" (Schliesser 2017, p. 5). Because he is also interested in Smith's role as a public thinker, he restricts himself to Smith's published corpus, or at least that part of his work that Smith himself did not mark for destruction (Schliesser 2017, pp. 15–18). By moving, by his own recognizance (ibid., p. 20), from an analysis of abstract (unobservable) human nature as manifested in the (observable) passions to Smith's analysis of social institutions (i.e., a systematic analysis focusing on *TMS* and *WN*), he strips away most of the rhetorical/strategic concerns that inform our reconsideration. Specifically, Schliesser, like Otteson, does not provide the unifying frame—or maybe be better: thread—that we propose (last but not least through game-theoretic modeling) and he does not appreciate how central information asymmetries are to Smith's thinking.

In his intro (p. 17 in particular), Schliesser acknowledges that his is not the first book that focuses on Smith and systems and enumerates in particular the work of Skinner (1996), Phillipson (2010), Fitzgibbons (1995), and Hill & Montag (2015).

While the first three in particular are classics, and while we agree with Aspromourgos (2009) that Skinner's book is "the most balanced, overall account of Smith's economics and wider thought" (p. 396), and while indeed Skinner did stress the importance of "language, rhetoric, and the communication of ideas" (see the title of his opening chapter 2), his focus is, by his own acknowledgment, firmly fixed on the contribution of Smith's scientific work (the published and unpublished) to the development of political economy (Skinner 1996, p. 30).

McKenna (2006), of course, did pay attention to the parallels in Smith's rhetoric lectures and his moral philosophy, identifying as the common thread throughout Smith's *LRBL* and *TMS* the concept, and problem, of propriety (ibid., p. 5). It is no coincidence that this term shows up in almost all chapter headings in McKenna's excellent study (to which we owe a lot for our own understanding of the unity of Smith's

[13] "[T]hat is, I interpret Smith's writings in light of each other."

work), including chapters 4 and 5 which are titled programmatically "Propriety in Smith's Rhetoric Lectures" and "Propriety in The Theory of Moral Sentiments." While it is puzzling that McKenna does not acknowledge the work of Otteson—McKenna's book was published several years after Otteson's book and related articles—in our judgment he draws out the importance of Smith's ideas on rhetoric for our understanding of Smith's moral philosophy rather persuasively (e.g., Conclusions to chapter 4, pp. 109–110). But he, too, does not provide the unifying frame that we propose (last but not least through game-theoretic modeling) and he does not seem to appreciate how central information asymmetries are to Smith's thinking.

Montes (2019), echoing McKenna to a considerable extent, has identified sympathetic persuasion as the "foundational and connecting principle of Smith's understanding of society" (p. 13) and discusses its use through Smith's work on morals (i.e., *TMS*), economics (i.e., *WN*), and jurisprudence (i.e., *LJ*). He, too, does not provide the unifying frame that we propose here, nor does he seem to appreciate how central information asymmetries are to Smith's thinking. And for that matter, how useful the game-theoretic framing of the implied principal–agent interaction can be.

Montes (2016), in which he acknowledges McKenna's contribution, concludes a discussion of the motives on display in *WN* and *TMS* respectively, with the following intriguing quote: "A proper understanding of the meaning of Smith's virtues, the moral character of self-interest and the neglected importance of self-command, is necessary to recover the classic connection between political economy and moral philosophy" (p. 52). We submit that our chapter 3 is a most suitable point of departure for some such undertaking and indeed would go a long way toward that charge.

Pack (1991, chapter 6) is a short but very perceptive assessment of the importance of Smith's rhetorical chops and how they translated into the *WN*. Specifically, Pack identifies, as we do (see our chapter 2), the *WN* as a tremendous work of persuasion based on Smith's Socratick method because he expected hostile reactions to his attack on the mercantile system of Great Britain. He also, pre-shadowing Fleischacker (2004, 2021), notes that the *WN* deserves credit as both a tract and a treatise: "This [the Socratick method] seems to be the approach of *The Wealth of Nations*. Although it is a scientific work, it is also clearly a work of intense persuasion. [...] The style of *The Wealth of Nations* seems to be calculated and deliberately crafted to form a seamless whole. It may be viewed as modelled on an enormously long Socratic dialogue where the audience is smoothly carried on to the arguments against the British mercantile system. [...] This form of exposition sneaks up on the reader, which encourages the reader to nod along in agreement. [...] It is not until almost page 400 that Smith begins his calculated attack on the mercantile system in earnest. The last ten pages of the book tell Britain to terminate its present relations with the North American colonies, and either to let them into the empire on an equal footing or, if that is not politically feasible, to let them go" (Pack 1991, pp.108–109). Through a careful analysis of the (social, political, and personal) context of publication of Smith's *WN* and of its particular structure, we substantiate Pack's claims, underlining the deeply rhetorical aspect of Smith's "very violent attack against the Commercial system of Great Britain" and the importance, for that matter, of the discussion of the American question at the very end of book.

Last but not least, we need to comment on Smith & Wilson's recently published book on Smith, called *Humanomics*. While behavioral and experimental economists have often used Smith's texts in a retrospective approach, identifying in it what they saw as anticipations of their own modern findings (see especially Ashraf, Camerer, and Loewenstein, 2005), Smith & Wilson (2019) rely on an "intensive approach" (Lapidus 2019), that is, they try to use Smith's texts to provide new insights for economics. They find in Smith an alternative to the *homo economicus* model and the associated Max U framework which still is the dominant paradigm in economics and which in their view prevents economists from better understanding human behavior especially in social interactions. Underlining Smith's views on sentiments, propriety, and the importance of social rules of conduct, they hope to offer a more "human" economics. They do not, however, pursue the questions that we pursue here.

3 Conclusion

> Reconstructing Smith's arguments on the basis of his language and its contexts can indeed provide us with a new Smith and a fresh understanding of his analysis of commercial society; and in the process he will certainly re-emerge as a critic, not simply of 'mercantilism' or 'feudalism,' but also of features of a commercial society whose anatomy he has at the same time taught us how to read.
>
> (Tribe 1999, p. 630)

While others have stressed the importance of rhetoric (see our review in chapter 2), few others have demonstrated that there is value in using game theory to frame Adam Smith's work in these terms (in fact Weingast 2018, is the only person that we know), and to the best of our knowledge no one has combined rhetoric and game theory to explore Smith's work through the combined conceptual lenses of rhetoric *and* game theory.

Our exploration of Smith's work through the conceptual lenses of rhetoric and game theory does not just add to better motivation of modern concepts (recall the 3rd epigraph at the beginning of this introduction, West 1990, p. 1) but allows us to unearth important reasoning routines that Smith adopted early and carried through for the remainder of his life and his work. We think of these (in particular the second routine) as the universal teachings that Fleischacker (2004, pp. xvi, xvii) has identified as being in need of extraction since Smith relies (too) often in his view on local teaching and anecdotal evidence (see the interesting discussion in chapters 1 and 2 of Fleischacker (2004) and there in particular pages 36–44 on types of evidence that Smith musters in the *WN*). As he points out, "Many of the difficulties in Smith's views and arguments arise from the fact that he was dealing with questions that remain difficult for us today" (ibid., p. xvi). Sorting them would be facilitated by separating the local and universal teachings.

By looking at Smith's oeuvre through the conceptual lenses of rhetoric and game theory—an approach that is both explicit (the rhetoric and related issues of information asymmetry) and implicit (the related issue of interactive decision-making) in Smith's work, and by identifying sets of "reasoning routines" that run through Smith's work from the very beginning, we show that there is considerable consistency across his body of (unpublished and published) work. This allows us to provide a simple and unifying explanation for observations that have puzzled other scholars, and of course it is also pleasing to our, and hopefully our readers', minds.

Acknowledgements We thank Ken Binmore, Dave Collings, Sheila Dow, Ryan Hanley, Geoff Harcourt, Steve Meardon, Leonidas Montes, and Spencer Pack for very useful feedback on early versions of this introduction.

References

Allison GT (1969) Conceptual Models and the Cuban Missile Crisis. Am Pol Sc Rev 63(3):689–718

Ashraf N, Camerer CF, Loewenstein G (2005) Adam Smith, Behavioral Economist. J Econ Perspect 19(3):31–45

Aspromourgos T (2009) Adam Smith: A Moral Philosopher and His Political Economy. Eur J Hist Econ Thought. 16(2):392–397

Banerjee S (2018) Improving Spatial Coordination Rates under the Agglomeration Bonus Scheme: A Laboratory Experiment with a Pecuniary and a Non-Pecuniary Mechanism (NUDGE). Am J Agric Econ 100(1):172–197

Berry CJ (2003) Review of James R. Otteson: Adam Smith's Marketplace of Life. J of Scott Phil 1(2):184–187

Binmore K (1990) Essays on the Foundations of Game Theory. Basil Blackwell, Cambridge MA

——— (1991) Game Theory and the Social Contract. In: Selten R (ed) Game Equilibrium Models II: Methods, Morals, and Markets. Springer, Berlin, pp 85–163

——— (1992) Fun and Games: A Text on Game Theory. DD Heath, Lexington

——— (1994) Playing Fair. Game Theory and the Social Contract, vol 1. MIT Press, Cambridge MA

——— (1997) Just Playing. Game Theory and the Social Contract, vol 2. MIT Press, Cambridge MA

Brown V (1994) Adam Smith's Discourse. Routledge, London

——— (2016) The Lectures on Rhetoric and Belles Lettres. In: Hanley R (ed) Adam Smith. His Life, Thought, and Legacy. Princeton University Press, Princeton, pp 17–32

Bruni L, Sugden R (2000) Moral Canals: Trust and Social Capital in the Work of Hume, Smith, and Genovesi. Econ Philos 16:21–45

Bryce JC (1985 [1983]) Introduction to *Lectures on Rhetoric and Belles Lettres*. In: Smith (1985). pp 1–37

Collings D, Ortmann A (1997) Review essay: Vivienne Brown (1994), Adam Smith's Discourse: Canonicity, Commerce and Conscience. In: Biddle J, Samuels W (eds) Research in the History of Economic Thought and Methodology, vol 15. JAI Press, Stamford, pp 329–336

Devetag G, Ortmann A (2007) When and Why? A Critical Survey of Coordination Failure in the Laboratory. Exp Econ 10:332–344

Diatkine D (2019) Adam Smith. La découverte du capitalisme et de ses limites. Seuil, Paris. English edition: Diatkine D (2021) Adam Smith and the Wealth of Nations: The Discovery of Capitalism and its Limits (trans: Diatkine D, Sowels N). Palgrave Macmillan, Evry

——— (2021) Adam Smith and the Wealth of Nations: The Discovery of Capitalism and its Limits. Palgrave Macmillan, Cham

Dow S (2009) Knowledge, Communication and the Scottish Enlightenment. Revue de philosophieeconomique 10(2):1–23

Eckstein W (1926) Intro to Adam Smith, Theorie der ethischenGefuehle. Felix Meiner Verlag, Hamburg

——— (1927) Adam Smith als Rechtsphilosoph. Archiv für Rechts- und Wirtschaftsphilosophie 20(3):378–395

EPS — See Smith (1982 [1980])

Fitzgibbons A (1995) Adam Smith's System of Liberty, Wealth, and Virtue: The Moral and Political Foundations of "The Wealth of Nations". Clarendon Press, Oxford

Fleischacker S (2004) On Adam Smith's Wealth of Nations. Princeton University Press, Princeton

——— (2016) Adam Smith and the Left. In: Hanley R (ed) Adam Smith. His Life, Thought, and Legacy. Princeton University Press, Princeton, pp 478–493

——— (2021) Adam Smith. Routledge, London & New York

Friedman D (1991) Evolutionary Games in Economics. Econometrica 59(3):637–666

Garsten B (2011) The Rhetoric Revival in Political Theory. Annu Rev Polit Sci 14:159–180

HA — Smith (1982)

Hanley RP (ed) (2016) Adam Smith, His Life, Thought, and Legacy. Princeton University Press, Princeton

Hill L (2021) Adam Smith as Political Problem Solver. The 'Project of an Empire' and the American War of Independence. Adam Smith Rev 12:183–202

Hill M, Montag W (2015) The Other Adam Smith. Stanford University Press, Stanford

Huehn MP, Dierksmeier C (2016) Will the Real A. Smith Please Stand Up! J Bus Ethics 136(1):119–132

Kalyvas A, Katznelson I (2001) The Rhetoric of the Market: Adam Smith on Recognition, Speech, and Exchange. Rev Polit 63(3):549–580

Kapust D, Schwarze M (2016) The Rhetoric of Sincerity: Cicero and Smith on Propriety and Political Context. Am Polit Sci Rev 110:100–111

Kennedy G (2005) Adam Smith's Lost Legacy. Palgrave Macmillan, London

——— (2010 [2008]) Adam Smith: A Moral Philosopher and His Political Economy. Palgrave Macmillan, London

——— (2017) An Authentic Account of Adam Smith. Palgrave Macmillan, London

Kreps DM (1990) Corporate culture and economic theory. In: Alt J, Shepsle KA (eds) Perspective on Positive Political Economy. Cambridge University Press, Cambridge MA, pp 90–143

Lapidus A (2019) Bringing them alive. Eur J Hist Econ Thought 26(6):1084–1106

LRBL — Smith (1985)

Liu G, Weingast B (2021) Deriving 'General Principles': Adam Smith's Pervasive Use of Equilibrium and Comparative-Statics Analysis. Adam Smith Rev 12:134–165

McCloskey DN (2021) Bettering Humanomics: A New, and Old, Approach to Economic Science. University of Chicago Press, Chicago

McKenna SJ (2006) Adam Smith: The Rhetoric of Propriety. State University of New York Press, Albany

Meardon SJ, Ortmann A (1996a) Self-Command in Adam Smith's Theory of Moral Sentiments: A Game-Theoretic Reinterpretation. Ration Soc 8(1):57–80

——— (1996b) Yes, Adam Smith was an Economist (A Very Modern One Indeed). Reply to Brown. Ration Soc 8(3):348–352

Meek R (1976) Social Science and the Ignoble Savage. Cambridge University Press, Cambridge

Montes L (2003) Das Adam Smith problem: its origins, the stages of current debate, and one implication for our understanding of sympathy. J Hist Econ Thought 25(1):63–90

——— (2014) Adam Smith in Context. A Critical Reassessment of Some Central Components of His Thought. Palgrave Macmillan, London

——— (2016) Adam Smith: Self-Interest and the Virtues. In: Hanley R (ed) Adam Smith. His Life, Thought, and Legacy. Princeton University Press, Princeton, p 138–156

——— (2019) Adam Smith's Foundational Idea of Sympathetic Persuasion. Camb J Econ 43(1):1–15

Oncken A (1897) The Consistency of Adam Smith. Econ J 7(27):443–450

Ortmann A (1996) Review of Binmore K (1994). South Econ J 62(4):1120–1122

——— (1997) Review of Binmore (1997). South Econ J 64(1):355–358

——— (1999) The Nature and Causes of Corporate Negligence, Sham Lectures, and Ecclesiastical Indolence: Adam Smith on Joint-stock companies, Teachers, and Preachers. Hist Polit Econ 31(2):297–315

——— (2008) Prospecting Neuroeconomics. Econ and Philos 24(3):431–448

Ortmann A, Meardon SJ (1995) A game-theoretic re-evaluation of Adam Smith's Theory of Moral Sentiments and Wealth of Nations. In: Rima IH (ed) The Classical Tradition in Economic Thought. Perspectives on the History of Economic Thought Vol XI. Edward Elgar, Brookfield, pp 43–61

Ortmann A, Walraevens B (2012) Review of Kennedy G (2008), Adam Smith: A Moral Philosopher and His Political Economy, and Nicholas Phillipson, Adam Smith, An Enlightened Life. Hist Econ Ideas 20(1):185–191

——— (2015) Review of Christopher J. Berry, Maria P. Paganelli, & Craig Smith (2013), The Oxford Handbook of Adam Smith. Eur J Hist Econ Thought 22(2):340–343

——— (2018 [2014]) Adam Smith's Rhetorical Strategy in The Wealth of Nations against the Commercial System of Great Britain. Available via SSRN. https://papers.ssrn.com/sol3/papers.cfm?abstract_id=3300236. Posted 18 December 2018

Ortmann A, Walraevens B, Baranowski D (2019) Schumpeter's Assessment of Adam Smith and the *Wealth of Nations:* Why he Got it Wrong. J Hist Econ Thought 41(4):531–551

Ortmann A, Weber A (2007) Thomas Schelling und die Theorie der Self-Command. In: Pies I, Leschke M (eds) Thomas Schellings strategische Ökonomik. Mohr-Siebeck, Tubingen, pp 121–134

Otteson JR (2002a) Adam Smith's Marketplace of Life. Cambridge University Press, Cambridge

——— (2002b) Adam Smith's First Market: The Development of Language. Hist Philos Q 19(1):65–86

——— (2002c) Adam Smith's Marketplace of Morals. Archiv fuer Geschichte der Philosophie 84(1):190–211

——— (2016) Adam Smith and the Right. In: Hanley R (ed) Adam Smith. His Life, Thought, and Legacy. Princeton University Press, Princeton, p 478–493

Pack SJ (1991) Capitalism as a Moral System: Adam Smith's Critique of the Free Market Economy. Edward Elgar, Aldershot

——— (2010) Aristotle, Adam Smith and Karl Marx: On Some Fundamental Issues in 21st Century Political Economy. Edward Elgar, Cheltenham

Paganelli MP (2020) The Routledge Guidebook to Smith's Wealth of Nations. Routledge, London & New York

Phillipson N (2010) Adam Smith: An Enlightened Life. Yale University Press, New Haven

Price LL (1893) Adam Smith and his Relation to Recent Economics, Econ J 3:239–254

Raphael DD, Macfie A (1982) – intro *TMS*

Rasmussen D (2017) The Infidel and the Professor. David Hume, Adam Smith and the Friendship that shaped Modern Thought. Princeton University Press, Princeton

Riedl A, Rohde I, Strobel M (2015) Efficient Coordination in Weakest-Link Games. Rev Econ Stud 83(2):737–767

Ross IS (2010 [1995]) The Life of Adam Smith. Oxford University Press, Oxford.

Sagar P (2017) Beyond Sympathy: Smith's Rejecti on of Hume's Moral Theory. Brit J Hist Phil 25(4):681–705

Sagar P (2021) Adam Smith and the Conspiracy of the Merchants. Glob Intel Hist 6(4):463–483

Sandmo A (2016) Adam Smith and Modern Economics. In: Hanley R (ed) Adam Smith. His Life, Thought, and Legacy. Princeton University Press, Princeton, pp 231–246

Schliesser E (2017) Adam Smith: Systematic Philosopher and Public Thinker. Oxford University Press, Oxford

Sen A (2016) Adam Smith and Economic Development. In: Hanley R (ed) Adam Smith. His Life, Thought, and Legacy. Princeton University Press, Princeton, pp 281–302

Shearmur Jeremy, Klein, Daniel B, (1997) Good Conduct in a Great Society: Adam Smith and the Role of Reputation. In: Klein DB (ed) Reputation: Studies in the Voluntary Elicitation of Good Conduct. University of Michigan Press, pp 29–45. Available at SSRN: https://ssrn.com/abstract=464023

Skinner AS (1996) A System of Social Science: Papers Relating to Adam Smith, 2nd ed. Clarendon, Oxford

Smith A (*TMS*), The Theory of Moral Sentiments. Raphael DD, Macfie AL (eds) (1982b). Liberty Classics, Indianapolis (Glasgow edition: 1976)

——— (*HA*), The Principles which lead and direct Philosophical Enquiries illustrated by the History of Astronomy, pp 33–105 in *EPS*

——— (*LRBL*), Lectures on Rhetoric and Belles Lettres. Bryce JC, Skinner AS (eds) (1985) Liberty Classics, Indianapolis (Corresponding Glasgow edition: 1983)

——— (*WN*), An Inquiry into the Nature and Causes of the Wealth of Nations. Campbell RH, Skinner AS (eds) (1981). Liberty Classics, Indianapolis (Corresponding Glasgow edition: 1976)

——— (*Corr*), Correspondence of Adam Smith. Mossner E, Ross I (eds) (1987) Liberty Classics, Indianapolis (Glasgow edition: 1977)

——— (*EPS*), Essays on Philosophical Subjects. Wightman W, Bryce J, Ross I (eds) (1982). Liberty Classics, Indianapolis, pp 269–351 (Corresponding Glasgow edition: 1980)

Smith VL, B Wilson (2019) Humanomics. Moral Sentiments and The Wealth of Nations for the Twenty-First Century. Cambridge University Press, Cambridge

Stewart D (1982 [1795]) Account of the Life and Writings of Adam Smith, LL.D. In: Smith A (*EPS*) Essays on Philosophical Subjects. Wightman W, Bryce J, Ross I (eds). Liberty Classics, Indianapolis, pp 269–351

Tirole J (1988) The Theory of Industrial Organization, MIT Press, Cambridge

TMS — *See* Smith (1982 [1976]

Tribe K (1999) Adam Smith: Critical Theorist? J Econ Lit 37(2):609–632

——— (2008) "Das Adam Smith Problem" and the Origins of Modern Smith Scholarship. Hist Eur Ideas 34(4):514–525

Tullock G (1985) Adam Smith and the Prisoners' Dilemma. *Q J Econ 100 (issue supplement)*:1073–1081

Vanderschraaf P (1998) The informal game theory in Hume's account of convention. Econ Philos 14:215–247

——— (1999) Hume's Game-theoretic Business Ethics. Bus Ethics Q 9(1):47–67

Walraevens B (2010) Croissance et progrès chez Adam Smith. These de doctorat en sciences economiques, Universite Paris 1 Panthéon Sorbonne

Weingast BR (2018) How Adam Smith Negotiated Leave from Oxford: A Game-Theoretic Account. Available via SSRN. https://papers.ssrn.com/sol3/papers.cfm?abstract_id=3162425

West EG (1976) Adam Smith. The Man and His Works. Liberty Press, Indianapolis

——— (1990) Adam Smith and Modern Economics. From Market Behavior to Public Choice. Edward Elgar, Aldershot

Wiggins SN (1991) The economics of the firm and contracts: A selective survey. J of Instit and Theor Econ (JITE)/Zeitschrift für die gesamte Staatswissenschaft 147:603–661

WN — see Smith (1981 [1976])

CHAPTER 2

The Rhetorical Structure of Adam Smith's *Wealth of Nations* (and What Caused It)

1 Introduction

Adam Smith's deep and long-lasting interest in rhetoric is now well-known.[1] His lecture notes (Smith 1985) on the topic are widely acknowledged to be a rudimentary version of a book he had thought about both early and in the twilight of his career (see Stewart1795, in Smith 1982, p. 275, p. 320; see also pp. 6–7, pp. 132–133, and chapter 13 in Phillipson 2010 and there in particular p. 261). Some scholars have tried to place these lectures into the history of rhetoric, highlighting their originality and richness (Bevilaqua, 1968; Howell 1975; Bryce 1983; McKenna 2005; Salber Philips 2006). Others have investigated if and how Smith's rhetoric shows up in his works, for example in his *The Theory of Moral Sentiments*[2] (Griswold 1991; Brown 1994; Collings & Ortmann 1997; McKenna 2005; Hanley 2009), and how his rhetorical theory informs his views about practical judgment in legal and commercial transactions (Longaker 2014). Several studies have focused on rhetorical aspects of specific parts or topics of the *Wealth of Nations*[3] already. For example, Endres (1991) studied the rhetoric of chapter V

[1] For general introductions to Smith's analysis of rhetoric and language, see Swearingen (2013) and McKenna (2016).

[2] *TMS*.

[3] *WN*.

A. Ortmann and B. Walraevens, *Adam Smith's System*, Palgrave Studies in the History of Economic Thought,
https://doi.org/10.1007/978-3-030-99704-5_2

of Book IV on bounties, while Peaucelle (2012) and Herzog (2013) focused on Smith's analysis of the division of labour and the famous pin factory example. Kennedy (2017) analyzed Smith's use of metaphors in his works, and especially his "invisible hand" metaphor. Likewise, Dellemotte & Walraevens (2015) worked on the rhetoric of Smith's depiction of the conflicts between masters-manufacturers and workers, and Gore (2011) studied the sophistry of merchants.[4] Kennedy (2008) and Walraevens (2010) underlined the importance of the concept of persuasion in Smith's economic thought, when Montes (2019) made it more extensively a foundational concept of Smith's ideal of a free and civilized society. Pack (1991, chapter 6), Bazerman et al. (1993), Brown (1994), and Fleischacker (2004, Chapter 1) provide more general statements about the style and rhetoric of Smith's *WN*. And Dow (2009) tries to show how different views of Smith's use of rhetoric have led to different interpretations of his economic thought.

However, none of these authors attempted to analyze, with the help of Smith's own teachings, the rhetorical structure of the whole book, as we do here. Against Brown (1994), we try to show that Smith's concepts of rhetoric, as they are presented in his *Lectures on Rhetoric and Belles Lettres*,[5] can be fruitfully applied to his own works, and especially to *WN*. We show specifically that the structure of *WN* was influenced by the political context of writing and publication of the book. Like Fleischacker (2004), we understand *WN* as both a "tract" and a "treatise" and, while we appreciate the *WN* as a treatise and analytic achievement, below we focus on its function as a tract. Contra Fleischacker, we believe the structure of the *WN* itself to be rhetorical. Smith's critique of the commercial system was, in other words, carefully and strategically presented and, in our view, Book V ("Of the Revenue of the Sovereign or Commonwealth"), as much as it is a treatise on optimal and just taxation and spending (*WN*, V.ii.b.7, p. 827), is also a book focused on the threat the Mercantilist system posed to the future of the British Empire, the topic of the very last pages of the *WN*. That Book V should be considered a key book of the *WN* in this regard is a novel interpretation in the literature (but see Ortmann & Meardon 1995).

[4] See also Kellow (2011).

[5] *LRBL*.

To buttress our claim, we analyze the context of Smith's writing of the *WN* and make use of the rhetorical insights that Smith developed in *LRBL* to make inferences about the purpose of the *WN and* about its structure which is, in our view, determined by Smith's intention to undertake "a very violent attack against the commercial system of Great-Britain" (*Corr.* 208, p. 251), an "attack" that was originally motivated by Smith's assessment of the developments in Scotland but which was later enriched and completed by his interest for the "recent disturbances in the colonies" of North America.[6] Ross writes that "As a result [of his intended 'attack'], much that he had to say about the relationship of the British Government with the American colonies was polemic, and demonstrated the manoeuvres of Smith the rhetorician" (2010, p. 266). We agree with Ross on this point and try to substantiate this argument below. We also draw out how it affected the structure of the *WN*. We buttress this argument furthermore with an analysis of the political and social changes sweeping through England and Scotland while Smith was writing the *WN,* with an emphasis on the years he spent in London, which was "the greatest mercantile city in the world" and the "seat of government" of Great Britain (*WN,* V.iii.35, p. 918; see also Flavell 2010), prior to the publication of the book. In other words, London was the heart of the commercial system and, as such, it was the perfect place for staying informed about the situation in the colonies and for observing this emergent system in action. It also meant that what started out as a treatise increasingly took on the nature of a tract. So much so, in fact, that this was a concern of some of Hume's friends before and after publication (see Phillipson 2010, pp. 239–241 for a good discussion). One consequence of this shift in focus was that it took Smith three years longer to finish the *WN* than he had planned. Another consequence was how it impacted the writing of, and order of presentation in, the *WN*. While Smith's interest in the American colonies, and the fate of the British Empire, has been dealt with by several commentators,[7] none of them showed that it affected the way he wrote the *WN*.

[6] See also Hill (2021). Of course, Smith was not alone in being interested in "the American question" (Phillipson 2010, chapter 12). Simiqueli claims that "the independence of the American colonies figures as one of the main topics of discussion among the enlightened Scots" (2017, p. 19).

[7] See recently Diatkine (2019) and Hill (2021).

In line with others (e.g., Fleischacker 2002, 2004, and Phillipson 2010), we conclude that *WN* should be read as a very political book—and as both a treatise and a tract (see also Fleischacker 2004)—deeply embedded in its time and place for a very specific reason: to address (one of) the most pressing political issues of the day in Great Britain, the fate, threatened as it was by mercantile interests, of the Empire. At the end of Book IV, the reader was led to the idea that the consequences of the prevailing mercantile system were mainly to slow the rate of growth. With Book V, Smith led the reader to the idea that the consequences were even more dangerous. Smith's decision to finish his book with the hot topic of the day in his country was well thought through. It was eminently rhetorical and informed by Smith's own rhetorical tenets. Indeed, Smith was concerned, in theory and in practice, with how best to persuade others, be it in writing or discourse. Persuasion, he argued (1983, p. 96), depended heavily upon the subject matter and the circumstances, but also on the character and manner of both speaker (writer) and listener (reader), as well as the rapport they have.[8] More specifically, Smith stressed that hostile listeners or readers require a speaker or writer to argue in roundabout ways ("rhetorical") rather than "didactical" ways. Didactical, to Smith, meant a sober presentation of the pros and cons of an argument. Rhetorical, in contrast, entailed the acknowledgment of reasoning that is strategic. Below we explain why Smith thought it necessary to argue, as pertains to the structure of the *WN*, rhetorically rather than didactically and who the hostile listeners or readers were whose approval he could not take for granted. We examine the political and social changes sweeping through England and Scotland at the time Smith was writing the *WN* and how this may have factored into Smith's three-year delay in finishing the book. In brief, Smith had come to understand that the differential growth rates in England and Scotland

[8] See also Bryce (1983, p. 7 and p. 13). Rae reported that Smith had divulged to a third party that sometimes he would select one of his students as an unsuspecting gauge of the extent to which he managed to captivate the class: "I had him constantly under my eye. If he leant forward to listen all was right, and I knew that I had the ear of my class; but if he leant back in an attitude of listlessness I felt at once that all was wrong, and that I must change either the subject or the style of my address" (Rae 1895, p. 57). The attention that Smith paid to others' perception of his performance—an attention very much reflected in the spectator construction of *TMS* (Meardon & Ortmann 1996a, 1996b)–clearly paid off as by all accounts Smith was considered a good teacher (Stewart 1795 in Smith 1982; Ortmann 1997, 1999).

corresponded to the extent of Mercantilist philosophies and practices. More importantly, he realized that the progress of the American colonies illustrated economic systems that came closer to natural liberty and that their higher growth rates were likely no coincidence.[9] But Smith also realized how Mercantilist philosophies and practices were interacting with colonial policy, specifically in North America, both of which he showed were a key source of the worsening debt situation Hume had years earlier starkly analyzed as a threat to the existence and sovereignty of the state and, in fact, the whole idea of an Empire.[10] The example of the American colonies thus offered itself for Smith both to explain the possible benefits of his ideal system of natural liberty *and* the dangers of the mercantile system. That was why Smith defined in Book V of the *WN* a new system of taxation and public expenditure that would save Great Britain from bankruptcy by requiring Ireland and the American colonies to pay taxes to the mother country commensurate with the costs of direct and indirect defence and governance. Following the 1707 example of Scotland, in return Ireland and the colonies would have representation in the British Parliament. Thus, Smith decided, purposefully, to conclude the *WN* on the dramatic, *political* consequences of the mercantile system and on how to deal with it.[11]

Our chapter is organized as follows. In part 2, we explain how, when, and why the *WN* turned into "a very American book" (Fleischacker 2002, p. 903). Then, in part 3, we study how Smith made his case against the Mercantilist system by marshaling his own key insights about rhetorical theory and practice, as they are presented in his *LRBL*. We conclude by summarizing our case for the importance of Book V and by outlining why it matters to understand the rhetorical structure of the *WN*.

[9] As Skinner (1996, p. 227) succinctly puts it: "America, in short, had acquired the status of an experiment which 'confirmed' Smith's theses, one that could be allowed to remain in the *Wealth of Nations* as a kind of permanent exhibit".

[10] Van de Haar (2013)'s chapter on empire and international relations in Smith is more focused on the latter than on the former and misses the link between the colonial wars, the mercantile system, the importance for Smith of the American question, and his views for the future of the British Empire, which are all related, as we show here.

[11] For more details on the political consequences of the mercantile system for Smith, see Diatkine (2019, chapter 5).

2 Why Smith Attacked the Mercantilist System

In this first part of the chapter, we study the fundamental role that the American colonies played in Smith's conceptualization of the different systems of political economy, in his involvement in the issue of the British Empire, and in the three-year delay of the publication of the *WN*. These topics are closely related, as we shall see presently.

2.1 How the WN Turned into "a Very 'American' Book" (Fleischacker 2002, p. 903)

In a nutshell: Scotland, in the run-up to the publication of Smith's major works, was a low-wage country in, following the 1707 Act of Union with England, "the biggest free-trade zone in Europe at the time" (Devine 2006, p. 54). Driven in part by its wage advantage and in part by the innovation and leadership of its landed elite, business classes, and ecclesiastical and educational institutions (Devine 2006, pp. 61–62), Scotland (and in particular the Scottish Lowlands) staged an industrial and agricultural revolution that truly deserved the name (Devine 2006, p. 107; see also pp. 105–123). This revolution triggered a period of extraordinary urbanization between 1760 and 1830 which surpassed even England and Wales (and Ireland; see Devine 2006, pp. 152–169). Smith leveraged his first-hand knowledge of these developments in Scotland (Kirkcaldy,[12] Edinburgh,[13] and Glasgow[14]) and England (Oxford and London) to understand the drivers of this Revolution by examining the different conditions undergirding the developments in England and Scotland, with the former more stifled than the latter by constraints that conspired against a natural system of liberty. Developments in the American colonies made it clear that even Scotland, which by all accounts was less corrupted by vested interests, had a long way to go toward a system of natural

[12] "Kirkcaldy. It was there that he went to school, there he returned for the long vacations that he enjoyed as a student and professor at Glasgow, and there that he wrote much of the Wealth of Nations between 1767 and 1773" (Phillipson 2010, p. 10).

[13] " … Edinburgh was to remain close to the centre of his field of vision for the rest of his life as a city he valued for its intellectual life and its cultural politics" (Phillipson 2010, p. 72).

[14] "And although Smith always preferred Glasgow's collegiate culture and the peace and quiet of Kirkcaldy to the more ***mouvemente*** life of the capital, …" (Phillipson 2010, p. 72).

liberty. From the growth rates and emergent state of opulence, it seemed that the American colonies presented a far better example from a policy point of view (*WN*, IV.vii.b.1–2, pp. 564–565; IV.vii.b.6, p. 567). As Smith notes, "there are no colonies of which the progress has been so rapid than that of the English in North America" (*WN*, IV.vii.b.15, p. 571).

In addition, England had just emerged from what is known, among other names, somewhat misleadingly as the Seven-Years War (1754–1763), a veritable world war that was fought in Europe and elsewhere and involved numerous countries in shifting alliances. While Great Britain emerged—due to its superior naval power—as a major territorial winner, expanding its sphere of influence in Canada, Spanish Florida, the Caribbean, Senegal, and the Indian subcontinent, her wins came at the cost of a crippling debt load. Smith recorded a 69% increase in public debt for the British government (from £72 to £122 million) during the war (*WN*, V.iii.45, p. 922). Who was to pay for this war and the war with the American colonies, and how, were the political questions of the day.

Interestingly for our purpose, upon Smith's return from continental Europe in 1766, the Chancellor of the Exchequer, Charles Townshend, asked Smith for his opinion on how to deal with the fiscal consequences of the Seven-Years War.[15] Questions of taxation and spending, and of an optimal economic system at home and abroad, had thus gained importance and urgency. These questions also informed notions of what the relation between Great Britain and its American colonies should be. As mentioned, Smith's early thinking on this was strongly influenced by the 1707 Act of Union and the benefits it had for Scotland.[16] Also,

[15] "(Smith's) involvement with colonial affairs as an advisor was more personal and prolonged. We do not know if [Smith] recommended the Townshend duties that were later to play a major part in the Boston tea party in 1773, but we can be fairly certain from the treatment given to public debt and taxation in Book V of the *Wealth of Nations*, and his speculative plan for a 'states-general of the British Empire' in Book IV, that Smith supported Townshend's resolve to make the American colonies contribute a larger share of their revenues to cover debts incurred in their governance and defence" (Winch 2013, p. 4).

[16] "By a union with Great Britain, Ireland would gain, besides the freedom of trade, other advantages much more important, and which would much more than compensate any increase of taxes that might accompany that union. By the union with England, the middling and inferior ranks of people in Scotland gained a compleat deliverance from the power of an aristocracy which had always before oppressed them. By a union with Great Britain the greater part of the people of all ranks in Ireland would gain an equally

in the run-up to the publication of the *WN*, the consensus was that any solution to the conflict with the American colonies would be Great Britain's to choose. While Smith was skeptical that the conduct of the war would lead to victory,[17] Wedderburn, even shortly after the publication of the *WN*, had little doubt that Great Britain would prevail.[18] "The American question" (Phillipson, 2010, chapter 12) with which Smith was deeply concerned,[19] even after the publication of the *WN*,[20] thus had many interwoven facets: the (in)dependence of the American colonies, the future of the British Empire, the question of how to move England closer to utopia,[21] and the design of an optimal economic organization (Pincus 2012). To conclude, the American colonies played a key role in Smith's analysis of economic policy because they represented both the worst of mercantile policies[22] and the closest example of a nation following the precepts of the system of natural liberty.

compleat deliverance from a much more oppressive aristocracy" (*WN*, V.iii.89, p. 944). See also (*Corr.*, Appendix B).

17 "The American Campaign has begun awkwardly. I hope, I cannot say that I expect, it will end better. England, tho' in the present times it breeds men of great professional abilities in all different ways, great Lawyers, great watch makers and Clockmakers, etc. etc., seems to breed neither Statesmen nor Generals" (*Corr.* 158, Smith to Strahan, June 3, 1776).

18 "I have a strong persuasion that in spite of all our wretched Conduct, the mere force of government clumsily and unsteadily applied will beat down the more unsteady and unmanageable Force of a democratical Rebellion" (*Corr.* 159, Wedderburn to Smith, June 6, 1776).

19 In a letter to Smith dated 8 February 1776, Hume writes: "The Duke of Bucleugh tells me, that you are very zealous in American Affairs. My notion is, that the matter is not so important as is commonly imagind" (*Corr.* 149, p. 185).

20 See for example the already mentioned (fn 11) 1778 memorandum for Alexander Wedderburn.

21 "To expect, indeed, that the freedom of trade should ever be entirely restored in Great Britain, it is absurd as to expect that an Oceania or Utopia should ever be established in it. Not only the prejudices of the publick, but what is much more unconquerable, the private interests of many individuals, irresistible oppose it ..." (*WN*, IV.ii.43, p. 471).

22 For a similar idea, see Evensky (2016, p. 80).

2.2 *When Did the WN Turn into "a Very 'American' Book" (Fleischacker 2002, p. 903): A Conjectural History of the Writing and Publication of WN*

To understand this, we need to know what Smith knew about the developments in the American colonies, and when exactly he knew about them. Regarding when, the evidence suggests that Smith came to London in the Spring of 1773 in anticipation of having the *WN* published soon.[23,24] Yet it took almost three years for the book to be printed, and another three months for it to be published.[25] His friend Hume complained of the delay in publication and warned him that "if you wait till the Fate of America be decided, you may wait long" (*Corr.* 149, p. 185; see also Rasmussen 2017, pp. 154–159). All the indications are that the delay was because Smith wanted to better grasp what was happening in the American colonies[26] (e.g., *Corr.* 158, p. 195). Angst about how it might be received may also have played a role; in Hume's words: "the Perusal of it has taken me from a State of great Anxiety. It was a Work of so much Expectation, by yourself, by your Friends, and by the Public, that I trembled for its Appearance..." (*Corr.* 150, p. 149).[27]

[23] "In the spring of 1773 Smith decided to end his Kirkcaldy retreat and to finish *The Wealth of Nations* in the capital. He needed company and American news" (Phillipson 2010, p. 209). "In 1773–1776 Smith was in London revising *The Wealth of Nations* - somewhat unexpectedly, too, since he came down from Kirkcaldy with the intention of publishing at once" (Eliot 1924, p. 70).

[24] In a letter dated September 3, 1772 to William Pulteney, Smith wrote: "My Dearest Pulteney I received your most friendly letter in due course, and I have delayed a great deal too long to answer it. Tho I have had no concern myself in the Public calamities, some of the friends for whom I interest myself the most have been deeply concerned in them; and my attention has been a good deal occupied about the most proper method of extricating them. In the Books which I am now preparing for the Press ..." (*Corr.* 132, p. 163).

Letter from Hume to Smith, dated November 23, 1772: "Come hither for some weeks about Christmas; dissipate yourself a little; return to Kirkcaldy; finish your work before Autumn; go to London; print it; return and settle in this town, which suits your studious, independent turn even better than London: ..." (*Corr.* 134, p. 166).

[25] See *Corr.* 149, p. 185.

[26] For a similar idea, see Ross (2010, chapter 16). Evensky claims, without textual support or further investigation, that Smith's three-years delay in the publication of the WN was intended by him "primarily to further develop Book IV..." (2016, p. 79).

[27] We owe this alternative explanation to Margaret Schabas. On Hume's authority, there is some validity to her suggestion but we believe that the balance of the evidence suggests

Fleischacker points out that the evidence for the connection between Smith and Franklin is suggestive only, he concludes that Smith's book was a template for the Founders' mechanism to design problems and solutions. Although Fleischacker's (2002) reflections on Smith's reception among the founders contain some tantalizing evidence about what Smith knew, more persuasive evidence is provided by Atiyah (2006) and Eliot (1924), who scrutinize the interactions between Smith and Franklin.[28] Atiyah (2006), perhaps somewhat self-servingly, plays up the considerable interaction between the Edinburgh intelligentsia and Franklin, an interaction that was likely not just restricted to that locale. But here too our previous caveat applies. Eliot (1924) sees it as his task to test the claim made by others, including Franklin's biographer, that Smith was strongly influenced by Franklin; that they were close friends and in frequent communication. Surely that was possible, as "Franklin was sent to England twice on missions to Parliament, as representative or agent of Pennsylvania, and by appointment, of other colonies; from 1757 to 1762, and again from December 1764 to 1775, inclusive" (p. 67). Eliot does not find much evidence of Franklin and Smith interacting directly (but acknowledges the possibility during the years they overlapped in London, for example) or indirectly through overlapping circles of close friends.[29] Of course, the absence of evidence is not evidence of absence. There are other ways Smith could have received information about the American question. Reading Rasmussen (2017) for example (e.g. pp. 114 – 115), it seems clear that Franklin and Hume had excellent rapport and numerous

strongly that Smith really felt apprehensive about his own knowledge which of course might have fed some angst.

[28] Chaplin (2006), Flavell (2010) and Morrison (2012, p. 416) are other references of relevance here. Flavell musters considerable evidence that London was before, and even after the Declaration of Independence, qua its cultural amenities and thousands of Americans those brought to Europe, Franklin being one of them, "an American City in Europe" (so the title of the prelude). Drawing apparently on Chaplin's book, she argues that Franklin "in his travels through both Scotland and England met other well-known philosophers, intellectuals and entrepreneurs – David Hume, Adam Smith, James Watt, Matthew Boulton – all eager to meet 'the best philosopher of America'" (p. 207) but there are no specifics about what Smith might have learned from Franklin and when.

[29] See also Ross (2010, chapter 16). Eliot points out that the key facets of Smith's thinking, especially his claim that it was ultimately labor that created value, were to be found years before the publication of *WN* in Franklin's publications. But it is possible that Franklin had just plagiarized Petty on that topic. We thank Tony Aspromourgos for pointing this out to us.

interactions and, given the extraordinarily close friendship between Hume and Smith documented in Rasmussen's book, it seems safe to assume that considerable knowledge spillover happened between Franklin and Smith, via Hume. In the end, it is only so interesting whether Smith interacted with one specific person, even if that person was eminent.

In sum, Smith had been thinking about the American question at least since returning from his 1764 to 1766 trip to continental Europe (Winch 2013, p. 4), and he worked to understand Great Britain's options, given that Mercantilist interests dominated the public debate about the best policy toward the colonies. As a matter of fact, Morrison (2012) suggests that Smith's interest in these matters went back even further. According to him (Morrison 2012, p. 406), from the beginning of the 1760s, Smith was a privileged interlocutor and recurrent advisor to Lord Shelburne, one of the leading figures of British politics during the Imperial crisis in the 1770s and 1780s and Prime Minister of Great Britain from 1782 to 1783, who acknowledged explicitly his conversion to some of Smith's principles as well as the fact that it took him considerable time to get converted.[30] This partially supports the claim of Morrison (2012) that "Smith was lobbying leading policymakers to abandon the Mercantilist project in America since the 1760s" (2012, p. 401). Recognizing that the territorial wins came at a cost unsustainable to the public purse,[31] but realizing that he was too far away from the action to feel confident in his judgment, Smith postponed the publication of the *WN*.[32]

Phillipson (2010, chapters 10 and 11) writes persuasively of the importance of Smith's stays in London during eight months in 1766–1767 and between 1773 and 1776. He makes it clear that Smith "was able to move in political circles at a time when the future of Anglo-American relations, the role of the East India Company in the government of India and public finance and taxation were under discussion, all matters of importance

[30] "I owe to a journey I made with Mr. Smith from Edinburgh to London the difference between light and darkness... The novelty of his principles made me unable to comprehend them at the time, but he urged them with so much ***eloquence***, that they took a certain hold which, though it did not arrive at full ***conviction*** for some few years after, I can truly say has constituted ever since the happiness of my life" (Morrison 2012, p. 395, our italics).

[31] For another point of view on this issue, see Morrison (2012).

[32] In Morrison's view, "Smith delayed publishing his treatise to make explicit connections between the predictions of his theory and the colonists' violent rejection of mercantilist imperialism" (2012, p. 407).

to the WN" (2010, p. 201). It is noteworthy that, in Smith's *Lectures on Jurisprudence*[33] (dated 1762 and 1766), we find no mention of the "mercantile system," nor of the "agricultural system" or the "system of natural liberty," while hindrances to the freedom of internal and foreign commerce and the false belief in the monetary foundation of wealth are repeatedly denounced. Moreover, in his *LJ*, Smith neither deals with the American colonies, nor does he analyze the issue of public debt. It means that Smith's enemy in *WN*, the pernicious system of merchants and manufacturers persuading legislators to make laws favoring them at the expense of the interest of society, was not yet clearly "conceptualized."[34] For this task, in line with Morrison (2012, p. 407), we conjecture that he needed to further investigate the American colonies.

That Smith spent three years in London before publishing *WN* is, for us, the key; there, "in the greatest mercantile city in the world" and "seat of the government" of Great Britain (*WN*, V.iii.35, p. 918), he could be a spectator of the dangerous collusion between the political elite and the economic powers, and exchange ideas with both groups in intellectual clubs and salons of which he was a well-known member. In a letter to Smith dated January 4, 1776, Hume writes that "it [*WN*] is probably much improved by your last Abode in London" (Smith *Corr.* 150, pp. 186 - 7). In other words, while Smith undoubtedly had the premises of the system of natural liberty in mind very early, it was only after his trip to France and his meeting with key members of the Physiocratic School and Turgot that he started on its theoretical *conceptualization* and that of its antagonistic counterpart, the mercantile system. It is noteworthy that the first to use the expression "mercantile system" was Mirabeau, one of the leading figures of the Physiocrats, who Smith might have met during

[33] *LJ*.

[34] As Phillipson writes, "it seems fairly certain that Smith's principal task was to reflect on the principles of political economy he had developed at Glasgow in the light of those of Quesnay and his disciples, and to develop and refine the vast stock of historical illustrations on which the effectiveness of his advocacy would depend. He had already established the principle that the opulence of a nation was to be measured in terms of the flow of consumable goods and not its reserves of gold and silver. …

Moreover, he had outlined a theory of natural liberty, which argued that a system of free markets and free exchange would optimize a nation's wealth, and he had raised the provocative and question-begging issue of why the progress of opulence had been so slow in Europe. But while he had offered an account of many of the economic, political and moral factors on which the progress of opulence depended, he had not yet worked these factors into a system which explained precisely how they interacted" (2010, p. 205).

his stay in Paris. But it is Smith who first developed that concept in the *WN*. Completing his system of political economy required a conceptualization of the different discourses prevailing at that time and of their influence on economic and political reality, a task still to be accomplished and for which the colonies of North America were essential.[35]

Moreover, it is noteworthy, as we stated earlier, that Smith had initially not been deeply concerned with the increase of public debt in Great Britain, despite the publication in 1752 of Hume's essay *On Public Credit* (Hume 1986). Therefore, Book IV (and chapter 3 of Book V) is entirely new and, presumably, written after Books I–III. The delay in the publication of the WN presumably granted him more time to better understand the mercantile system, to address its dangerous economic and political consequences, and to prepare the structure of his attack carefully, knowing that the American question was the polemic debate of the day in Great Britain. The *WN* is a book deeply embedded in the political realities of its time and place. So much so that Blair, otherwise full of praise for the *WN*, saw it "too much like a publication for the present time" (*Corr.* 151, p. 188), while Roebuck wrote to Smith in November 1775 that "the meeting of Parliament is the proper time for the publication of such a work as yours" and that "it might also have been of general use in influencing the Opinion of many in this American contest" (*Corr.* 147, p. 184). Smith carefully chose the publication date of *WN* to make a deep impact on public opinion and politics.

2.3 The Mercantile System, Colonial Policy, and Public Debt

Smith thus purposely left Utopian theorizing about the British Empire to the final pages of his book. His immediate goal was to discuss public

[35] In Phillipson's words: "what his theory and his attack on the commercial system had lacked was any strong example of a nation whose economic progress had actually followed the route laid out in an essentially conjectural analysis. He had naturally called attention to Scotland's remarkable economic and political progress since the creation of its free-trade union with England to illustrate his Glasgow lectures, and he made copious use of Scottish examples to illustrate various themes of the Wealth of Nations. But Scotland, still encumbered by the constraints of feudal system, was not the perfect example of the sort of natural progress Smith had envisaged. His masterstroke was to introduce the experience of colonial America as the classic, and indeed the only possible, example of a society whose progress had been rapid and natural by comparison with that of Europe" (2010, p. 228).

credit and the consequences of war on public finance, the most topical of all the subjects discussed in the *WN*. In his essay ***On Public Credit***, Hume insisted on the increasing and unsustainable public debt of Great Britain. In his words, "either the nation must destroy public debt, or public debt will destroy the nation" (Hume 1986, pp. 360–361). Using a similarly dramatic tone, Smith claimed that "the progress of the enormous debts which at present oppress ... all the great nations of Europe ... will in the long run probably ruin" them (*WN*, V.iii.10, p. 911). Smith doubted that Great Britain could support another significant increase of its public debt (*WN*, V.iii.58, p. 929). The contribution of Smith's analysis with regard to Hume[36] on this issue was to identify the connections between public debt and the mercantile system on the one hand, and its relationship to the American colonies on the other. Generally speaking, increasing public debt in Europe was, for Smith, the result of repeated conflicts between nations being wrongly "jealous" of each other's opulence.[37] War was the consequence of applying the deceitful principles that rationalized the mercantile system with its view of international commerce as a zero-sum game and the related doctrine of the positive balance of trade. While for Smith commerce "ought naturally to be, among men as among nations, a bond of union and friendship, [it] has become the most fertile source of discord and animosity" (*WN*, IV.iii.c.9, p. 493). As regards public debt, the "sophistry of the mercantile system" makes a dangerous and erroneous "apology" of it, claiming that "in the payment of the interest of the publick debt ... it is the right hand which pays the left" (*WN*, V.iii.52, pp. 926–927).[38] In contrast with this partisan view of public debt, Smith explains in the last chapter of *WN*, the detrimental effects it has on national opulence and, most importantly, on political sovereignty. Regarding Great Britain, Smith attributes the alarming rise in public debt to the successive wars for defending its North American colonies (*WN*, IV.vii.c.64, p. 615; V.iii.41–45, pp. 921–922; V.iii.88, p. 944; V.iii.92, p. 946). Usually, he writes, "the common advantages which every empire

[36] On Hume's analysis of public debt, see Paganelli (2010).

[37] The issue of the "jealousy of trade" was also investigated by Hume in his eponymous essay and in *Of the Balance of Trade*. On jealousy of trade in Hume and Smith, see Hont (2005, 2015) and Walraevens (2017).

[38] This metaphor was used by Melon in his *Political Essay on Commerce* and was already denounced by Hume (1986, p. 356).

derives from the provinces subject to its dominion, consists...in the military force which they furnish for its defence; and ... in the revenue which they furnish for the support of its civil government" (*WN,* IV.vii.c.11). However, "the English colonists have never yet contributed any thing towards the defence of the mother country, or towards the support of its civil government" but "they themselves, on the contrary, have hitherto been defended almost entirely at the expence of the mother country" (*WN,* IV.vii.b.20, p. 573).[39] The increase in public debt is likely to have dramatic *political* consequences for Great Britain, Smith argues. If nothing is done to secure new revenues from Ireland and the American Colonies, in particular, and to reduce public expenditure (*WN*, V.iii.92, p. 946), the British Empire is likely to collapse. Smith therefore pleaded for a union of the Empire in the spirit of the 1707 Act of Union with Scotland.

Smith's plan for a new British Empire is based on the following reasoning. Knowing that the security of the colonies has had huge consequences on Great Britain's public finance,[40] Smith thinks "it is not contrary to justice that ... America should contribute towards the discharge of the publick debt of Great Britain" (*WN*, V.iii.88, p. 944). In his view, the British Empire to this point has been a dream, existing nowhere but in the minds of men (*WN*, V.iii.92, p. 947). Were American colonies considered true "provinces" of the Empire, Smith claims, they should stop being the "free-riders" of the Empire, reaping the benefits of the protection of the mother country without bearing the costs for that protection. Political union with Great Britain, which in Smith's opinion would be mutually beneficial (WN, V.iii.88, p. 944) and natural (*WN*, IV.vii.c.77, p. 624), would grant the colonies new rights and duties. In return for the payment of taxes to Great Britain, the colonies would get "a fair and equal representation" in the British Parliament, that being in proportion to their contribution to the revenue of the Empire (*WN*, IV.vii.c.75, p. 622; IV.vii.c.77, p. 624; V.iii.68, p. 933). They

[39] "Great Britain is, perhaps, since the world began, the only state which, as it has extended its empire, has only increased its expence without once augmenting its resources" (*WN,* IV.vii.c.73, p. 621).

[40] "That publick debt has been contracted in defence, not of Great Britain alone, but of all the different provinces of the Empire; the immense debt contracted in the late war in particular, and a great part of that contracted in the war before, were both properly contracted in defence of America" (*WN*, V.iii.88, p. 944).

would also be relieved of regulations concerning colonial trade (*WN*, IV.vii.c.44, p. 606) of which "the merchants who carry it on, it must be observed, have been the principal advisers" and by which "the interest of the colonies was sacrificed to the interest of those merchants"[41] (*WN*, IV.vii.b.49, p. 584).[42] It is because of "the groundless jealousy of the merchants and manufacturers of the mother country" that this monopoly of the colony trade, an "unjust" policy, "a manifest violation of the most sacred rights of mankind," was instituted (*WN*, IV.vii.b.44, p. 582).

In Smith's words, this plan for the British Empire should be regarded as "a new Utopia" (*WN*, V.iii.68, p. 934),[43] in the same way as the demand for a complete restoration of the perfect liberty of commerce in Great Britain is, both being closely related, as we shall see (*WN*, IV.ii.43, p. 471). In both cases "the private interest of many powerful individuals, the confirmed prejudices of great bodies of people seem, indeed, at present, to oppose to so great a change such obstacles as it may be very difficult, perhaps altogether impossible, to surmount" (*WN*, V.iii.68, p. 934; IV.ii.43, p. 471). Smith anticipated the powerful merchants and manufacturers would oppose until the end the monopoly of the colony trade, of which they were the main, not to say only, beneficiaries, as Smith repeatedly denounced.[44] Besides, they were the owners of British public debt from which they drew considerable interest, so they had no interest in a great reduction of public debt. But it was not only the political power of the mercantile class which was an obstacle to the freedom of commerce

[41] Simiqueli (2017) convincingly shows that Smith's project of Empire is informed by the distinction he made between two types of ancient colonies: the Greek *apoikia* and the Roman *colonia*.

[42] Smith underlines the economic benefits for Great Britain and the colonies of a free trade between them in (*WN*, IV.vii.c.48, p. 608). The American colonies could also reap political benefits from the union with Great Britain, Smith argues. In particular, due to the distance with the mother country, the spirit of faction (a great source of corruption of moral sentiments and political instability) would be undermined (WN, V.iii.90, p. 945).

[43] Note, though, that for Simiqueli, "we can say that Smith foresees the foreseeable, or imagines the imaginable – his reflection on the colonies belongs to the context in which he writes, and it attempts to address the specific problems within this scenario…More than formulating 'principles of imperial government regarded as applicable in all circumstances' (Benians 1925 268), what we have here is a pragmatic response to an objective demand…" (2017, p. 34).

[44] "To promote the little interest of one little order of men in one country, it hurts the interest of all other orders of men in that country, and of all men in all other countries" (*WN*, IV.vii.c.60, p. 612). See also (*WN*, IV.vii.c.67, p. 618).

between Great Britain and its American colonies. The monopoly of the colony trade had broken "that natural balance which would otherwise have taken place among all the different branches of British industry" (*WN*, IV.vii.c.43, p. 604). So much so that "Great Britain resembles one of those unwholesome bodies in which some of the vital parts are overgrown, and which, upon that account, are liable to many dangerous disorders..." (ibid.). Smith concluded his medical metaphor with the idea that "a small stop in that great blood-vessel, which has been artificially swelled beyond its natural dimensions, and through which an unnatural proportion of the industry and commerce of the country has been forced to circulate, is very likely to bring on *the most dangerous disorders upon the whole body politick*" (ibid., pp. 604–605, *our italics*). That is why "the expectation of a rupture with the colonies...has struck the people of Great Britain with more terror than they ever felt for a Spanish armada, or a French invasion" (ibid., p. 605). For Smith, the only thing that could prevent this danger was to bring about "some moderate and gradual relaxation of the laws which give to Great Britain the exclusive trade to the colonies, till it is rendered in a great measure free" in order to "restore that natural, healthful, and proper proportion which perfect liberty necessarily establishes" (*WN*, IV.vii.c.44, p. 606). However, "to open the colony trade all at once to all nations, might not only occasion some transitory inconveniency, but a great permanent loss to the greater part of those whose industry or capital is at present engaged in it" (ibid.). "Such are the unfortunate effects of all the regulations of the mercantile system," Smith laments, that "they not only introduce very dangerous disorders in the state of the body politick, but disorders which it is often difficult to remedy, without occasioning ... still greater disorders" (ibid.). It is thus to "the wisdom of future statesmen and legislators to determine" how "the colony trade ought gradually to be opened" and "in what manner the natural system of perfect liberty and justice ought gradually to be restored" (ibid.). The monopoly of the colony trade was used by Smith as the best example of the misdeeds of the mercantile system on economic growth (*WN*, IV.vii.c.49, p. 608; IV.vii.c.56, pp. 610–601) and on the body politic. The mercantile policy of Great Britain with its colonies was very costly, economically and politically, leading to lower rates of growth, wars, and public debts. Yet "to propose that Great Britain should voluntarily give up all authority over her colonies...would be to propose such a measure as never was, and never will be adopted by any nation in the world" (*WN*, IV.vii.c.66, p. 616). To avoid the fall of the

British Empire, a new social contract was needed between the mother country and its American colonies. Smith's project of empire, as utopian as it seemed to be, tried to provide a mutually beneficial and just union between them. As he noted, "That this union, however, could be easily effectuated, or that difficulties and great difficulties might not occur in the execution, I do not pretend. I have yet heard of none, however, which appear insurmountable. The principal perhaps arose, not from the nature of things, but from the prejudices and opinions of the people both on this and on the other side of the Atlantic" (*WN*, IV.vii.c.77, p. 625).[45] Smith's whole Book IV was an attempt to deconstruct old prejudices and pernicious opinions about wealth and commerce. His project of Empire was aimed to influence the opinion on the "American question"[46] and to show how detrimental the mercantile system could be, both economically and politically. As such, it was a rhetorical project.

Smith's critique of and attack on the commercial system of Great Britain didn't stop at the end of Book IV, as many readers tend to assume. Rather, it reaches its climax in the discussion on the British Empire which was rhetorically placed at the very end of the *WN*, presumably in order to definitely get the agreement of his reader against the mercantile system. As Pack rightly captured, "When one writes a book of this length, placement certainly matters" (p. 84, fn. 35). We next turn to how Smith's principles of rhetoric informed his critique of the mercantile system, and his related treatment of the American colonies and the British Empire in *WN*.

[45] Hill (2021) (convincingly) argues that the project of union (or imperial parliament) with the American colonies exposed and supported by Smith in *WN* might not have been the solution he personally favored above all other options (which would be a complete separation with complete freedom of trade), but rather a second-best solution knowing the interests, pride, and prejudices of people and politicians on both sides of the Atlantic. Smith's stance on this issue thus exhibits his gradualist and pragmatist approach of politics, and—we stress—it also illustrates Smith's savvy use of rhetorical strategies.

[46] See John Roebuck quoted above (*Corr.* 147, p. 184) and William Robertson, writing to Smith on April 8, 1776: "Many of your observations concerning the Colonies are of capital importance to me. I shall often follow you as my Guide and Instructor" (*Corr.* 153, p. 192).

3 How Smith Attacked the Mercantilist System

In the first part of the chapter, we explained how Smith's interest in the American question informed his conceptualization of the different discourses of political economy and might have led him to postpone the publication of the *WN* to have a better grasp on this issue and to make a biggest impact on public opinion, in which it was fiercely debated. Yet Smith clearly understood that more than proper timing was needed to persuade his readers to adopt his plan for a new British Empire. In this second part, we turn our attention to how Smith organized his attack against the mercantile system of Great Britain, that is, on the rhetorical structure of his argumentation per se. To do this, we need first to recall some of Smith's principles of rhetoric.

3.1 Smith's Early and Everlasting Interest for Rhetoric

The evidence shows that rhetoric was always on Smith's mind, in theory and in practice. He taught private lectures on rhetoric and belles lettres in Edinburgh from 1748 to 1751 at a very early stage of his career, before even his first professorial appointment (Phillipson 2010, chapter 5). Prior to these lectures, he had studied six years at Oxford's Balliol College, where he developed a deep interest in ancient and modern languages (Stewart 1795 in Smith 1982, p. 272). When, in January 1751, he was appointed professor of Logic and Metaphysics at the University of Glasgow, his teaching continued to include large portions of his lectures on rhetoric (Stewart 1795 in Smith 1982, p. 274; see also Phillipson 2010, chapter 6). Even though he was appointed to the more prestigious chair of Moral Philosophy within a year, Smith went on teaching rhetoric in private classes as a complement to his courses in moral philosophy (Ross 2010, p. 128; Phillipson 2010, p. 127). In a letter to La Rochefoucauld, Smith even expressed his intention to publish a book in which rhetoric would have a major place (*Corr.* 248, p. 287). Unfortunately for us, it might have been part of the manuscripts he asked to burn at his death.

Smith's long-lasting interest in rhetoric and languages was part of his larger investigation into the powers of the human mind and the principles of human nature. Both themes were prominent in the work of Hutcheson and Hume, arguably Smith's most important influences throughout his life, especially while he attended the University of Glasgow between 1737 and 1740 and in the decade of his intellectual formation that followed (Phillipson 2010, 2013; Rasmussen 2017).[47] In particular, Smith paid extraordinary attention to how best to communicate one's thoughts and understood that different circumstances required different discourses. Communicative effectiveness, he argued (*LRBL*, p. 96), was contextual and depended on the subject matter, circumstances, character, and manner of both speaker (writer) and listener (reader), and the rapport they had. More precisely, Smith praised a clear, plain style, devoid of ornaments, tropes, or figures of speech that might ruin communicative efficiency (*LRBL*, pp. 25–26, p. 29, and pp. 55–56). We note that his critique of impediments to the free exchange of ideas and sentiments parallels his aversion to Mercantilist policies (Ortmann & Walraevens 2021; Chapter 7 this book). Besides, Smith stressed, when faced with a particularly hostile listener or reader whose agreement could not be presumed, it is necessary to argue in a "rhetorical" manner rather than a "didactical" one.

Smith not only had theoretical insights about successful rhetorical strategies, but practical insights as well. As Rosen explains, "In Smith's day, University of Glasgow professors were paid a fixed annual retainer financed out of university endowment, and seniority eventually gave entitlement to a university house, part of which could be rented to students to supplement income. The greater part of income arose out of fees paid directly to teachers by students" (Rosen 1987, p. 562; see also Ortmann 1997, 1999). Smith was an avid supporter of such incentive compatible mechanisms; his lectures were well attended, and his reputation was high.

3.2 The Targets of His "Very Violent Attack" (Corr. *208, p. 251)*

In Book III of the *WN*, Smith provides his readers, against the backdrop of more positive developments in Scotland and the American colonies, with a historical sketch of the slow and unnatural progress of opulence in Europe. He opened Book IV by defining political economy "as a branch of the science of a statesmen or legislator" which proposes "to enrich both the people and the sovereign" (*WN*, IV.Introduction.1, p. 428),

[47] Smith, according to Millar (as reported in Stewart), believed: "The best method of explaining and illustrating the various powers of the human mind, the most useful part of metaphysics, arises from an examination of the several ways of communicating our thoughts by speech, and from an attention to the principles of those literary compositions which contribute to persuasion or entertainment" (Stewart 1795 in Smith 1982, p. 274).

and he claimed that two systems of political economy had been devised to enrich the people: the system of commerce and that of agriculture (*WN*, IV.introduction.2, p. 428). Book IV then presented a tight, critical scrutiny of both systems (of which 8 chapters, or almost 90%, are devoted to a critique of Mercantilism and only one, accounting for less than 10%, to a critique of the agricultural system) followed by a brief summary (less than 1% of Book IV) of Smith's own system of political economy: the system of natural liberty. That brief summary can be seen as a light version of Books I–II and chapter 1 of Book III, which account for about 30% of the *WN*. The two-page summary of the system of natural liberty in Book IV is, after the lengthy detour of Books III and IV, a reminder of the point of departure of Book IV and an attempt to set the stage for his subsequent analysis. Rhetoric at work.

For Smith, this detour was not just academic. In Book III, he documented the differential growth rates across nations. In Book IV, he attacked quite forcefully[48] the Mercantilist system, and in the last pages of Book V he launched his ultimate, decisive argument against it. We argue that Smith's decision to launch a "very violent attack" against the mercantile system (*Corr.* 208, p. 251)[49] and the rhetorical sequencing of Books I–II, III, IV, and V cannot be fully appreciated without considering the distinction between didactic discourse and rhetorical discourse that Smith very explicitly made.

To anyone who reads his *Lectures on Rhetoric and Belles Letters*, Smith is known as someone who developed his arguments plainly and carefully (*LRBL*, p. 35–36, 40, 89, 146–147; see also Collings & Ortmann (1997) and Fleischacker (2004), but see Kellow (2011)). Smith applied his criteria for the perfection of style to his own work.[50] He recognized that the relationship between listener (reader) and speaker (author) was often a principal-agent relationship[51] that sometimes required the speaker

[48] For example, Ferguson (*Corr.* 154, p. 193) attested: "You have provoked, it is true, the church, the universities, and the merchants ...".

[49] According to Stewart, Smith's "remarks with respect to the jealousy of commerce are expressed in a tone of indignation, which he seldom assumes in his political writings" (Stewart 1795 in Smith 1982, p. 216).

[50] For a different point of view, see Brown (1994, pp. 15–18). For a discussion of her work, see Collings & Ortmann (1997).

[51] "We have shewn how fare they have acted agreably to that Rule, which is equally applicable to conversation and behaviour as writing. For what is that makes a man agreable

(author) to "keep as far from the main point to be proved as possible, bringing on the audience by slow and imperceptible degree to the thing to be proved" (*LRBL*, p. 146). We claim that the *WN*, in the way that it was structured and that its books were sequenced, was one such rhetorical enterprise; its original purpose was to attack, in a strategic way, a dysfunctional and, above all, dangerous system of commerce nowadays routinely labeled Mercantilism.

3.3 *The Theory Underlying the "Very Violent Attack"* (Corr. *208, p. 251): Didactic Discourse and Rhetorical Discourse*

A method for dealing successfully with a hostile audience is given in Smith's *Lectures on Rhetoric and Belles Lettres* from 1762 to 1763. There, Smith partitioned discourse into several categories and sub-categories. The first division was based on purpose: if one's purpose is to relate facts, the Narrative or Historical style ought to be chosen. If one wishes to prove a proposition, then one should choose Didactic or Rhetorical discourse. With the Didactic proof, the speaker (author) treats his subject scientifically and impartially, carefully weighing the pros and cons of his argument. The Rhetorical proof, on the other hand, is designed to be a persuasive device. Going further, Smith broke down the Rhetorical proof into two sub-categories, the Aristotelian and the Socratick, which "are adapted to the two conterary cases in which an orator may be circumstanced with regard to his audience, they may either have a favourable or unfavourable opinion of that which he is to prove" (*LRBL*, p. 147). In the Aristotelian Rhetorical proof, the speaker (author) states his main point up front and goes on to justify it. In the Socratick proof, the speaker (author) initially hides his point, leading the reader along his path of

company, is it not, when his sentiments appear to be naturally expressed, when the passion or affection is properly conveyed and when their thoughts are so agreable and naturall that we find ourselves inclined to give our assent to them. A wise man too in conversation and behaviour will not affect a character that is unnaturall to him; if he is grave he will not affect to be gay, nor if he be gay will he affect to be grave. He will only regulate his naturall temper, restrain within just bounds and lop all exhuberances and bring it to that pitch which will be agreable to those about him. But he will not affect such conduct as is unnaturall to his temper tho perhaps in the abstract they may be more to be wished" (*LRBL*, p. 133).

reasoning toward a conclusion.[52] The latter method, Smith explains, "is the smoothest and most engaging manner" (*LRBL*, p. 147), and is best suited to persuading an antagonistic crowd.

The Wealth of Nations has elements of both Didactic and Rhetorical proofs, as others have argued before (Muller 1993; Brown 1994; Fleischacker 2004).[53] In some parts, Smith lays out principles of nature such as the propensity to truck, barter, and exchange which leads to the division of labour and increased productivity; the desire to better our condition which sustains the accumulation of capital; or the natural right every man has to choose how to use his capital or faculties as he sees proper, a principle that allows an efficient allocation of resources. These are supposed to be universal, uncontroversial principles and as such, nothing more than a Didactic proof is needed. On the other hand, the *WN* is a fight against old prejudices about commerce, a reaction to Mercantilism and an attempt to steer policy in a different direction. The *WN* was thus inherently and deliberately polemic. In this sense, the *WN* is in some parts, but most importantly in its sequencing of books and chapters, an exercise in persuasion that utilizes, we claim, Smith's own rhetorical teachings, and, more specifically, the argumentation of the Socratick kind. As Smith makes clear in *LRBL*, the objective of Didactic argumentation is instruction and conviction. A secondary end is persuasion. Undoubtedly, Smith wanted to be both persuasive and instructive.

[52] "As there are two methods of proceeding in didacticall discourses, so there are two in Deliberative eloquence which are no less different, and are adapted to very conterary circumstances. The 1st may be called the Socratick method, as it was that which, if we may trust the dialogues of Xenophon and Plato, that Philosopher generally made use. In this method we keep as far from the main point to be proved as possible, bringing on the audience by slow and imperceptible degrees to the thing to be proved, and by gaining their consent to some things whose tendency they can't discover, we force them at last either to deny what they had before agreed to, or to grant the Validity of the Conclusion. This is the smoothest and most engaging manner. The other is a harsh and unmannerly one where we affirm the thing we are to prove, boldly at the Beginning, and when any point is controverted beginn by proving that very thing and so on, this we may call the Aristotelian method as we know it was that which he used" (*LRBL*, pp. 146–147).

[53] Fleischacker (2004; see in particular pp. 10–11) is remarkable; in that he stresses the "same roundabout, qualified way of making points" runs from sentences over passages all the way to "the structure of the WN as a whole".

3.4 *How to Address the Audience: Smith's Application of His Theoretical Insights in His Critique of the Mercantilist System*

Anticipating the chilly reception, his work might receive from vested interests in government and commerce (an anticipation that was well-founded; e.g., prominently Fleischacker 2004, pp. 261–262; Teichgraeber 1987), and aware of his rhetorical purpose, Smith used the method of exposition most appropriate and persuasive for hostile audiences, the Socratick Rhetorical method,[54] to sequence the five books of the *WN* in order to unfold his argumentation against the mercantile system. He first outlined the optimality of a rigorously developed system assuming away problems of public good provision or externalities—a system whose descendants still reign in today's textbooks on economic principles. In the first two books of the *WN*, Smith highlights the economic benefit of letting people freely express and satisfy their natural desires to exchange (the first three chapters of Book I on the division of labour) and to better their condition (Book II on the accumulation of capital).[55] Once they are free to use their faculties and employ their capital as they see fit, the economy will follow the natural, optimal order of progress toward opulence (Book III, chapter 1).

Then in chapters 2 to 4 of Book III of the *WN* (i.e., 90% of that book), Smith described the history of Europe's slow and unnatural progress toward opulence, against the backdrop of more positive developments

[54] "These 2 methods are adapted to the two conterary cases in which an orator may be circumstanced with regard to his audience, they may either have a favourable or unfavourable opinion of that which he is to prove. That is they may be prejudiced for or they may be prejudiced against. In the 2nd Case we are to use the Socratic method, in the 1st the Aristotelian. I do not mean by this that we are to suppose that in any case the Orator and his audience are to hold a dialogue with each other, or that they are to go on by granting small demand < s > or by boldly denying what the other affirms; but only that when the audience is favourable we are to begin with the proposition and set it out Roundly before them as it must be most for our advantage in this case to shew at the first we are of their opinion, the arguments we advance gain strength by this precaution. On the other hand if they are prejudiced against the Opinion to be advanced; we are not to shock them by rudely affirming what we are satisfied is dissagreable, but are to conceal our design and beginning at a distance bring them slowly on to the main point and having gained the more remote ones we get the nearer ones of consequence" (*LRBL*, p. 147).

[55] Dellemotte (2002) has shown how the natural propensity to trade, barter, and exchange and the desire to better our condition, are derived from the universal desire of mutual sympathy.

in Scotland and the American colonies. Book IV was mainly devoted to a critique of Mercantilism which concludes, after a brief digression on the agricultural system, with a brief summary of Smith's own system of political economy: the system of natural liberty. As a result, in Books I through III, Smith alluded to the damage done by an economic system catering to vested interests, but he refrained from saying outright that the Mercantilist system was responsible for the damage. That restraint was abandoned in Book IV of the *WN*, where Smith launched his "very violent attack" on the mercantile system. Yet it was in Book V that the attack finds its apogee, when Smith shows that it threatens the British Empire.

If we look more closely at the unfolding of Smith's critique of the mercantile system in WN, we should begin with chapter 8 of Book I, in which Smith highlights how capital owners can collude to defending their class interests and obtain privileges from legislators.[56] Later in Book I, he underlined that "the clamour and sophistry of merchants and manufacturers easily persuade them that the private interest of a part, and of a subordinate part of the society, is the general interest of the whole" (*WN*, I.x.c.25, p. 144). Again, in the last lines of Book I, he attacked the merchants and manufacturers and their collusion with politicians, but he does not refer to the "mercantile system" yet.[57]

In chapters 2 to 4 of Book III, Smith detailed next how Europe did not follow the natural path toward growth and progress because of the

[56] "We rarely hear, it has been said, of the combinations of masters; though frequently of those of workmen. But whoever imagines, upon this account, that masters rarely combine, is as ignorant of the world as of the subject. Masters are always and every where in a sort of tacit, but constant and uniform combination, not to raise the wages of labour above their actual rate. To violate this combination is every where a most unpopular action, and a sort of reproach to a master among his neighbours and equals. We seldom, indeed, hear of this combination, because it is the usual, and one may say, the natural state of things which nobody ever hears of...The masters upon these occasions are just as clamorous upon the other side, and never cease to call aloud for the assistance of the civil magistrate, and the rigorous execution of those laws which have been enacted with so much severity against the combinations of servants, labourers, and journeymen" (*WN*, I.viii.13, p. 84).

[57] "The proposal of any new law or regulation of commerce which comes from this order, ought always to be listened to with great precaution, and ought never to be adopted till after having been long and carefully examined, not only with the most scrupulous, but with the most suspicious attention. It comes from an order of men, whose interest is never exactly the same with that of the publick, who have generally an interest to deceive and even to oppress the publick, and who accordingly have, upon many occasions, both deceived and oppressed it" (*WN*, I.xi.p. 10, p. 267).

harmful prescriptions of the mercantile system for economic policy, as detailed in Book IV. It is only in Book IV, "Of Systems of Political Economy,"[58] that Smith explicitly critiqued the mercantile system. Taking up the theme he introduced at the very end of Book I, Smith presented this system as a partial and deceitful discourse on political economy sponsored by capital owners for defending their personal interests and persuading legislators to favor them (even though they were aware that it went against the general interest of society). The architecture of Book IV, we claim, is part of Smith's rhetorical strategy: 8 chapters out of 9 are spent describing and critiquing the Mercantilist system whose wrong theoretical principles on money and the balance of trade led to the implementation of unfair and inefficient economic policies.[59] The last chapter was devoted to the agricultural system because it was theoretically closer to Smith's system of natural liberty[60] and thus prepared the ground for its explicit introduction. Book IV ended with a rehash of Smith's system of political economy, the system of natural liberty laid out in Books I and II. At this point, the reader was not given the opportunity to judge Smith's view of Mercantilism from the outset; instead, he was taken along step by step to that opinion in Book IV and ultimately in the final pages of Book V.

An enriched view of Smith's philosophical critique of the different systems of political economy is given once we apply to them, again, Smith's own rhetorical categories. Indeed, he saw both the mercantile and the agricultural systems as being persuasive yet partial and wrong discourses on political economy. To use Smith's concepts, the mercantile

[58] Smith's criticism of Mercantilism in Book IV grew sharper with time. In the third edition of *WN* appears a new chapter ("Conclusion of the Mercantile System", WN, IV.viii, pp. 642–662) and a number of new passages relating the legislative influence of mercantile interests to "extortion," (*WN*, IV.viii.3-4, pp. 643–644) and explaining how such influence functions at the expense of the poor. For example: "It is the industry which is carried on for the benefit of the rich and powerful, that is principally encouraged by our mercantile system. That which is carried on for the benefit of the poor and the indigent, is too often, either neglected, or oppressed" (*WN*, IV.viii.4, p. 644).

[59] Smith devotes only one chapter to the agricultural system because it is less pernicious for economic growth than the mercantile system and it has never been implemented.

[60] "In representing the wealth of nations as consisting, not in the unconsumable riches of money, but in the consumable goods annually reproduced by the labour of the society; and in representing perfect liberty as the only effectual expedient for rendering this annual reproduction the greatest possible, its doctrine seems to be in every respect as just as it is generous and liberal" (*WN*, IV.ix.38, p. 678).

system was a "rhetorical discourse" (*LRBL*, i.150, p. 62) because, first, it was a partial, self-serving discourse. As a rhetorical discourse, it "endeavours by all means to perswade us; and for this purpose it magnifies all the arguments on the one side and diminishes or conceals those that might be brought on the side conterary to that which it is designed that we should favour" (ibid.). In Smith's words, "merchants and masters-manufacturers complain much of the bad effects of high wages in raising the price, and thereby lessening the sale of their goods at home and abroad. They say nothing concerning the bad effects of high profits. They are silent with regard to the pernicious effects of their own gains" but "they complain only of those of other people" (*WN*, I.ix.24, p. 115).

The commercial system was political economy from the point of view of the capital owners, giving undue and inefficient encouragements to industry and foreign trade against agriculture. And it was deceitful rhetoric in that merchants and manufacturers tried to persuade the legislators and public opinion that the interest of their class was aligned with the interest of society. The mercantile system was the "sophistry" of the merchants on political economy.[61] It distorted the natural allocation and "balance" of the capital of society, creating "disorders" which were difficult to overcome because of the collusion between merchants and legislators. In his introduction to Book IV, Smith claimed that political economy aimed "to enrich both the people and the sovereign" (*WN*, IV, introduction, p. 428). Yet he noted that he tried to show in Book IV "that the mercantile system has not been very favourable to the revenue of the great body of the people," while Book V demonstrated that "it seems not to have been more favourable to the revenue of the sovereign" either (*WN*, V.ii.k.25, p. 881).

With the system of natural liberty, Smith, by contrast, envisioned a system of political economy in which the wealth of the nation was maximized by free trade, giving no encouragement to a specific sector and letting capital follow its natural course, so that it would enrich both the great body of the people and the sovereign. This system was impartial with regard to agriculture, industry, and foreign commerce, giving "equal treatment" to each class or order of citizens (*WN*, IV.vii.c.87, p. 629). The system of natural liberty was intended by Smith to be seen as a "didactic discourse" (*LRBL*, i.150, p. 149) of a philosopher or impartial

[61] For more details on sophistry in the WN, see Gore (2011).

spectator who takes a distanced, well-informed, unbiased view on political economy, treating each sector and class of society with equality and impartiality. In the didactic discourse, the "design" is "to set the case in the clearest light; to give every argument its due force, and by this means persuade us no farther than our unbiased judgments is convinced" (*LRBL*, ii.13, p. 89). "Instruction" is here the main end (*LRBL*, i.150, p. 149). "Scarce any nation has dealt equally and impartially with every sort of industry," Smith lamented (*WN*, introduction and plan of the work, p. 11). In other words, the "wise" legislator he called for in order to implement the system of natural liberty and to reform the British Empire, is nothing but an impartial spectator of the economy.

4 Conclusion

Our reading of the *WN*, and in particular the sequencing of its books, suggests a contextually sensitive and strategically written book, with a special emphasis on the often overlooked Book V and its final pages on the future of the British Empire threatened by mercantile interests in the colonies. It is in this book that Smith addresses the incentive-compatible organization of joint-stock, educational, and ecclesiastical organizations (Ortmann 1999) as well as the ways of addressing externalities and dealing with the provision of various public goods.

But Smith was also clearly alarmed by the "enormous debt of Great Britain" (*WN*, V.iii.61, p. 932) resulting from recent wars for acquiring new and defending old colonies and, above all, for preserving the mercantile interests associated with them, especially in North America. Smith conspicuously saw the crisis of the British Empire as a crisis of the Mercantilist system (Pincus 2012). While most readers of the *WN* focused on Book III and IV's presentation of the dire economic consequences of the Mercantilist system, Book V, especially chapter 3 of this book, which closes the *WN*, is crucial to understanding the ultimate, dramatic political consequences of that system: the ruin of the State and the downfall of the Empire, and thus was essential for Smith to gain the assent of his readers against the mercantile system. That this issue was dealt with at the very end of the entire book is no coincidence. As such, it was both the final point of Smith's "very violent attack against the commercial system of Great Britain" in *WN* and the last thought he left his readers with. And what is better to close a book than the hot topic of the day in his country? Smith clearly wanted to publicly take part in this debate (after having been a private advisor of several politicians) and to share with his readers, the point of view of a well-informed, impartial spectator on this topic.

Proposing an optimal and fair system of taxation based on "fiscal justice" by identifying "unjust," "oppressive," and "inconvenient" taxes, defining "proper" subjects of taxation (*WN*, V.iii.58, p. 928) and public expenditure, "more equal" taxes, and "distributing the weight of it more equally upon the whole" therefore became a fundamental issue for preserving the integrity, opulence, and sovereignty of the British Empire (*WN*, V.iii.67, p. 933). Great Britain desperately needed additional sources of revenue. Hence, Smith's project for a new British Empire was based on a union with American colonies, very likely inspired by the 1707 Act of Union between England and Scotland. In return for the payment of taxes and in proportion to the amount paid, the colonies would be granted—as Scotland had been—a number of seats in the British Parliament, and the monopoly of the colonial trade would also be abolished in line with the prescriptions of Smith's system of natural liberty. Therefore, his plan for a new British Empire was both the final point of his critique of the mercantile system *and* of his plea for the system of natural liberty.

Smith realized that the constitutional reforms he called for were unlikely to go through. The merchants and manufacturers who benefitted from the monopoly of the colonial trade owned the greatest share of public debt (*WN*, V.iii.7, p. 910; V.iii.35, p. 918), and were the principal advisors to legislators on these issues, would immediately oppose such changes as they would oppose the implementation of the system of natural liberty. Yet, even though he was realistic about the immediate implementability of what he considered the best solution (knowing the interests and prejudices and people and politicians on both sides of the Atlantic), Smith was determined to lay out preventative options to a course that was destined to lead to the failure of the British Empire.

These elements make the *WN* a very American and political book, as others have noted before (Fleischacker 2004). But we add, and have made the case above, that its purpose also affected the way it was structured and written, indeed very much in line with the rhetorical strategies that Smith had offered in his earlier work on rhetoric. Smith knew the opposition he would face from many legislators, statesmen, and merchants-manufacturers who were involved and quite influential in these debates. We thus tried to show in what way the sequencing of the

WN and the progressive critique of the mercantile system, finding its apogee in the project of Empire which closes the book, can be seen as a rhetorical answer to the hostile audience Smith knew he would face in writing a book criticizing the all-powerful merchant class and the legislators supporting their interests. Smith used what he referred to in his *LRBL* as the Socratick method of presentation, which is best suited to a presumably hostile and prejudiced readership, to make his case against this class. In doing so, his own theoretical insights on rhetoric proved essential. The reader discovers slowly, approaching the end, the unsavoury truth of the Mercantilist system whose principles had been applied across Europe and whose most serious threat is revealed in the final chapter of the *WN:* it will "in the long-run probably ruin all the great nations of Europe" (*WN,* V.iii.10, p. 911). The colonial policy of Great Britain was threatening the whole Empire. The future was in America, Smith understood. With or without Great Britain.

Acknowledgements This manuscript builds on previous work of the first author with S. J. Meardon. Ortmann & Meardon (1995) stressed the importance of acknowledging the rhetorical structure of Adam Smith's *The Wealth of Nations* and, around the same time, they wrote a related manuscript focusing on its rhetorical structure. The present manuscript is so distinct in arguments and supporting facts that S. J. Meardon felt it was not appropriate to still be listed as co-author. We appreciate his insightful comments on a recent version of the present manuscript. We also thank Tony Aspromourgos, Christopher Berry, Geoffrey Harcourt, Lisa Herzog, Gavin Kennedy, Nicholas Phillipson, Margaret Schabas, Vernon L. Smith, and the participants at the *History of Economic Thought Society* Australia conference 2015 for their feedback. The usual caveat applies. This chapter is an updated version of the version that we posted on ssrn on 28 December 28, 2018 at https://papers.ssrn.com/sol3/papers.cfm?abstract_id=3300236; we have not updated the 2018 version on ssrn because we refer to it in Ortmann, Walraevens, & Baranowski (2019) and because we like to document our thinking about these issues at that point.

References

Atiyah M (2006) Benjamin Franklin and the Edinburgh Enlightenment. Proc Am Philos Soc 150(4):591–606

Bazerman C (1993) Money Talks: The Rhetorical Project of Adam Smith's *Wealth of Nations*. In: Henderson W et al (eds) Economics and Language. Routledge, New York, pp 173–199

Benians E (1925) Adam Smith's Project of an Empire. Camb Hist J 1(3):249–283

Berry CJ, Paganelli MP, Smith C (eds) (2013) The Oxford Handbook of Adam Smith. Oxford University Press, Oxford

Bevilaqua C (1968) Adam Smith and Some Philosophical Origins of Eighteenth Century Rhetorical Theory. Mod Lang Rev 63(3):559–568

Brown V (1994) Adam Smith's Discourse: Canonicity, Commerce and Conscience. Routledge, New York

Bryce JC (1985 [1983]) Introduction to *Lectures on Rhetoric and Belles Lettres*. In: Smith (1985) pp 1–37

Chaplin JE (2006) The First Scientific American: Benjamin Franklin and the Pursuit of Genius. Basic Books, New York

Collings D, Ortmann A (1997) Review Essay: Vivienne Brown (1994), Adam Smith's Discourse: Canonicity, Commerce and Conscience. In: Biddle J, Samuels W (eds) Research in the History of Economic Thought and Methodology, vol 15. JAI Press, Stamford, pp 329–336

Dellemotte J (2002) Gravitation et sympathie. L'essai smithien d'application du modèle newtonien à la sphère sociale. Cahiers d'Economie Politique 42:49–74

Dellemotte J, Walraevens B (2015) Adam Smith on the Subordination of Wage-Earners in Commercial Societies. Eur J Hist Econ 22(4):692–727

Devine TM (2006) The Scottish Nation 1700–2007. Penguin Books, London

Diatkine D (2019) Adam Smith. La découverte du capitalisme et de ses limites, Seuil, Paris. English edition: Diatkine D (2021) Adam Smith and the Wealth of Nations: The Discovery of Capitalism and its Limits (trans: Diatkine D, Sowels N). Palgrave Macmillan

Dow S (2009) Knowledge, Communication and the Scottish Enlightenment. Revue de philosophie économique 10(2):1–23

Eliot TD (1924) The Relations between Adam Smith and Benjamin Franklin Before 1776. Political Sci Q 39(1):67–96

Endres A (1991) Adam Smith's rhetoric of economics: an illustration using 'smithian' compositional rules. Scott J Polit Econ 38(1):76–95

Evensky J (2016) *The Wealth of Nations*. In: Hanley R (ed) Adam Smith. His Life, Thought and Legacy. Princeton University Press, Princeton, pp 67–88

Flavell J (2010) When London Was the Capital of America. Yale University Press, New Haven

Fleischacker S (2002) Adam Smith's Reception among the American Founders, 1776–1790. William Mary Q 59:897–924

——— (2004) On Adam Smith's Wealth of Nations. Princeton University Press, Princeton

Gore DC (2011) Sophists and Sophistry in the *Wealth of Nations*. Philos Rhetor 44(1):1–26

Griswold C (1991) Rhetoric and Ethics: Adam Smith on Theorizing About the Moral Sentiments. Philos Rhetor 24(3):213–237

Hanley R (2009) Adam Smith and the Character of Virtue. Cambridge University Press, Cambridge

Herzog L (2013) The Community of Commerce: Smith's Rhetoric of Sympathy in the Opening of the *Wealth of Nations*. Philos Rhetor 46(1):65–87

Hill L (2021) Adam Smith as Political Problem Solver. The 'Project of an Empire' and the American War of Independence. Adam Smith Rev 12:183–202

Hont I (2005) Jealousy of Trade: International Competition and the Nation State in Historical Perspective. Cambridge University Press, Cambridge

——— (2015) Politics in Commercial Society: Jean-Jacques Rousseau and Adam Smith. Harvard University Press, Cambridge

Howell S (1975) Adam Smith's Lectures on Rhetoric: An Historical Assessment. In: Skinner A, Wilson T (eds) Essays in honour of Adam Smith. Oxford University Press, Oxford, pp 11–43

Hume D (1986 [1777]) Essays: Moral, Political and Literary. Liberty Fund, Indianapolis

Kellow G (2011) Things Familiar to the Mind: Heuristic Style and Elliptical Citation in the *Wealth of Nations*. Hist Hum Sci 24(1):1–18

Kennedy (2008) Adam Smith: A Moral Philosopher and His Political Economy. Palgrave Macmillan, New York

——— (2017) An Authentic Account of Adam Smith. Palgrave Macmillan, London

Longaker MG (2014) Adam Smith on Rhetoric and Phronesis, Law and Economics. Philos Rhetor 47(1):25–47

McKenna S (2005) Adam Smith: the Rhetoric of Propriety. State University of New York Press, New York

——— (2016) Adam Smith and Rhetoric. In: Hanley R (ed) Adam Smith. His Life, Thought and Legacy. Princeton University Press, Princeton, p 387–404

Meardon SJ, Ortmann A (1996a) Self-Command in Adam Smith's Theory of Moral Sentiments: A Game-Theoretic Re-Interpretation. Ration Soc 8(1):57–80

——— (1996b) Yes, Adam Smith was an Economist (A Very Modern One Indeed). Reply to Brown. Ration Soc 8(3):348–352

Montes L (2019) Adam Smith's Foundational Idea of Sympathetic Persuasion. Camb J Econ 43(1):1–15

Morrison JA (2012) Before Hegemony: Adam Smith, American Independence, and the Origins of the First Era of Globalization. Int Organ 66(3):395–428

Muller J (1993) Adam Smith in his time and ours. Princeton University Press, Princeton

Ortmann A (1997) How to Survive in Postindustrial Environments: Adam Smith's Advice for Today's Colleges and Universities. J Higher Educ 68(5):483–501

——— (1999) The Nature and Causes of Corporate Negligence, Sham Lectures, and Ecclesiastical Indolence: Adam Smith on Joint-Stock Companies, Teachers, and Preachers. Hist Polit Econ 31(2):297–315

Ortmann A, Meardon SJ (1995) A game-theoretic re-evaluation of Adam Smith's Theory of Moral Sentiments and Wealth of Nations. In: Rima IH (ed) The Classical Tradition in Economic Thought. Perspectives on the History of Economic Thought Vol XI. Edward Elgar, Brookfield, pp 43–61

Ortmann A, Walraevens B (2012) Adam Smith, Philosopher and Man of the World. Review of Gavin Kennedy (2008) Adam Smith: A Moral Philosopher and His Political Economy, and Nicholas Phillipson (2010) Adam Smith, An Enlightened Life. Hist Econ Ideas, 20(1):185–191

——— (2021) Adam Smith's Reasoning Routines and the Deep Structure of his Oeuvre. Working Paper: https://papers.ssrn.com/sol3/papers.cfm?abstract_id=3992914

Ortmann A, Walraevens B, Baranowski D (2019) Schumpeter's Assessment of Adam Smith and 'The Wealth of Nations': Why He Got It Wrong. J Hist Econ Thought 41(4):531–551

Pack S J (1991) Capitalism as a Moral System. Adam Smith's Critique of the Free Market economy. Edward Elgar Publishing, Aldershot

Paganelli MP (2010) The Moralizing Role of Distance in Adam Smith: The Theory of Moral Sentiments as Possible Praise of Commerce. Hist Polit Econ 42(3):425–441

Peaucelle J-L (2012) Rhetoric and Logic in Smith's Description of the Division of Labour. Eur J Hist Econ Thought 19(2):385–404

Phillipson N (2010) Adam Smith: An Enlightened Life. Yale University Press, New Haven

——— (2013) Adam Smith: A Biographer's Reflections. In: Berry CJ, Paganelli MP, Smith C (eds) The Oxford Handbook of Adam Smith. Oxford University Press, Oxford, pp 23–35

Pincus S (2012) Rethinking Mercantilism: Political Economy, the British Empire, and the Atlantic World in the Seventeenth and Eighteenth Centuries. William Mary Q 69(1):3–34

Rae J (1895) Life of Adam Smith. Macmillan, London. Available via Econlib. http://www.econlib.org/library/YPDBooks/Rae/raeLSCover.html. Accessed 28 Jan 2022

Rasmussen DC (2017) The Infidel and the Professor: David Hume, Adam Smith, and the Friendship that Shaped Modern Thought. Princeton University Press, Princeton

Rosen S (1987) Some Economics of Teaching. J Labor Econ 5:561–575

Ross IS (2010) The Life of Adam Smith, 2nd edn. Oxford University Press, Oxford

Salber Philips M (2006) Adam Smith, Belletrist. In: Haakonssen K (ed) The Cambridge Companion to Adam Smith. Cambridge University Press, Cambridge, pp 57–78

Simiqueli RR (2017) Apoikia and Colonia: Smith's Comments on the 'Recent Disturbances' in the Colonies. Adam Smith Rev 9:19–37

Skinner AS (1996) A System of Social Science: Papers Relating to Adam Smith, 2nd edn. Clarendon Press, Oxford

Smith A[62] (*CL*), Considerations Concerning the First Formation of Languages, pp 201–226 in *LRBL*

——— (*Corr*), Correspondence of Adam Smith. Mossner E, Ross I (eds) (1987) Liberty Classics, Indianapolis (Glasgow edition: 1977)

——— (*EPS*), Essays on Philosophical Subjects. Wightman W, Bryce J, Ross I (eds) (1982). Liberty Classics, Indianapolis, pp 269–351 (Corresponding Glasgow edition: 1980)

——— (*HA*), The Principles which lead and direct Philosophical Enquiries Illustrated by the History of Astronomy, pp 33–105 in EPS

——— (*LJ*), Smith A (*LJ*), Lectures on Jurisprudence. Meek RL, Raphael DD, Stein PG (eds) (1982a). Liberty Classics, Indianapolis (Corresponding Glasgow edition: 1978)

——— (*LRBL*), Lectures on Rhetoric and Belles Lettres. Bryce JC, Skinner AS (eds) (1985) Liberty Classics, Indianapolis (Corresponding Glasgow edition: 1983)

——— (*TMS*), The Theory of Moral Sentiments. Raphael DD, Macfie AL (eds) (1982b). Liberty Classics, Indianapolis (Corresponding Glasgow edition: 1976)

——— (*WN*), An Inquiry into the Nature and Causes of the Wealth of Nations. Campbell RH, Skinner AS (eds) (1981). Liberty Classics, Indianapolis (Corresponding Glasgow edition: 1976)

Stewart D (1982) [1795] Account of the Life and Writings of Adam Smith, LL.D. In: Smith A (EPS) Essays on Philosophical Subjects. Wightman W, Bryce J, Ross I (eds). Liberty Classics, Indianapolis, pp 269–351

Swearingen CJ (2013) Adam Smith on Language and Rhetoric: The Ethics of Style, Character, and Propriety. In: Berry CJ, Paganelli MP, Smith C (eds)

[62] We follow in our reference to Smith's work what has emerged as standard convention (abbreviations such as *CL*, *Corr.*, *EPS*, *HA*, and so on). We refer to the Liberty version of the Glasgow edition of Smith's oeuvre. Typically the Liberty version were available a few years later, so we also indicated the original publication date of the corresponding Glasgow edition.

The Oxford Handbook of Adam Smith. Oxford University Press, Oxford, pp 159–174

Teichgraeber R (1987) 'Less Abused than I had Reason to Expect': The Reception of *The Wealth of Nations* in Britain, 1776-90. Hist J 30(2):337–366

Van de Haar E (2013) Adam Smith on Empire and International Relations. In: Berry CJ, Paganelli MP, Smith C (eds) The Oxford Handbook of Adam Smith. Oxford University Press, Oxford, pp 417–442

Walraevens B (2010) Adam Smith's Economics and the Lectures on Rhetoric and Belles Lettres: The Language of Commerce. Hist Econ Ideas 18(1):11–32

——— (2017) Jealousy of Trade in Hume and Smith. Hist Econ Ideas 25(2):11–36

Winch D (2013) The Political Economy of Empire. Keynote Address Presented at Charles Gide Association Symposium on 'les economistes et les colonies', Martinique, November 2013

CHAPTER 3

Self-Command in Adam Smith's Theory of Moral Sentiments: A Game-Theoretic Reinterpretation

Stephen J. Meardon and Andreas Ortmann

1 Introduction

The *New York Times*[1] reported that former tennis star John McEnroe has now taken up art dealing. In addition to documenting McEnroe's new professional tribulations, the reporter made the following personal observations:

> When he talks it is easy to feel his pent-up energy. His speech is quick, his concentration intense. *The demons that have exploded on the court still lurk within, but age and experience seem to have taught him control.*

[1] Emphasis added. *The New York Times*, 27 March 1994, Section 9, pp. I, 8.

The original version of this chapter was revised: Chapter author name in this chapter has been corrected. The correction to this chapter is available at https://doi.org/10.1007/978-3-030-99704-5_9

A. Ortmann and B. Walraevens, *Adam Smith's System*, Palgrave Studies in the History of Economic Thought,
https://doi.org/10.1007/978-3-030-99704-5_3

The self-command that McEnroe seems to have learned was acquired only after a lengthy, and often losing, struggle. That struggle is universal and timeless; Adam Smith (1982 [1759]) analyzed it in his *Theory of Moral Sentiments* (*TMS*) and discussed its importance to society. Smith considered both the evolution of society's general rules of morality (How did we get the notion that court-side tantrums are bad?) and the difficulties in a person's decision to violate or to respect those rules (Why, for most of his life up to now, did McEnroe decide to throw tantrums anyway? Why has he now apparently stopped?).

Elsewhere (Ortmann and Meardon 1995a) we have addressed Smith's ideas on the origin and evolution of the general rules of morality. Here we take the general rules as given, and are concerned only with the decision to violate or respect them. Our reading of Smith's work shows he believed this decision is made rationally; he expressed it as a struggle between two calculating inner selves with different preferences over psychic and emotional payoffs. Specifically, our reinterpretation of *TMS* in the following pages shows that Smith's theory of self-command can be modeled as an asymmetric game whose structure is identical to "endogenous quality" or "reputation" games in the game theory literature (Kreps 1990). Reviewing *TMS* in this light is useful for two broad purposes:

First, to better understand the explanatory power and limits of an asymmetric, intrapersonal, rational-choice model of self-command. To this end, we contrast our model with earlier efforts to model selfcommand that explicitly or implicitly use symmetric "prisoner's dilemma"-type games. Framing self-command in *TMS* as an asymmetric, intrapersonal, rational-choice model places Smith's theory in the company of computational theories of action and offers new insights about the relation between altruism and self-interest. Our finding is that one need not incorporate any concept of altruism into an explanation of why and how individuals practice self-command; self-command can be explained sufficiently in terms of self-interest and rational choice.

Second, to better understand Smith as an early theorist capable of employing the conceptual tools inherent in such a model. In this and related papers, we show how throughout Smith's work, one finds pervasive concern with issues of information asymmetry, strategic interaction, and reputational enforcement[2]—precisely the same concerns shared by

[2] Ortmann and Meardon (1995b) provides an overview of this paper and Ortmann and Meardon (1993, 1995a). The latter two papers bring similar game-theoretic approaches to bear on the evolution of the general rules of morality in *The Theory of Moral Sentiments* and problems of public goods provision and externalities in *The Wealth of Nations*.

modem game-theorists and current practitioners of many other fields.[3] Our game-theoretic reinterpretation also illustrates that Smith's work contains the same tension that has led to the eductive and evolutive approaches to non-cooperative game theory Binmore 1990).

Remarkably, whereas these two approaches are often viewed as conflicting, our reinterpretation shows that Smith used them as complements.

Two points must be stressed from the beginning:

1. We distinguish sharply between the individual's decision of action and his understanding that one act is "right" while the other is "wrong." Smith wrote that "it is altogether absurd and unintelligible to suppose that the first perceptions of right and wrong can be derived from reason" (1982, 320). The model presumes the *decision* to act rightly or wrongly is made rationally; but Smith did not claim, nor do we claim, that the individual's *conception* of right and wrong is necessarily the product of his reasoning.
2. When we eventually point toward an equilibrium where self-command is indeed attained (like McEnroe's present conduct the individual acts "rightly"), we do not deny the possibility of a person acting passionately, impulsively or otherwise "wrongly." Such actions—McEnroe's past actions—can and do happen. What cannot happen is the emergence of an equilibrium where a person engages consistently in such actions while deceiving himself about their impropriety. Once age and experience have taught us well to distinguish right from wrong, departures from right behavior will seldomly—though still occasionally—be made.

This chapter is organized as follows: first, based on an analysis of Smith's five classes of passions, we discuss the nature of payoffs to be received in the intrapersonal game of self-command. Next we complete the formalization of the game by presenting the players and their choice sets, and by quantifying their payoffs. We then show that the resulting game is an endogenous quality or reputation model whose mechanics and insights are well-documented in the game-theory literature. Finally,

[3] From modern micro-economic theory (Holmstroem and Tirole 1989; Tirole 1988; Kreps 1990) to modern macro-economic policy (Barro 1990) and the political economy of institutions and decisions (Ostrom 1990).

we comment on other related discourses, including some relevant experimental evidence.

2 Passions, Passive Feelings, and Active Principles

According to Smith, self-command is the practice of using "active principles" to moderate one's actions when the "passive feelings" that would motivate them are too strong, too violent, or would otherwise compel one to act inappropriately. Active principles and passive feelings consist of different classes of passions Smith identifies the five classes of "original passions" in part I, section II of *TMS*[4]; in order of discussion, they are:

1. *"Passions which take their origin from the body"*: Smith names hunger and sexual appetite-"naturally the most furious of all passions" (1982, 28), as well as pain.
2. *"Passions which take their origin from a particular turn or habit of the Imagination"*: Smith names love, disappointment in love and "secondary passions… which arise from the situation of love" (1982, 33).
3. *"Unsocial Passions"*: Smith quotes "hatred and resentment, with all their different modifications" (1982, 34) as prime examples. These, too, are derived from the imagination.
4. *"Social Passions"*: Smith names "generosity, humanity, kindness, compassion, mutual friendship and esteem, all the social and benevolent affections,.." (1982, 38). Later (1982, 163) Smith adds politeness, justice, truth, chastity, fidelity etc., to the list.
5. *"Selfish Passions"*: Smith lists "grief and joy, when conceived upon account of our private good or bad fortune" (1982, 40).

Passive feelings are the passions which we can't easily control, which are felt almost mechanically, and which in themselves motivate actions: the bodily passions, imaginative passions, selfish passions, and, most importantly for our purposes, the unsocial passions such as hatred and resentment. By contrast, active principles consist of the social passions

[4] Passions are sensations, feelings, or emotions—Smith often uses these terms synonymously—that are excited by some external action or occurrence.

(such as generosity and compassion). Since these passions are generated by will and may thus have an underlying motive, they are of a very different nature from those representing passive feelings.

The relationship between the discussions of passive feelings and active principles (1982, 137), on the one hand, and the five classes of passions (1982, 27–43), on the other, may have remained widely unrecognized due to their separation in the text by 100 pages. Yet by emphasizing the willfulness of the social passions, the distinction between passive feelings and active principles is critical in laying the groundwork for an intrapersonal, rational-choice model of self-command.

> When our passive feelings are almost always so sordid and selfish, how comes it that our active principles should often be so generous and so noble? . . . It is not the soft power of humanity, it is not that feeble spark of benevolence which Nature has lighted up in the human heart, that is thus capable of counteracting the strongest impulses of self-love. It is a stronger power, a more forcible motive, which asserts itself upon such occasions. It is reason, principle, conscience, the inhabitant of the breast, the man within, the great judge and arbiter of our conduct. It is not the love of our neighbor, it is not the love of mankind, which upon many occasions prompts us to the practice of those divine virtues. It is a stronger love, a more powerful affection, which generally takes place upon such occasions; the love of what is honourable and noble, of the grandeur, and dignity, and superiority of our characters. (1982, 137)

Note carefully: Smith tells us that "It is *not* the soft power of humanity, it is *not* that feeble spark of benevolence.... It is *not* the love of our neighbor, it is *not* the love of mankind ..." which motivates us to act properly. Rather, it is "reason, principle, conscience ..." We cannot do much about most of our passions, our passive feelings. It is human nature to feel even the worst of them. We *can* do something about our actions, however. Though we may feel pulled by urgent desires, reason often tells us that it would not be in our interest to follow them; we would incur a high cost, we would sacrifice "the superiority of our characters," if we did. In such cases we must rely on our active principles in order to resist our short-run impulses, thereby bringing us the long-run payoffs of "grandeur" and "dignity."

In a person's struggle to master his passive feelings with active principles lies the key to the game-theoretic model of Smith's theory of self-command. Smith specifies an incentive problem: the trade-off between the psychic and emotional payoffs of acting according to one's passive feelings, versus those of using one's active principles. Implicit is the assumption of rational (self-interested) decision-making. As we shall see, Smith also specifies the "players" and their choice sets. First, however, we can further refine our understanding of the payoffs.

3 Praise-Worthiness and Blame-Worthiness, and How to Extract Them

The "love of ... the grandeur, and dignity, and superiority of our characters" is, at a more basic level, the love of the feeling of praise-worthiness that accompanies knowing we have such characters. According to Smith (1982, 114), people practice self-command to obtain feelings of self-approbation, or praise-worthiness, and to avoid feelings of self-disapprobation, or blame-worthiness.

Praise-worthiness and blame-worthiness are social constructs; the general rules of morality—or moral standards—that determine what is praise-worthy, and what is blame-worthy, evolve through repeated social interaction among many people.[5] However, just as a firm with small market share has a negligible role in determining market price, each individual plays a negligible role in defining society's moral standards. We can thus simplify the model of the individual's decision to obey or violate them by taking the standards themselves as given.

To take the moral standards as given, however, is entirely different from taking any individual's understanding of them as given. How, then, does one come to understand what is praise-worthy and what is blame-worthy? It is by observing the passions of others as they are triggered by external actions and occurrences that one learns the general rules of morality.

Studying the passions of others is a problem in itself, however. Passions are unobservable; what we observe in others are the expressions of those passions, which may come in the form of words, gestures, or actions. Thus the observer who would try to take note of another person's passions

[5] Few of the general rules of morality are ever put in writing—they are informal rules learned by similar example, based on an implicit understanding of what is proper and improper. Morality, for the most part, cannot be legislated for the same reason that high quality of goods cannot be legislated-third-party enforcement costs are simply too high. It is the common knowledge and general acceptance of general rules which constitutes the social fabric; without it, society could not exist.

in order to better understand the general rules faces a signal extraction problem; a person must use his imagination to try to understand another's passions.

> As we have no immediate experience of what other men feel, we can form no idea of the manner in which they are affected, but by conceiving what we ourselves should feel in the like situation. Though our brother is upon the rack, as long as we ourselves are at ease, our senses will never inform us of what he suffers. They never did, and never can, carry us beyond our own person, and it is by the imagination only that we can form any conception of what are his sensations. (Smith 1982, 9)
>
> ... it is by changing places in fancy with the sufferer, that we come either to conceive or to be affected by what he feels ... (Smith 1982, 10)

This, then, is how we solve the signal extraction problem and learn the rules of morality. After the match in which McEnroe threw his racket at the ballboy and heard a loud and unanimous "boo" from the crowd, he may have taken a moment to imagine himself in the place of a person in the grandstand. Observing such an action from her point of view would have disgusted him, too—he might even have been inclined to "boo" himself. He then knew (though he may have figured it out at a much earlier age) that "booing" signifies disgust, and throwing one's racket at people is improper behavior. By the same process, hearing the crowd applaud as he bowed toward Princess Diana after losing his first Wimbledon championship final, he may have determined that the applause signified appreciation, and exceptional courtesy toward royalty is proper behavior. This process of "finding in a vast variety of instances that one tenor of conduct constantly pleases in a certain manner, and that another as constantly displeases the mind" (Smith 1982, 320) is how we adopt the general rules that guide our behavior.

Once we know the rules of morality, in order to accrue the payoffs of praise-worthiness or blame-worthiness, we need to know both before and after we act whether our action will be or was in harmony with the rules. In these cases, we use a similar method as we used to learn the rules, with one difference: instead of imagining ourselves in the place of a real observer (who might have a bias that would invalidate her judgment), we pretend to be in the place of a purely imaginary, impartial one. Smith calls this imaginary viewer we create and consult to judge our own conduct the "impartial spectator," "the man within the breast," or simply "the man within"; it is his voice that tells us whether our behavior has been praise-worthy or blame-worthy (1982, 130–131).

If we succeed in being praise-worthy, and avoid being blame-worthy, then we have tempered our passive feelings with active principles—we have by way of reasoning internalized society's rules of conduct:

> The man of real constancy and firmness, the wise and just man who has been thoroughly bred in the great school of self-command, in the bustle and business of the world, exposed, perhaps, to the violence and injustice of faction, and to the hardships and hazards of war, maintains this control of his passive feelings upon all occasions; and whether in solitude or in society, wears nearly the same countenance, and is affected very nearly in the same manner. He has never dared to forget for one moment the judgement which the impartial spectator would pass upon his sentiments and conduct. He has never dared to suffer the man within the breast to be absent one moment from his attention. With the eyes of this great inmate he has always been accustomed to regard whatever relates to himself. This habit has become perfectly familiar to him. He has been in the constant practice, and, indeed, under the constant necessity, of modelling, or of endeavouring to model, not only his outward conduct and behaviour, but, as much as he can, even his inward sentiments and feelings, according to those of this awful and respectable judge. He does not merely affect the sentiments of the impartial spectator. He really adopts them. (Smith 1982, 146–147)

Smith was quite aware, however, that the knowledge of when and how to use the active principles is not instilled perfectly in every person. Such knowledge implies a reasonable ability to gauge present and future trade-offs that is obtained over time, perhaps with great effort or many instances of trial and error. For example, "A very young child has no self-command," Smith wrote. But as it ages the child "enters into the great school of self-command, it studies to be more and more master of itself, and begins to exercise over its own feelings a discipline which the practice of the longest life is very seldom sufficient to bring to complete perfection" (1982, 145).

Nor can people who lack "real constancy and firmness," and who have not "been thoroughly bred in the great school of self-command," gauge the relevant trade-offs. By making these qualifications, Smith addresses the important issue of the opportunity cost of rational, foresightful behavior.[6] A person who has not yet learned well the lessons of the "great school" will perceive a lower opportunity cost of acting improperly. Furthermore, opportunity costs may vary for different people of similar ages and past experiences depending on the particularities of their social or occupational contexts.

In sum, as a person ages and learns to practice self-command, blameworthy behavior will occur less frequently—but "even the practice of the longest life" (Smith 1982, 145) is unlikely to avoid it altogether. Smith thus explains why McEnroe has mellowed with age; he also suggests that while restraint might usually be expected hereafter, a few minor tantrums may yet lie ahead.

4 Modeling Self-Command

To model "the constant necessity, of modeling, or of endeavouring to model, not only his outward conduct and behaviour, but, as much as he can, even his inward sentiments and feelings" (Smith 1982, 147), Smith suggested that the problem consists of two different "selves" seeking satisfaction: the Man Today and the Man Tomorrow, or (as we shall use) the Man Yesterday and the Man Today. In each case, he talks first about the man who is inflamed by passion and is about to act, and then about the man who must afterward face the consequences of that action.

> The man of to-day is no longer agitated by the same passions which distracted the man of yesterday: and when the paroxysm of emotion, in the same manner as when the paroxysm of distress, is fairly over, we can identify ourselves, as it were, with the ideal man within the breast, ... (Smith 1982, 157–158)

The Man Today exists both as real person after the Man Yesterday, and as imaginary construct within the mind of the Man Yesterday. Smith makes clear that even as the Man Yesterday is in the midst of the most furious unsocial passions, "his own mind forebodes" (p. 161) the consequences of succumbing to them. This notion of the imaginary construct allows us to downplay the intertemporal aspect of the Man Yesterday and the Man Today.

[6] For an interesting argument along these lines, see also Smith (1937 [1776], 669–670 and 674).

Smith models this intrapersonal struggle as a binary choice game.[7] The Man Yesterday has the two options of acting "properly" or "improperly," of allowing himself or not allowing himself to be distracted by passions or paroxysms of emotion and distress. The Man Today's options are to evaluate the Man Yesterday's actions either "routinely" or "really" (at high emotional cost). As we will show presently, the scenario lends itself naturally to a 2 X 2 strategic form game matrix in which the Man Yesterday is the row player and the Man Today is the column player.

Following Smith's example, we base the Man Yesterday's payoffs on the voice of the Man Today inside the mind of the Man Yesterday, and the Man Yesterday's eagerness to succumb to his passions. The Man Today's payoffs come also from the internal voice, but do not include rewards for passionate action, and include in addition rewards for atonement that come only to the sequentially existent Man Today and thus are not considered by the Man Yesterday. Thus, on the one hand, we allow the Man Yesterday to feel distressed by what he does even as he feels the satisfaction of succumbing to passion; and, on the other, we allow the Man Today to be a distinctly separate player with payoffs that are not entirely subsumed by those of the Man Yesterday.

In particular, payoffs come in four components: blame-worthiness, passion, praise-worthiness, and atonement. The players' payoffs are built from different subsets of the four components. Both the Man Yesterday and the Man Today incur the cost of feeling blame-worthy, but only the Man Yesterday is rewarded by the passionate yet improper action that causes feelings of blame-worthiness. Both the Man Yesterday and the Man Today are rewarded with feelings of praise-worthiness, but only the Man Today can be rewarded with the particular kind of praiseworthiness that accompanies atonement (the real evaluation of an improper action). The numerical cost or reward associated with each of the four components may vary (in consistent manner) cell-by-cell, but the following rules always hold:

1. Blame-worthiness is a cost borne equally by both players.
2. Praise-worthiness is a reward granted equally to both players.

[7] Two-sided simultaneous-move intrapersonal prisoner's dilemma games have been modeled and defended by Kavka (1991, 1993), among others. Modeling the acquisition of self-command as a one-sided simultaneous-move intrapersonal prisoner's dilemma can be justified theoretically on the same grounds.

3. Passionate action is a reward granted only to the Man Yesterday.
4. Atonement for passionate action is a reward granted only to the Man Today.

On our way to the strategic game form, Matrix 1, we next discuss cell-by-cell the construction of payoffs. We let the Man Yesterday be the row player: the proper action is his first row choice and the improper action is his second row choice. The Man Today will be the column player: the routine evaluation is his first column choice and the real evaluation is his second column choice. To structure the discussion, we consider the payoff cells in order of the Man Today's choice, examining each of the two possible outcomes of that choice depending upon the choice of the Man Yesterday. We can do so moving clockwise around the payoff matrix, beginning with the upper-right comer; thus we start off in the context of the Man Today's real evaluation, and finish with his routine evaluation. In each cell, we bear in mind the example of McEnroe and the ballboy as one possible illustration of the cell's scenario.

5 Real Evaluation

> At the very time of acting, at the moment in which passion mounts the highest, he hesitates and trembles at the thought of what he is about to do: he is secretly conscious to himself that he is breaking through those measures of conduct which, in all his cool hours, he had resolved never to infringe, which he had never seen infringed by others without the highest disapprobation, and of which the infringement, his own mind forebodes, must soon render him the object of the same disagreeable sentiments. Before he can take the last fatal resolution, he is tormented with all the agonies of doubt and uncertainty; he is terrified at the thought of violating so sacred a rule, and at the same time is urged and goaded on by the fury of his desires to violate it. (Smith 1982, 161)

5.1 Proper Action

Despite his fury, McEnroe decides not to attack the ballboy—and as Dick Enberg interviews him after the match, he can think of little else but what a good sport he is for having restrained himself (That little else he does think of is that a true sportsman would be thinking of something more sportsman-like.)

If the Man Yesterday acts properly, the real evaluation Smith describes in the above quotation is wasted effort. There is some reward to feeling good about oneself, but it is balanced by the cost of evaluating. One might think of the cost of this evaluation as a dose of blame-worthiness accompanying feelings of praise-worthiness: praise worthiness because the action of the Man Yesterday is found to be proper; blame-worthiness because to carefully evaluate a proper action is to knowingly indulge oneself in vanity.

The real evaluation of the proper action:

> costs both players (-1) for blame-worthiness;
> rewards both players (+1) for praise-worthiness;
> rewards the Man Yesterday (0) for succumbing to passion;
> rewards the Man Today (0) for atonement.

5.2 Improper Action

McEnroe attacks the ballboy, and during the interview repents in tears before a captive national audience.

If the Man Yesterday acts improperly, the real evaluation is illustrated by "[m]en of the most detestable character, who, in the execution of the most dreadful crimes, had taken their measures so coolly as to avoid even the suspicion of guilt" (Smith 1982, 118), but who nevertheless confess their crimes. They do so because they have made a real evaluation of an improper action; in doing so, they feel terrible for what they have done, but they also feel praise-worthy for evaluating the action and thereby atoning for their crimes. Again, for both players the costs of this evaluation and the benefits may balance each other.

Smith explains the Man Today's payoff for atonement as follows:

> By acknowledging their guilt, by submitting themselves to the resentment of their offended fellow-citizens, and, by thus satiating that vengeance of which they were sensible that they had become the proper objects, they hoped ... to reconcile themselves, at least in their own imagination, to the natural sentiments of mankind, to be able to consider themselves as less worthy of hatred and resentment; to atone, in some measure, for their crimes; ... (1982, 118–119)

The real evaluation of the improper action:

costs both players (- 3) for blame-worthiness;
rewards both players (0) for praise-worthiness;
rewards the Man Yesterday (+3) for succumbing to passion;
rewards the Man Today (+3) for atonement.

6 Routine Evaluation

It is so disagreeable to think ill of ourselves, that we often purposely turn away our view from those circumstances which might render that judgment unfavorable....Rather than see our own behaviour under so disagreeable an aspect, we too often, foolishly and weakly, endeavour to exasperate anew those unjust passions which had formerly misled us; we endeavour by artifice to awaken our old hatreds, and irritate afresh our almost forgotten resentments; we even exert ourselves for this miserable purpose, and thus persevere in injustice, merely because we once were unjust, and because we are ashamed and afraid to see that we were so. (Smith 1982, 158)

6.1 Improper Action

McEnroe attacks the ballboy, and kids himself that 'it could have happened to anyone'.

If the Man Yesterday acts improperly, the routine evaluation does not involve enough honest introspection to admit wrongdoing. In this case, a routine evaluation is effectively an act of self-deceit, which minimizes—but does not eliminate—the feelings of blame-worthiness borne by both players.

The routine evaluation of the improper action:

costs both players (-1) for blame-worthiness;
rewards both players (0) for praise-worthiness;
rewards the Man Yesterday (+3) for succumbing to passion;
rewards the Man Today (0) for atonement.

6.2 Proper Action

McEnroe doesn't attack the ballboy; not only is he entirely aware of the emotional payoffs of venting Juror versus practicing restraint, but he is well-accustomed and eager to experience the lasting contentment of knowing he behaved well and can continue to do so.

If the Man Yesterday acts properly, the routine evaluation is illustrated by "the man of real constancy and firmness" we met earlier. The "habit" of evaluating his behavior "has become perfectly familiar to him" (Smith 1982, 146–147). With little thought or effort, he has determined the Man Yesterday's actions to be proper.

The routine evaluation of the proper action:

costs both players (0) for blame-worthiness;
rewards both players (+1) for praise-worthiness;
rewards the Man Yesterday (0) for succumbing to passion;
rewards the Man Today (0) for atonement.

Aggregating the payoffs just suggested, Smith's game of self-command can be represented as follows[8]:

Matrix 1. The game of self-command

		Man Today	
		routine	real
Man Yesterday	proper	1, 1	0, 0
	improper	2, -1	0, 0

[8] Note that for the Man Yesterday, the proper choice is associated with praiseworthiness and the improper choice is associated with blame-worthiness; for the Man Today, the diagonal entries are associated with praise-worthiness and the off-diagonal entries are associated with blame-worthiness. The upper-left cell lies at the inter section of praise-worthy choices for both players; this cell represents respect for the general rules of morality. The lower-left cell lies at the intersection of blame-worthy choices for both players and defines the breakdown in social fabric. As Smith tells us, the "very existence of human society" depends upon the game's outcome gravitating toward the upper-left cell (1982, 163). Such gravitation is the evolutionary bedrock upon which rests the period-by-period calculation in the game of self-command.

If the payoffs seem arbitrary, consider that we are not trying to quantify precisely the psychological costs and benefits of succumbing to passion and practicing self-command. We simply attempt to provide some intuition for possible parameterizations. The preceding explanation of payoff cells suggests an intuitive story, faithful to Smith's text that underlies the payoffs in a game form representing the main features of his model.

The parameterization derived in the previous pages of the game played between the Man Yesterday (the row player) and the Man Today (the column player) turns out to be structurally identical to an endogenous quality or reputation game where the row player (the agent) can choose high quality or low quality and the column player (the principal) can choose between monitoring or not monitoring. Such games have been extensively studied in the game theory literature. The parameterization in Matrix 1 can be found, for example, in Kreps (1990) and Rasmusen (1989).[9] Its key feature is that the row player (Man Yesterday or agent) has a weakly dominant strategy (improper or low effort). Making standard assumptions of individual rationality and common knowledge, such a situation would lead the column player (Man Today or principal) to choose the real evaluation or monitoring option. In a one-shot game, then, game theory would predict the Nash equilibrium for the lower right cell of the payoff matrix—an outcome that is not Pareto optimal.

Of course, as we have documented, the game played between the Man Yesterday and the Man Today is a repeated game. It is a well-established result in the game theory literature (Kreps 1990, 65–77) that the outcome of an endogenous quality or reputation game depends crucially on how often it is played. Specifically, for reasonably low rates of time preference, it is easy to show that a Nash equilibrium of an indefinitely repeated game may give a result that is Pareto optimal.

Consider what the row player must be thinking if the current game is indefinitely repeated: he is still faced with a choice between proper and improper behavior, but he now has to assess the payoff gains of such behavior *over an indefinite period of time*. Assuming both players use a

[9] A closely related parameterization can be found in Friedman (1991) and Pitchik and Schotter (1987). Their parameterization leads to a mixed strategy equilibrium in one-shot games. If monitoring costs are high and the temptation to provide low quality is strong, the mixed-strategy Nash equilibrium will approach the one to be identified presently.

trigger strategy,[10] the row player knows that if he chooses to receive the initially high payoff of 2 units by choosing "improper" while the column player chooses "routine," he will forever after receive the low payoff of zero when the column player catches on in the next round and plays "real" (and continues to do so in all future rounds). Each player must weigh not only the payoffs in the current round, but the sum of all payoffs in future rounds as well. Formally, the payoff considerations for the row player are represented by:

$$1. \sum_{i=1}^{\infty}\left(\frac{1}{(1+r)^{i-1}}\right) > 2 + \sum_{i=2}^{\infty}\left(\frac{0}{(1+r)^{i-1}}\right)$$

These payoff considerations may be reduced to:

$$2. \ 1 + \frac{1}{r} > 2$$

The short-term rewards of passionate action are a pittance relative to the long-term sacrifice of payoffs. The threat of losing the series of payoffs for proper behavior may very well prevent the row player from engaging in improper behavior. In shifting the players' awareness of the game from one-shot to indefinitely repeated, a new Nash equilibrium emerges.

The reader may object that the assumption of trigger strategies, and hence the model, is unrealistic. We agree that the assumption of trigger strategies is unrealistic—but it is a simplifying assumption only, and can be relaxed. The folk theorem suggests there are numerous Nash equilibrium strategies in the indefinitely repeated game, many of which are Pareto optimal. Furthermore, most such strategies typically allow occasional departures from praise-worthy (proper, routine) behavior. The prediction of game theory in the indefinitely repeated case of our game—*especially* when the assumption of trigger strategies is relaxed—is thus consistent with Smith's theory of self-command, which allows even "the man of real constancy and firmness" to slip up now and then. In equilibrium, the

[10] Meaning that the row player will react to the column player's choice of "real" by choosing "improper" forever afterward, and similarly the column player will react to the row player's choice of "improper" by forever choosing "real." In this way, the column player protects himself from any future damaging (improper, routine) outcomes; he also punishes the row player, denying him the higher payoffs he could earn from (proper, routine) or (improper, routine) outcomes.

discipline imposed by concern for long-term payoffs of praise-worthiness makes such slip-ups the exceptions rather than the rule.

The trade-off between short-term and long-term payoffs is the punchline of a rich class of models representing phenomena as varied as (asymmetrically structured) seller–buyer transactions of goods of adjustable quality or employee–employer relations ("reputation games"), or (symmetrically structured) price competition between oligopolists, attempts at collusion, and problems of public goods provision and externalities ("hawk-dove games"), to mention a few. Note that an outside observer, watching any single one of the indefinitely repeated encounters of players with these payoffs, might come to the conclusion that the players are "altruistic" and not out for their self-interests when in fact they are.

To postulate, as Smith and we do, that self-command is selfinterested in the sense of concern for long-term emotional payoffs, is not without controversy, though. There exists a large body of literature debating one aspect or another of this central issue. Among the topics are "the economic way of looking at behavior" (Becker 1993), the delineation of self-interest and altruism, and the related issue of commitment devices and enforcement mechanisms. We now discuss our model's implications along these lines in the context of specific works we consider particularly relevant.

7 Related Literature and Recent Experimental Results on Self-Regarding and Other-Regarding Behavior

7.1 *The Question of Self-Interested Players, and the Evidence*

By framing the acquisition of self-command as a reputation game, we have asserted that the relevant decisions are made rationally and are motivated by self-interest. Others would argue that the explanatory power of self-interest as a motive for self-command is more limited, and altruism more powerful than admitted in models such as ours.

Amartya Sen (1977) equates "commitment" with concern for duty. In his usage of the words, neither can be motivated by self-interest:

> One way of defining commitment is in terms of a person choosing an act that he believes will yield a lower level of personal welfare to him than an alternative ... we can expand the definition of commitment to include cases in which the person's choice, while maximizing anticipated personal welfare, would be unaffected under at least one counterfactual condition in which the act chosen would cease to maximize personal welfare This broader sense may have particular relevance when one acts on the basis of a concern for duty which, if violated, could cause remorse, but the action is really chosen out of the sense of duty rather than just to avoid the illfare resulting from the remorse that would occur if one were to act otherwise. (p. 327)

Note in the above quote that the remorse caused by violation of duty is what Smith would call "blame-worthiness." Sen says behavior motivated by the desire to avoid remorse lies outside the scope of commitment and duty, properly defined. Smith, to the contrary, says duty includes precisely such behavior.

The gap between the approaches of Smith and ourselves on the one hand, and Sen on the other, is narrowed, but not closed, when the semantic issues are cleared up.

First, in contrast with Sen, we distinguish commitment and duty as two very different things. We prefer to use the more intuitive definition of commitment as pre-commitment, and do not concern ourselves with it any further. (We are interested in the agent's decision of selfcommand when he has the whole domain of actions to choose from, not when he has limited his choices to a subset of that domain by prior action.) Duty, then, is abiding by the general rules of morality (Smith 1982, 161–162). The motivation for doing so is not directly important to the definition, and may include self-interest.

Second, in addition to defining duty such that self-interest is allowed to be a motive, we further view self-interest in the context of *TMS* as duty's *leading* motive—as it underlies the desire for praise-worthiness and aversion to blame-worthiness. After overcoming our semantic differences, this is where we part ways with Sen. We do not find it necessary, as Sen believes it is, to look beyond self-interest for the motivation of dutiful action. When it appears that the agent is "choosing an act that he believes will yield a lower level of personal welfare," in Smith's and our view, this is not the case. Either a short-run view was taken in defining "welfare," or payoffs were defined strictly materially. To better understand the choice, the time horizon allowed for observing payoffs should be broadened and psychic and emotional payoffs should be admitted. Feelings of praise-worthiness and blame-worthiness are very real payoffs in a repeated game, and it is for their concern, Smith tells us that we do our duty.

Jane Mansbridge, from whose work we culled the second quote in the prefix to this chapter, is equally skeptical of the rational-choice approach, if not more so. The essays in Mansbridge (1990) "spell out some of the varieties of altruism and how these differ from narrow self-interest" (p. xi). Her book "aims to make thinking about self-interest more subtle, showing that when people... define their own interests and when they act to pursue those interests, they often give great weight to their moral principles ..." In this paper and elsewhere, we argue that many moral principles are social constructs informed by self-interested behavior.[11]

Amitai Etzioni (1986) takes moral norms like duty as given and a point of departure for "The Case for a Multiple-utility Conception."[12] Like Mansbridge, Etzioni claims that the rational actor paradigm is too parsimonious to accommodate "authentic altruism" and that the prevailing imperialist attempts at looking at all kinds of behavior in the economic way "violates the rules of sound conceptualization. Once a concept is defined so that it encompasses all the incidents that are members of a given category (in the case at hand, the motives for all human activities), it ceases to enhance one's ability to explain" (p. 162).

Without wanting to get drawn into the morass of a rather contentious debate, we like to state our belief that, as Mansbridge puts it, "[c]onceptually we know what we mean by altruism only by contrasting it with self-interest." In our interpretation, this insight translates into altruism being a residual category in which everything is put that cannot be explained by the approach we suggest in this paper. Whether "prosocial motivations" (Mansbridge 1990) or "authentic altruism" (Etzioni 1986) exist per se should, in our view, become an issue after the explanatory power of the rational-choice model has been exhausted.

Arguments against the economic way of looking at behavior are often based, as in the case of both Mansbridge and Etzioni, on anecdotal evidence and/or alleged evidence of systematic departures of subject

[11] Coleman (1990, 1993) uses a similar approach in sociology.

[12] Etzioni (1986). See also Brennan (1989) and Lutz (1993).

behavior from the predictions of game theory in experimental implementations of two- or one-sided prisoner's dilemma games, centipede games, bargaining games, and the like.[13] There are a variety of responses to such arguments, among them the introduction of incomplete information (as, for example, in Kreps et al. 1982), modifying the experiments that allegedly invalidated the original models. Another response is a close look at the design of experiments that contradict the predictions of game theory. In this context, it is important to note that recent research in experimental economics suggests that the earlier studies which motivated arguments against the economic way of looking at behavior were marred by serious design flaws.[14] We find the recent research rather convincing and agree with Vernon Smith's assessment, made even before much of the recent design criticism emerged, that "[experimental economics] documents a growing body of evidence that is consistent with the implications of rational models..“" (V.Smith 1991, 878). Smith's assessment relocates the argumentative burden.

7.2 *An Alternative Model of Self-Command—Commitment Devices*

Thomas Schelling (1984) recalls Smith's use of the existence of separate "selves" within each person: one of them, the "self" who must experience an action and its immediate effects, is more concerned with immediate pain or pleasure. The other, the "self" who can contemplate the action afterward undisturbed by the joy or grief that affected the first self, is more concerned with the long-term rewards or penalties of the action. Schelling thus understands the conflicting incentives people may face in isolated situations: "Two or more sets of values alternately replace each other..." However, because he uses a different definition of self-command and doesn't discuss the role of the moral faculty of the Man Yesterday in restraining one's passions in a repeated game, his particular two-player model cannot be used to explain Smith's theory of self-command. Schelling defines self-command as a commitment device imposed by one self on the other (perhaps by means of a third person) to prevent that

[13] For example, Marwell and Ames (1979, 1980, 1981).

[14] See, for example, Hoffman et al. (1993), Smith (1991), Smith and Walker (1993), Harrison (1992), Yezer et al. (forthcoming) and Ortmann and Tichy (1995). See also Sally (1995) for an important meta-study, though he does not address recent methodological developments.

other from acting in a manner the first believes to be improper. By self-command, Schelling thus means something quite different than does Smith—both in the meaning of the word and the method by which it is achieved. Schelling is quite aware of this. Acknowledging Smith's contribution to a theory of self-command, he explains: "In my usage, self-command is what you may not need to employ if you already have enough of what Adam Smith meant by it" (Schelling 1984, 3).

7.3 Is Game Theory Applicable to "Egonomics"?

In his insightful article, "Weakness of Will and the Free-rider Problem," Jon Elster (1985) investigates many of the above issues. He argues that there are essentially three different methods of self-command acquisition:

1. Commitment (the devices that Schelling discusses).
2. Concern for reputation and future payoffs (the kind of reputational enforcement discussed in the current paper).
3. (Self-induced) preference changes.

Elster notes that the first and second methods have analogies in interpersonal collective action problems (pp. 256–257), but questions whether game theory is an applicable tool of analysis to these sorts of intrapersonal relations—the study of which Schelling calls "egonomics." Elster claims that two common features of intrapersonal relations, asymmetry of time and indivisibility of persons, constitute problems which complicate the association of intrapersonal relations with interpersonal collective action problems. He adds, however, that "the interpersonal framework... [u]sed with caution,... still provides many insights" (p. 234). The problems Elster bring up must be addressed if one wants to apply game theory to "egonomics"; our model of Smith's theory of self-command does indeed address them.

We have modeled self-command as a game whose structure is identical to endogenous quality or reputation models well-known in the game theory literature. Elster, and to the best of our knowledge everyone else who has attempted to exploit the (partial) analogies between interpersonal collective action problems and weakness of the will, have identified the structure as symmetric, made by players with identical strategy sets.

In the present chapter, we have made the case for an asymmetric interpretation which seems much more intuitive, and, as a matter of fact, justifies a remark made by Elster:

> Note that this is not a question of presenting oneself as a cooperator to the other player, but of how one appears to oneself. Self-image is, as it were, an internal reputation effect. (Elster 1985, 265)

Our asymmetric model of Smith's theory of self-command overcomes, or at least attenuates, the two problems Elster mentions. "Asymmetry of time" is addressed by showing how a figure who is temporally the "second" player resides "within the breast" of the figure who is temporally the "first" player. The temporal distinction between the players can thus be downplayed; it is brought to light only to point out that this distinction does imply the two players do not share exactly the same sets of payoff components. Having two players with different payoffs, though, implies the internal players have different preference rankings—which addresses "indivisibility of players."

In the end, these solutions to Elster's two problems lead to a parameterization that confirms his intuition from the preceding quote. Even as one rushes to satisfy his passions, "his own mind forebodes" that doing so is immoral, blame-worthy, and will make him feel bad (affect this payoffs) here and now as well as in the future. If he is to choose restraint, his most compelling consideration will have to be the selfinterested concern for his feelings about himself, also both now and in the future; as Elster put it, "Self-image is ... an internal reputation effect."

8 Conclusion

Building on an analysis of his enumeration of five classes of original passions, we have shown how in *The Theory of Moral Sentiments* Adam Smith modeled the acquisition of self-command as a game whose structure is identical to endogenous quality or reputation models well-known in the game-theory literature.

Others have analyzed self-command only in terms of commitment devices. Others have also attempted to exploit the (partial) analogies between interpersonal collective action problems and intrapersonal problems of weakness of the will by relying upon symmetrically structured models with identical agents. Our approach is new, in that we analyze self-command in the absence of commitment devices, and we do so with a variant of a principal-agent model. Our formulation allows us to better address modeling problems arising from the two principal features of intrapersonal relations: asymmetry of time and indivisibility of persons. In doing so, we remain faithful to Smith's text.

Based on our examination of the five classes of original passions and the individual's desire for praise-worthiness and aversion to blameworthiness, we have determined that Smith analyzed the intrapersonal incentive problem in a manner that places him in the tradition of computational theories of action. With the support of recent experimental evidence, we have commented on how our game-theoretic approach to the acquisition of self-command ties into the debate over the relation between altruism and self-interest. Like Becker (1993), we have found explanatory power in a model that presumes motives others might consider "altruistic" are in fact self-interested.

Self-interested action in the indefinitely repeated game of selfcommand disallows an equilibrium where people consistently violate the general rules of morality and engage in self-deceit. Under standard assumptions, it points to an equilibrium where people generally respect the moral standards. The issue here is whether one can rely on selfcommand, or instead must rely on third-party enforcement, to ensure that people's actions will meet given moral standards. We have shown in this chapter that Smith provides a framework in which moral standards may, as a general rule, be upheld entirely with self-command acquired by internal reputational enforcement.

While highlighting the role of self-interest in decisions of whether to violate or respect the general rules of morality, and pointing toward an equilibrium where self-command can be attained through reputational enforcement, we have also acknowledged the learning process Smith emphasized in *TMS*. Like John McEnroe, people learn the lessons of the "great school of self-command" only with age and experience. In this sense, Smith found the eductive and evolutive approaches of modern game theory to be complementary: eductive decision-making may rest upon an evolutionary bedrock.

As people endeavor to learn the general rules of morality, they are bound to engage in blame-worthy behavior. Once they have learned the moral standards, they will generally be disciplined by the long-run rewards of praise-worthiness to practice self-command. Yet we also may see occasional lapses. The internal reputation effect is powerful, but for the individual or society to rely on it alone would be too optimistic. With age and experience, McEnroe has calmed down—but his demons still lurk within, ready to erupt.

Acknowledgements The authors acknowledge with thanks the permission granted by Oxford University Press to cite from Adam Smith's *Theory of Moral Sentiments*, edited by D.D. Raphael and A.L. Macfie (1976). We thank participants at the 1993 H.E.S. meetings and 1994 A.E.A. meetings for comments and suggestions that improved this paper. The usual disclaimer applies.

References

Barro RG (1990) Macroeconomic Policy. Harvard University Press, Cambridge

Becker GS (1993) The Economic Way of Looking at Behavior. J Polit Econ 101(3):385–409

Binmore K (1990) Essays on the Foundations of Game Theory. Basil Blackwell, Cambridge

Brennan TJ (1989) A Methodological Assessment of Multiple Utility Frameworks. Econ Philos 5(2):198–208

Coleman JS (1990) Foundations of Social Theory. Belknap Press of Harvard University Press, Cambridge

——— (1993) The Rational Reconstruction of Society. Am Sociol Rev 58(1):1–15

Elster J (1985) Weakness of the Will and the Free-rider Problem. Econ Philos 1(2):231–265

Etzioni A (1986) The Case for a Multiple-utility Conception. Econ Philos 2(2):159–183

Friedman D (1991) Evolutionary Games in Economics. Econometrica 59(3):637–666

Harrison GW (1992) Theory and Misbehavior of First Prize Auctions: Reply. Am Econ Rev 82(5):1426–1443

Hoffman E, McCabe K, Smith V (1993) Further Results on Dictator and Ultimatum Games. Working Paper, University of Arizona

Hoffman E, McCabe K, Shachat K, Smith V (1994) Preferences, Property Rights, and Anonymity in Bargaining Games. Games Econ Behav 7(3):346–380

Holmstroem BR, Tirole J (1989) The Theory of the Firm. In: Schmalensee Rm Willig RD (eds) Handbook of Industrial Organization, vol 1. Elsevier Science, New York, pp 66–133

Kavka GS (1991) Is Individual Choice less Problematic than Collective Choice? Econ Philos 7(2):143–165

——— (1993) Internal Prisoner's Dilemma Vindicated. Econ Philos 9(1):171–174

Kreps DM (1990) Game Theory and Economic Modelling. Oxford University Press, Oxford

Kreps DM, Milgrom P, Roberts J, Wilson R (1982) Rational Cooperation in the Finitely Repeated Prisoner's Dilemma. J Econ Theory 27(2):245–252

Lutz MA (1993) The Utility of Multiple Utility: A Comment on Brennan. Econ Philos 9(1):145–154

Mansbridge JJ (1990) Beyond Self-interest. University of Chicago Press, Chicago

Marwell G, Ames RE (1979) Experiments on the Provision of Public Goods. I. Resources, Interest, Group Size, and the Free Rider Problem. Am J Sociol 84(6):1335–1360

——— (1980) Experiments on the Provision of Public Goods. II. Provision Points, Stakes, Experience and the Free Rider Problem. Am J Sociol 85(4):926–937

——— (1981) Economists Free Ride, Does Anyone Else? J Public Econ 15(3):295–310

Ortmann A, Meardon SJ (1993) A Game-theoretic Re-evaluation of Adam Smith's Wealth of Nations. Working Paper, Bowdoin College

——— (1995a) Adam Smith on the Origin and Evolution of Moral Sentiments: A Gametheoretic Re-evaluation. Mimeo, Bowdoin College

——— (1995b) A Game-theoretic Re-evaluation of Adam Smith's Theory of Moral Sentiments and Wealth of Nations. In: Rima I (ed) The Classical Tradition in Economic Thought. Edward Elgar Pubilshing, Brookfield, pp 43–61

Ortmann A, Tichy L (1995) Understanding Gender Effects in the Laboratory: Two Hypotheses, a Double-blind Design, and Experimental Results. Working Paper, Bowdoin College

Ostrom E (1990) Governing the Commons: The Evolution of Institutions for Collective Action. Cambridge University Press, Cambridge

Pitchik C, Schotter A (1987) Honesty in a Model of Strategic Information Transmission. Am Econ Rev 77(5):1032–1036

Rasmusen E (1989) Games and Information: An Introduction to Game Theory. Basil Blackwell, Cambridge

Sally D (1995) Conversation and Cooperation in Social Dilemmas: A Meta-analysis of Experiments from 1958 to 1992. Ration Soc 7(1):58–92

Schelling TC (1978) Egonomics, or the Art of Self-Management. Am Econ Rev 68(2):290–294

——— (1984) Self-command in Practice, in Policy, and in a Theory of Rational Choice. Am Econ Rev 74(2):1–11

Sen AK (1977) Rational Fools: A Critique of the Behavioral Foundations of Economic Theory. Philos Public Aff 6(4):317–345

Smith A (1982) [1759] The Theory of Moral Sentiments. In: Raphael DD, Macfie AL (eds) Liberty Classics, Indianapolis

——— (1937) [1776] An Inquiry into the Nature and Causes of the Wealth of Nations. In: Cannan E (ed) The Modem Library, New York

Smith V (1991) Rational Choice: The Contrast Between Economics and Psychology. J Polit Econ 99(4):877–897

Smith V, Walker JM (1993) Monetary Rewards and Decision Cost in Experimental Economics. Econ Inq 31(2):245–261

Tirole, J (1988) The Theory of Industrial Organization. MIT Press, Cambridge

Yezer, AM, Goldfarb RS, Poppen PJ (1996) Does Studying Economics Discourage Cooperation? Watch What We Do, Not What We Say or How We Play. J Econ Perspect 10(1):177–186

CHAPTER 4

The Nature and Causes of Corporate Negligence, Sham Lectures, and Ecclesiastical Indolence: Adam Smith on Joint-Stock Companies, Teachers, and Preachers

Andreas Ortmann

In every profession, the exertion of the greater part of those who exercise it, is always in proportion to the necessity they are under of making that exertion.
Adam Smith, *WN*

Adam Smith discussed joint-stock companies and educational and ecclesiastical institutions—in that order—in part 3, chapter 1, book 5 of The Nature and Causes of the Wealth of Nations ([1776] 1937; hereafter cited as WN). It is unlikely that Smith's bunching and sequencing of these discussions was coincidental, as he typically developed his arguments carefully and strategically (Smith 1983, 89, 146–47).

I shall argue that Smith saw all three institutions adversely affected by similar incentive structures that were likely to produce poorly functioning organizations. Smith identified self-interest as the driving force of

A. Ortmann and B. Walraevens, *Adam Smith's System*, Palgrave Studies in the History of Economic Thought,
https://doi.org/10.1007/978-3-030-99704-5_4

the incentive misalignments that he diagnosed, and he considered what, if anything, could prevent these institutions from being afflicted by them.

I shall furthermore argue that in order to explain the misalignment of incentives, Smith looked at the particular raison d'etre of these institutions: their products. In analyzing them, Smith made the now wellknown distinction between inspection, experience, and credence goods[1] and discussed how the nature of a product can affect the internal organization of an institution; this distinction also motivated him to discuss joint-stock companies, teaching, and preaching in the order he did. Specifically, he argued that joint-stock companies typically function only if they restrict themselves to routinized activities-inspection goods of sorts. Such solutions are not available for teaching and preaching, which Smith identified as experience goods and credence goods, respectively. As we now know, and as Smith understood rather well, serious moral hazard and quality assessment problems afflict such goods and their production-preaching (the ultimate credence good) more so than teaching (a classic experience good). Throughout, Smith's long-standing interest in institutional arrangements—whether they be reputational or regulatory—informed his discussion on the prevention of incentive misalignment and the occurrence of negative organizational outcomes.

The balance of this chapters organized as follows: In Sect. 1, I sketch why promotion of manufacture, teaching, and preaching are problem isomorphs, and follow with a detailed discussion of Smith's analysis of joint-stock companies and educational and ecclesiastical institutions in Sects. 2 through 4. Next, I consider the commonalities of these three

[1] The distinction reflects the degree to which the quality of a good can be assessed before purchase, after purchase, or both. If a consumer must consume the product to determine its quality, it is said to have experience quality (Nelson 1970). Michael Darby and Edi Karni (1973) labeled those experience goods whose quality cannot be determined after consumption credence goods. Examples of experience goods are car repairs and health, day, or elder care, examples of credence goods are organic fruit or certain kinds of medical care and other prevention and repair services. In contrast, goods whose quality can be assessed prior to purchase are called inspection or search goods (Carlton and Perloff 1994; Tirole 1988). Note that labor (services) can be similarly classified. The effort that goes into routinized activities can be easily gauged. In contrast, effort is often difficult to observe or verify for non-routinized activities. Smith did not use the labels employed by the modern Industrial Organization literature, but he understood well that whether the quality of a good or service can be assessed before or after purchase feeds on the internal organization of an institution and its products.

discussions. I also argue that Smith's discussion of the pervasive incentive problems of joint-stock companies and educational and ecclesiastical institutions is an important example of a reasoning routine that Smith employed in a variety of contexts.

1 Promotion of Manufacture, Teaching, and Preaching as Problem Isomorphs: A Road Map

Adjustable quality is typical of experience and credence goods. One must experience such products or services (Nelson 1970; Tirole 1988) or may even have to accept their quality on faith if an assessment is prohibitively expensive or not possible at all (Darby and Karni 1973; Tirole 1988). The possibility that the seller of a good promises high quality (at a corresponding price) and then delivers low quality creates a moral hazard problem for the seller (Klein and Leffler 1981). Typically, the effort put into production determines the quality of a good or service. The possibility that an agent promises high effort (at a corresponding wage or salary) and then delivers low effort creates a moral hazard problem for the agent. Smith's arguments suggest that quality assessment problems and moral hazard problems are closely related.[2] The notions of adjustable quality and adjustable effort, and the resultant moral hazard, or principal-agent problems, are key concepts in the following discussion.

Smith's concern with the circumstances that spur industry or induce indolence led to his discussion of joint-stock companies and educational and ecclesiastical institutions. (The epigraph to this chapter summarizes Smith's view succinctly.) In discussing these institutions, Smith followed a basic pattern: He first pondered the raison d'être of the institution under consideration and its products. He then analyzed whether that institution ought to defray its own expense. Finally, he considered different payment modes and their consequences for the provision of goods such as teaching and preaching. In the next three sections, I shall use Smith's rhetorical pattern as template.

[2] One can indeed show that the underlying incentive problems in each are identical in strategic game form (Ortmann and Colander 1997). To describe such situations, Herbert Simon (1991) has coined the notion of "problem isomorphs". From here on I shall use the terms *quality* (of a good or service) and *effort* (of the production factor labor) interchangeably.

2 Smith on Joint-Stock Companies

2.1 Raison d'Etre

Smith's discussion of joint-stock companies appears in book 5, chapter 1, part 3, article 1, as part of a discussion "Of the Expense of Public Works and Institutions". It immediately follows his discussion of the provision and maintenance of such public infrastructure items as "good roads, bridges, navigable canals, harbors, etc." necessary for facilitating the commerce of society and increasing the wealth of the nation. Smith (*WN*, 690–91) acknowledged the protection of trade to be as essential to the defense of the commonwealth as the military. He considered joint-stock companies in particular to be "established for the public-spirited purpose of promoting some particular manufacture" (715).

2.2 Who is to Pay?

Smith left no doubt that "the greater part of such public works [as good roads, etc.] may easily be so managed, as to afford a particular revenue sufficient for defraying their own expense, without bringing any burden upon the general revenue of the society" (682). However, Smith also suggested there exist "Public Works and Institutions ... necessary for facilitating particular Branches of Commerce" which could not be managed this way, especially those institutions that helped to protect trade with "barbarous nations" (e.g., forts, garrisons, ambassadors, and regulated and joint-stock companies) (690). Their purpose and expense required that they be paid out of the general revenue or receive special property rights that would allow them to recapture their initial investment. Smith thus proposed two provision modes, one drawing on the general revenue and the other drawing on private funds.

Specifically, Smith suggested that some trade, due to its comparatively high risk, represented "an experiment which the state might not think prudent to make" (691). In such situations, governments relied on regulated and joint-stock companies to privatize the risk, typically in return for temporary monopoly rights (712).

2.3 Incentive Problems

Smith pointed out that while joint-stock companies had a "public-spirited purpose" and in the short run could be successful in promoting some particular manufacture, "they have in the long-run proved, universally, either burdensome or useless, and have either mismanaged or confined the trade" (691). This occurred whether or not they had been given monopoly rights (700).

Smith explained that within joint-stock companies, such an outcome was the inevitable consequence of misaligned incentives generated by the organizational form. When compared to private "co-partneries" (partnerships), joint-stock companies had two severe disadvantages. First, joint stock was transferable and thus facilitated the separation of management and ownership—an issue that Smith explicitly discussed (699). Second, joint stock limited the financial risk for owners, further blunting their incentives to monitor their agents. The "total exemption from trouble and from risk, beyond a limited sum", invited people to become "adventurers in joint stock companies" and thus channeled funds away from the more incentive-compatible organization form—the private partnership (699).

> The directors of such [joint-stock] companies, however, being the managers rather of other people's money than their own, it cannot well be expected, that they should watch over it with the same anxious vigilance with which the partners in a private co-partnery frequently watch over their own Negligence and profusion, therefore, must always prevail, more or less, in the management of such a company. (700)

Smith analyzed the fate of a number of joint-stock companies, sprinkling his discussion with important and thoroughly modern insights and conclusions. Smith noted, for example, that there was an inverse relationship between the number of proprietors in a company and the attention that they would pay to the business at hand (702–703).[3] He concluded, "that a joint-stock company should be able to carry on successfully any branch of foreign trade, when private adventurers can come into any sort of open and fair competition with them, seems contrary to all experience" (705). Looking at the evidence, Smith furthermore concluded that joint-stock companies, even those with monopoly rights, were likely to fall prey to the destructive dynamics of incentive misalignment. Smith illustrated

[3] He thus anticipated, by roughly two hundred years, group-size effects now well established in the literature (Isaac, Walker, and Williams 1995 ; Abrahamson and Park 1994 ; Yermack 1996).

this point in a lengthy discussion of the fate of the East India Company (705–12). He argued that this company became the victim of its initial success (monopoly profits): "The great increase of their fortune had, it seems, only served to furnish their servants with a pretext for a greater profusion, and a cover for greater malversation, than in proportion even to that increase of fortune" (709).

He thus anticipated, by roughly two hundred years, group-size effects now well established in the literature (Isaac, Walker, and Williams 1995 ; Abrahamson and Park 1994 ; Yermack 1996).

Smith then discussed failed attempts to modify the governance structure of the company, stressing that the incentive alignment problems were structural (710). Summarizing his discussion, and referring to evidence compiled by Abbe Andre Morellet, Smith concluded that incentive problems of joint-stock companies were ubiquitous. But he also identified a curious and intriguing exception: "The only trades which it seems possible for a joint stock company to carry on successfully, without an exclusive privilege, are those, of which all the operations are capable of being reduced to what is called a routine, or to such a uniformity of method as admits of little or no variation" (713).

In other words, a "routine" is a trade where quality or effort (or both) is not adjustable—the key characteristic of so-called inspection goods. Smith identified banking, insurance (from fire, sea risk, and capture in time of war), construction and maintenance of canals, and provision of water for cities as four trades where routinization was typical. While the characterization of banking and insurance as routine undertakings seems curious from today's perspective, it is relevant for my argument about the sequencing of Smith's discussion that in his assessment of the survivorship record of joint-stock companies, he identified the absence of adjustable quality and effort as the key distinguishing feature.

3 Smith on Educational Institutions

3.1 *Raison d'Etre*

Smith discussed educational institutions in book 5, chapter 1, part 3, and article 2. This discussion immediately follows Smith's treatment of joint-stock companies. Smith contended that education was good not only for individuals—for example, to counteract ignorance and stupidity, which he regarded as the somewhat inevitable consequence of the division of labor (734–35)—but also for society at large. Education, claimed Smith, made it possible for people to conceive of moral sentiments and to deduce "the ordinary duties of private life" (735); it thus created the possibility of social fabric. Education (science) was also "the great antidote to the poison of enthusiasm and superstition", a byproduct of fanatic preachers (748). Last but not least, Smith asserted that education guaranteed that citizens would retain the martial virtues valued by the sovereign.

3.2 *Who is to Pay?*

All these externalities of education notwithstanding, Smith argued that colleges and universities ought to furnish their own expenses, either from fees or honoraria paid directly to teachers, "this natural revenue" (716), or from a variety of public endowments. He noted that there is, however, typically no need for deriving higher education's revenues from the general revenues of society.[4]

3.3 *Incentive Problems*

In his discussion of educational institutions, Smith questioned whether public endowments affected the quality of teaching:

> Have those public endowments contributed in general to promote the end of their institution? Have they contributed to encourage the diligence, and to improve the abilities of the teachers? Have they directed the course of education towards objects more useful, both to the individual and to the public, than those to which it would naturally have gone of its own accord? (716)

[4] While Smith (*WN*, 735) favors the application of the benefit principle as a basic rule for higher education, he stresses that "the laboring poor, that is the great body of the people" may not have the means to become literate and numerate. "For a very small expense the public can facilitate and can even impose upon almost the whole body of the people, the necessity of acquiring those most essential parts of the education" (737). Such state intervention, Smith argues, is desirable because of the detrimental consequences of the division of labor on the human mind and, ultimately, the social fabric (734–35).

Smith answered his second question first:

> In every profession, the exertion of the greater part of those who exercise it, is always in proportion to the necessity they are under of making that exertion. This necessity is greatest with those to whom the emoluments of their profession are the only source from which they expect their fortune, or even their ordinary revenue and subsistence. The endowments of schools and colleges have necessarily diminished more or less the necessity of application in the teachers. Their subsistence, so far as it arises from their salaries, is evidently derived from a fund altogether independent of their success and reputation in their particular professions. (717)

Appealing to individual rationality, Smith thus postulated that the payment mode affected the quality of teaching, which was more likely to be high when its suppliers competed for emoluments.[5] "Sham-lectures" would simply not draw the crowds necessary for those who deliver them to survive in the profession; word of mouth would drive out the professor who shirks (720). With dwindling student numbers translating into loss of income, the credible threat of students voting with their feet would prompt teachers' exertion, assuring students and their parents that they are provided with a reasonable standard of instruction. The discipline of the market—the reputational enforcement of the quality of teaching—would force teachers to perform at a high level. If, however, salaries were independent of the quality of teaching, then high quality could not be expected. Smith singled out the University of Oxford as a place where, in consequence of such a payment mode, "the greater part of the public professors have, for these many years, given up altogether even the pretense of teaching" (718).

One might argue that surely those teachers who did not apply themselves would be identified by their peers or by some authority and be dismissed. Not so, said Smith. Peers did not intervene, as intervention would have been incentive-incompatible for them:

[5] "It is the interest of every man to live as much at ease as he can, and if his emoluments are to be precisely the same, whether he does, or does not perform some very laborious duty, it is certainly his interest ... either to neglect it altogether, or, if he is subject to some authority which will not suffer him to do this, to perform it in as careless and slovenly a manner as that authority will permit" (718).

> If the authority to which he is subject resides in the body corporate, the college, or university, of which he himself is a member, and in which the greater part of the other members are, like himself, persons who either are, or ought to be teachers; they are likely to make a common cause, to be all very indulgent to one another, and every man to consent that his neighbor may neglect his duty, provided he himself is allowed to neglect his own. (718)[6]

Again, appealing to individual rationality, Smith confirmed the viability of collusion among faculty.[7] Smith then addressed the obvious question of why persons extraneous to the faculty, say bishop, or governor, or minister of state, or their agents, that is, some independent supervisor, could not intervene and take care of professorial slackers. He suggested that, while supervisors could force a teacher to offer ascertain number of lectures, they did not have effective means to control their quality. To make matters worse, "an extraneous jurisdiction of this kind, besides, is liable to be exercised both ignorantly and capriciously" (718).

Smith thus provided a negative answer to his second question, claiming that endowments did not "encourage the diligence", nor "improve the abilities of teachers". In essence, Smith made a case for the reputational enforcement of teaching, which he identified as an experience good whose quality was hard to observe or verify. Third party enforcement through supervisors, Smith argued, was bound to be ineffective and likely to generate additional problems, such as administrators making decisions that they are not qualified to make. Such a shift of decision-making power would consequently lead to obsequiousness on the part of those potentially exposed to administrators' ignorance and capriciousness, and further detract from both the ability and the diligence of teachers (718–19).

Smith then turned to his third question, "Have [endowments] directed the course of education towards objects more useful, both to the individual and to the public, than those to which it would naturally have gone of its own accord?" Specifically, Smith considered whether endowments promoted curricular innovation. The answer was implicit in his discussion of the ways teachers engaged in the "pretense of teaching" (720)

[6] Cognoscenti will note that Smith used a Nash equilibrium to model the idea: "that his neighbor may neglect his duty, provided he himself is allowed to neglect his own".

[7] The notion of collusion is well established in Smith's work. See, for example, Smith's (*WN*, 66–68) intriguing discussion of the bargaining between workers and masters.

by reciting the works of others and in his discussion of the evolution of curricular content throughout the ages (722–27). The answer was explicit in his discussion of "the improvements which, in modern times, have been made in several different branches of philosophy" (727). Smith contended that "the improvements ... have not the greater part of them, been made in universities". In fact, "the richest and best endowed universities have been the slowest in adopting those improvements, and the most averse to permit any considerable change in the established plan of education". In contrast, poorer universities and their teachers, "depending upon their reputation for the greater part of their subsistence, were obliged to pay more attention to the current opinions of the world" (727).

Smith thus concluded that public endowments did not direct the course of education toward an improved curriculum that best served students, parents, and the public at large. Endowments then affected not only what faculty taught, but also how they taught it.[8]

Endowments perverted the raison d'etre of educational institutions. "The discipline of colleges and universities is in general contrived, not for the benefit of the students, but for the interest, or more properly speaking, for the ease of masters" (720). Thus, implicit in his analysis of the effects of public endowments on the quality of teaching and on the process of modernizing the curriculum was Smith's contention that public endowments failed to promote the goals of their institution.[9]

[8] A referee for this journal noted that the title of this section was "Smith on Educational Institutions", but that I discuss mostly colleges and universities. Smith indeed discussed educational institutions in general. However, he also argued that incentive problems were highly and positively correlated with endowments. Some universities had them, but most schools and colleges did not, or had "but a very small one" (*WN*, 716–17). Smith, incidentally, identified three other sources of incentive problems. First, professions such as law, physics, and divinity required "a certain number of years in certain universities" (719). Second, "the charitable foundations of scholarships, exhibitions, bursaries, &c. necessarily attach a certain number of students to certain colleges, independent altogether of the merit of those particular colleges" (719). Third, classes (and teachers) are mandated by a college. In all three cases, Smith was concerned about limitations of students' choice sets since these circumstances reduced teachers' incentives to worry about their reputations (See *WN*, 719–20 for a detailed discussion).

[9] According to his biographer, Smith received during his years at Glasgow College more than half of his salary from fees (Rae 1895, 48–49). This was in contrast to the payment mode at the University of Oxford, the consequences of which Smith had experienced as student. Recall Smith's scathing comment on that university's professors.

The key to Smith's argument was that student fees were the more appropriate incentive structure, as students would flock to those teachers who took teaching seriously and kept up with an ever-accelerating knowledge base. Those teachers who did not would face empty classrooms. "Sham-lectures" would simply not cut the mustard. In short, Smith invoked the market as the guarantor of effectiveness in higher education and as the enforcer of good teaching and curricular innovation. Reputational enforcement would work only when the greater part of teachers' salaries came from fees and honoraria. Salaries based on seniority, endowments, or similar schemes that were independent of teachers' success and reputation were unlikely to promote the raison d'etre of educational institutions.[10]

4 Smith on Ecclesiastical Institutions

4.1 Raison d'Etre

Smith discussed ecclesiastical institutions in book 5, chapter 1, part 3, and article 3, immediately following his discussion of educational institutions.

Throughout his discussion, Smith explicitly underlines the similarity of educational and ecclesiastical institutions, describing both as "institutions for the instruction of the people" (684) and potentially beneficial to society (768).

While he stressed the similarity of educational and ecclesiastical institutions, Smith also made clear their key difference: "[Religious instruction] is a species of instruction of which the object is not so much to render the people good citizens in this world, as to prepare them for another and a better world in the life to come" (740). In terms of our earlier distinction, Smith identified nonreligious instruction as an experience good and religious instruction as a credence good. A consumer of nonreligious instruction was likely to reap its benefits in this life. In contrast, one had to accept on faith the benefits of religious instruction.[11]

[10] As I have argued elsewhere, there are important lessons here for contemporary higher education (Ortmann 1997b).

[11] Smith was quite aware that religious instruction, as an added bonus, could have tangible benefits. Specifically, affiliation with a sect could provide a social context much needed for those fleeing the countryside and in danger of sinking into obscurity and darkness (*WN*, 747).

4.2 *Incentive Problems*

Smith's discussion of preachers' incentives parallels, often explicitly, his discussion of teachers' incentives:

> The teachers of the doctrine which contains this instruction, in the same manner as other teachers, either depend altogether for their subsistence upon the voluntary contributions of their hearers; or they may derive it from some other fund to which the law of their country may entitle them; such as a landed estate, a tythe or land tax, and established salary or stipend. Their exertion, their zeal and industry, are likely to be much greater in the former than in the latter. (740)

And two pages later,

> The parochial clergy derive, many of them, a very considerable part of their subsistence from the voluntary oblations of the people: ...
>
> The parochial clergy are like those teachers whose reward depends more or less upon their industry and reputation. (742)

Having established the outline of his argument, Smith examined the impact of "endowments" in more detail. The "teachers of a new religion" were bound to be hungry, had not given themselves up to indolence, and hence were able to "keep up the fervor of faith and devotion in the great body of the people", while the "clergy of an established and well-endowed religion" were likely to become unconcerned with their original mission, satiated and defenseless (740).[12]

Predictably, such a clergy would—like joint-stock companies bogged down by their incentive problems—"call upon the civil magistrate to persecute, destroy, or drive out their adversaries, as disturbers of the public peace" (741). This strategy often succeeded because civil magistrates believed that established religious institutions had a stabilizing effect.

In sum, endowments and independent provisions neither promoted the end of the institution nor encouraged the diligence and commitment

[12] "Such a clergy, when attacked by a set of popular and bold, though perhaps stupid and ignorant enthusiasts, feel themselves as perfectly defenseless as the indolent, effeminate, and full-fed nations of the southern parts of Asia, when they were invaded by the active, hardy, and hungry Tartars of the North" (*WN*, 741).

of preachers. They did not guide the course of religious education in a direction that it would not otherwise have gone of its own accord. Or did they?

David Hume (quoted in *WN,* 743) had argued that perhaps it was for the better that established religious institutions received preferential treatment; the diligence and passion that hungry preachers mustered was bound to be a problem:

> This interested diligence of the clergy is what every wise legislator will study to prevent; because, in every religion except the true, it is highly pernicious, and it has a natural tendency to pervert the true, by infusing into it a strong mixture of superstition, folly, and delusion. Each ghostly practitioner, in order to render himself more precious and sacred in the eyes of his retainers, will inspire them with the most violent abhorrence of all other sects, and continually endeavor, by some novelty, to excite the languid devotion of his audience. No regard will be paid to truth, morals, or decency in the doctrines inculcated. Every tenet will be adopted that best suits the disorderly affections of the human frame. Customers will be drawn to each conventicle by new industry and address in practicing on the passions and credulity of the populace. And in the end, the civil magistrate will find, that he has dearly paid for his pretended frugality, in saving a fixed establishment for the priests; and that in reality the most decent and advantageous composition, which he can make with the spiritual guides, is to bribe their indolence, by assigning stated salaries to their profession, and rendering it superfluous for them to be farther active, than merely to prevent their flock from straying in quest of new pastures. And in this manner ecclesiastical establishments, though commonly they arose at first from religious views, prove in the end advantageous to the political interests of society.

Not so, said Smith. As other authors (Anderson 1986; West 1990) have pointed out, Smith *(WN,* 742–46) countered Hume's argument with an efficient market hypothesis of religious ideas. The "interested and active zeal of religious teachers" could be dangerous only where "either but one sect [is] tolerated in the society, or where the whole of a large society is divided into two or three great sects; ... But that zeal must be altogether innocent where the society is divided into two or three hundred, or perhaps into as many as a thousand small sects, of which no one could be considerable enough to disturb the public tranquility" (745). Smith argued that the competition of hundreds of other preachers would ultimately bring about "candor and moderation" among the teachers of each little sect who,

> finding themselves almost alone, would be obliged to respect those of almost every other sect, and the concessions which they mutually find it both convenient and agreeable to make to one another, might in time probably reduce the doctrine of the greater part of them to that pure and rational religion, free from every mixture of absurdity, imposture, or fanaticism, such as wise men have in all ages of the world wished to see established. (745)

As he did for educational institutions, Smith thus favored reputational over third-party enforcement for ecclesiastical institutions.[13]

5 Discussion

For all three institutions, Smith identified self-interested behavior as the driving force of incentive misalignments, which he believed to be ubiquitous, pervasive, and likely to produce poorly functioning organizations. In all three cases, he argued, the public had a vested interest in the provision of the services of these institutions, and that indeed these services had enough social value to warrant support from general revenues. However, in all three cases Smith suggested that private provision was possible and generally desirable.

Looking at the reality of private provision, Smith noted that the incentive structures he observed were counterproductive in all three cases. The monopoly rights given to joint-stock companies, by creating monopoly profits, blunted managers' incentives in the same way that guaranteed income blunted the incentives of teachers and preachers. These implicit incentive structures detracted from the diligence that all three principal

[13] Smith *(WN,* 747) realized sects may nevertheless appeal to the anonymous and hence possibly amoral masses. He suggested two remedies: academic study and artistic exposure. He recommended the study of science and philosophy because "science is the great antidote to the poison of enthusiasm and superstition; and where all the superior ranks of people were secured from it, the inferior ranks could not be much exposed to it". He also promoted "public diversions" such as painting, poetry, music, and dancing because they drive out "that melancholy and gloomy humor which is almost always the nurse of popular superstition and enthusiasm" (748).

actors otherwise would have needed to apply and thus invited lack of diligence. Monopoly rights and endowments thus did not promote these institutions' ultimate raison d'etre. Monopoly rights did not advance the welfare of the country, nor did endowments direct the course of instruction toward objects more useful than those to which it would have naturally gravitated of its own accord. Institutions could, however, establish incentive structures that would prevent abuse and incentive misalignment, and Smith discussed alternative arrangements ("alterations") in all three cases. The discipline of markets, Smith argued, could induce both good teaching (and hence strengthen the social fabric) and free religious instruction of superstition, folly, and delusion (and hence strengthen the social fabric). Smith recognized as well that powerful forces made the implementation of such viable solutions difficult.

Why is this important and what can be learned that we did not already know? As indicated above, Smith understood exceptionally well the causality running from products to organizational form, the nature of moral hazard and quality assessment problems, and the comparative advantages of enforcement mechanisms.[14] Smith asserted that organizations, whether aiming for profit or paradise, are susceptible to the same afflictions, namely misaligned incentives. What distinguishes them is the nature of their wares and the incentive alignment problems they entailed. Incentive problems do not exist for routinized activities—inspection goods or services of sorts. However, if an institution's product is an experience or credence good, then incentive alignment problems are likely to occur—more so for those goods whose quality has to be accepted on faith than for those that can be experienced after purchase. Smith's sequencing of the discussion of joint-stock companies and educational and ecclesiastical institutions reflects his insight that the quality of these institutions' wares became increasingly less observable and hence entailed an increasing likelihood of misaligned incentives. Smith also recognized that the quality of experience or credence goods is best assured through reputational enforcement. Furthermore, third-party enforcement is likely to create additional incentive problems and thus be ineffective.

[14] Benjamin Klein and Keith Leffler (1981, 618 n. 5), whose article is generally considered the path-breaking work in this area, point out that Smith's discussion of efficiency wages in book 1 of *WN* anticipates the essence of their argument about the role of market forces in assuring contractual performance.

Previous authors have moved toward the interpretation suggested here, that joint-stock companies and educational and ecclesiastical institutions face similar problems, in that the self-interested behavior of the principal actors is likely to generate incentive-incompatible structures and poorly functioning organizations.[15] However, the claim in the present chapter is more comprehensive and basic. I contend that Smith classified these institutions' incentive misalignments as problem isomorphs whose major distinction resulted from the goods they produced.

It turns out that Smith had encountered such problem isomorphs before. As I have demonstrated elsewhere, Smith discussed principalagent problems in his Lectures on Rhetoric and Belles Lettres, The Theory of Moral Sentiments, and early in the Wealth of Nations (Collings and Ortmann 1997; Meardon and Ortmann 1996a, 1996b; Ortmann and Meardon 1995). When in articles 1–3 of part 1, chapter 1, book 5 of *WN*, Smith discussed the incentive problems of joint-stock companies, teaching, and ·preaching, he was thus on familiar ground. Being able to fall back on old reasoning routines, he intuitively recognized that they applied (March and Simon 1993).

That people's activities, be they physical or mental, become routinized over time is generally accepted in a variety of literature (Margolis 1982; Pentland and Rueter 1994; March and Simon 1993; Cosmides and Tooby 1992, 1997). Smith, as is well-known to readers of this book almost always tried to identify the commonalities of seemingly disparate phenomena and understood intuitively that self-command or moral conduct had the same incentive structure as preaching and teaching. The process whereby an economic agent (e.g., a teacher, preacher, or citizen) came to regard a socially worthy action (e.g., giving a lecture or sermon really worth attending, or contributing voluntarily to the provision of a public good) as in his self-interest resembles closely the process whereby the moral agent comes to regard the moral injunctions of the "impartial spectator" as synonymous with his own selfcommand. When Smith (WN, 717) stated that "in every profession, the exertion of the greater part of those who exercise it, is always in proportion to the necessity they

[15] Among the relevant works are Anderson and Tollison 1982, Anderson 1986, Rosen 1987, and West 1990. Gary Anderson (1986, 1079–80) in particular recognized that "the Roman church was a kind of spiritual equivalent of the East India Company monopoly, which Smith had extensively analyzed in the immediately preceding section in book V. Although he did not himself explicitly draw this analogy; the analogy is striking".

are under of making that exertion", he paraphrased the insight, expressed nearly two decades earlier in The Theory of Moral Sentiments, that in every situation, the exertion to act "morally" on the greater part of those who exercise it is always in proportion to the necessity that they are under of making that exertion (Meardon and Ortmann 1996a, 1996b). Forget about morality, forget about the provision of high-quality experience and credence goods if the incentive structures are not such that the necessary exertion pays off.

The incentive problem underlying self-command and moral conduct or (the origin and evolution of) standards of moral conduct, the promotion of particular manufacture, preaching, teaching, and all other services whose quality are adjustable are identical.[16] Smith, whenever he came across a problem of that kind, intuitively understood the nature of the problem and followed a consistent reasoning pattern. He identified the (empirically observable) problem, considered the particular circumstances that created it, and identified the institutional arrangements that could overcome the problem. As regards the latter point, Smith's grasp of the subtleties of reputational enforcement (information flows, whether the game is finitely or indefinitely played) is remarkable.

6 Concluding Remarks

The present article is not an exercise in Whiggery in the tradition of Paul Samuelson (1977, 1987 ; Heilbroner 1979; see also Fitzgibbons 1995, 171). I do not take the insights of the economics of the last fifty years as a yardstick by which to measure how modern Smith's work is. Rather, I use modern agency theory as the conceptual lens that informs my reassessment of Smith's work on joint-stock companies, teachers, and preachers.

The present chapter is a stepping-stone toward a reassessment of Smith's oeuvre that uses the conceptual lenses of noncooperative game theory to argue that Smith anticipated much of what modern reputational theories of firms and society elaborate on (Ortmann and Meardon 1995; Meardon and Ortmann 1996a, 1996b; Ortmann 1997a; Holmstroem and Tirole 1989; Kreps 1990; Binmore 1994, 1997). It suggests

[16] In fact, they can all be expressed game-theoretically as I have shown elsewhere in joint work with Stephen J. Meardon (Ortmann and Meardon 1995; Meardon and Ortmann 1996a, 1996b).

that Smith was a rather modern and innovative economist. Such interpretation is in sharp contrast to the verdicts of Joseph Schumpeter (1954) and Salim Rashid (1992).

Acknowledgements Thanks are in order to participants at the 1996 H.E.S. meetings for comments and suggestions that improved this article. Special thanks to John Calabrese, Stephen J. Meardon, Spencer Pack, Susan Tananbaum, and two referees of *Rationality & Society*.

References

Abrahamson E, Park C (1994) Concealment of Negative Organizational Outcomes: An Agency Theory Perspective. Acad Manage J 37(5):1302–1334

Anderson GM (1986) Mr. Smith and the Preachers: The Economics of Religion in the Wealth of Nations. J Political Econ 96(5):1066–1088

Anderson GM, Tollison RD (1982) Adam Smith's Analysis of JointStock Companies. J Political Econ 90(6):1237–1256

Binmore K (1994) Playing Fair. Game Theory and the Social Contract, vol 1. MIT Press, Cambridge MA

— (1997) Just Playing. Game Theory and the Social Contract, vol 2. MIT Press, Cambridge MA

Carlton, DW, Perloff, JM (1994) Modern Industrial Organization, 2nd edn. Harper Collins, New York

Collings D, Ortmann A (1997) Review essay: Vivienne Brown (1994), Adam Smith's Discourse: Canonicity, Commerce and Conscience. In: Biddle J, Samuels W (eds) Research in the History of Economic Thought and Methodology, vol 15. JAI Press, Stamford, p. 329–336

Cosmides L, Tooby J (1992) Cognitive Adaptations for Social Exchanges. In: Barkow JH

Cosmides L, Tooby J (eds) The Adapted Mind: Evolutionary Psychology and the Generation of Culture. Oxford University Press, New York, p. 163–228

— (1997) Are Humans Good Intuitive Statisticians after All? Rethinking Some Conclusions from the Literature on Judgement under Certainty. Cognition 58(1):1 73

Darby MR, Karni E (1973) Free Competition and the Optimal Amount of Fraud. J Law Econ 16(1):67–88

Fitzgibbons A (1995) Adam Smith's System of Liberty, Wealth, and Virtue: The Moral and Political Foundations of "The Wealth of Nations". Clarendon Press, Oxford

Heilbroner RL (1979) Modern Economics as a Chapter in the History of Economic Thought. Hist Political Econ 11(2):192–198

Holmstroem BR, Tirole J (1989) The Theory of the Firm. In: Schmalensee R, Willig RD (eds) Handbook of Industrial Organization, vol 1. Elsevier, New York, p 61–133

Isaac R, Walker JM, Williams A (1995) Group Size and the Voluntary Provision of Public Goods: Experimental Evidence Utilizing Large Groups. J Public Econ 54(1):1–36

Klein B, Leffler K (1981) The Role of Market Forces in Assuring Contractual Performance. J Political Econ 89(4):615–641

Kreps DM (1990) Corporate Culture and Economic Theory. In: Alt E, Shepsle KA (eds) Perspectives on Positive Political Economy. Cambridge University Press, Cambridge, p 90–143

March J, Simon H (1993) Organizations, 2nd edn. Blackwell, Cambridge MA

Margolis H (1982) Patterns, Thinking, and Cognition: A Theory of Judgement. University of Chicago Press, Chicago

Meardon SJ, Ortmann A (1996a) Self-Command in Adam Smith's Theory of Moral Sentiments: A Game-Theoretic Re-interpretation. Ration Soc 8(1):57–80

— (1996b) Yes, Adam Smith was an Economist (A Very Modern One Indeed): Reply to Brown. Ration Soc 8(3):348–352

Nelson P (1970) Information and Consumer Behavior. J Political Econ 78(2):311–329

Ortmann A (1997a) Adam Smith's Reasoning Routines. Paper presented at the 1997 ASSA Annual Meeting, New Orleans, LA, January 4–7 1997

— (1997b) How to Survive in Postindustrial Environments: Adam Smith's Advice for Today's Colleges and Universities. J Higher Educ 8(5): 483–501

Ortmann A, Colander D (1997) A Simple Principal-Agent Game for the Classroom. Econ Inq 35(2):443–450

Ortmann A, Meardon SJ (1995) A game-theoretic re-evaluation of Adam Smith's Theory of Moral Sentiments and Wealth of Nations. In: Rima IH (ed) The Classical Tradition in Economic Thought. Perspectives on the History of Economic Thought Vol XI. Edward Elgar, Brookfield, p 43–61

Pentland BT, Rueter HH (1994) Organizational Routines as Grammars of Action. Adm Sci Q 39(3):484–510

Rae J (1895) Life of Adam Smith. Macmillan, London. Available via Econlib. http://www.econlib.org/library/YPDBooks/Rae/raeLSCover.html. Accessed 28 January 2022

Rashid S (1992) Adam Smith and the Market Mechanism. Hist Political Econ 24(1):129–152

Rosen S (1987) Some Economics of Teaching. J Labor Econ 5(4):561–575

Samuelson, PA (1977) A Modern Theorist's Vindication of Adam Smith. Am Econ Rev 67(1):42–49

— (1987) Out of the Closet: A Program for the Whig History of Economic Science. J Hist Econ Thought 9(1):51–60
Schumpeter JA (1954) History of Economic Analysis. Oxford University Press, New York
Simon HA (1991) Models of My Life. Basic Books, New York
Smith A [1776] (1937) An Inquiry into the Nature and Causes of the Wealth of Nations. Cannan, New York
— (1983) Lectures on Rhetoric and Belles Lettres. Oxford University Press, Oxford
Tirole J (1988) The Theory of Industrial Organization. MIT Press, Cambridge
West E (1990) Adam Smith and Modern Economics: From Market Behavior to Public Choice. Edward Elgar Publishing, Brookfield
Yermack D (1996) Higher Market Valuation of Companies with a Small Board of Directors. J Financ Econ 40(2):185–211

CHAPTER 5

The Proper Role for Government, Game-Theoretically, for Smith

Andreas Ortmann, Stephen J. Meardon, and Benoît Walraevens

1 Introduction

In Meardon and Ortmann (1996a, 1996b), we showed how strategic or game-theoretic conceptions—previously developed by Smith in his *Lectures on Rhetoric and Belles Lettres* (*LRBL)*—pervade his *Theory of Moral Sentiments* (then *TMS*) and in particular its centerpiece, the

Meardon and Ortmann wrote a first draft of this manuscript in 1993 (It is referenced in Ortmann & Meardon 1995 as Meardon & Ortmann 1995b). Over the last couple of years Ortmann and Walraevens revised it numerous times.

The original version of this chapter was revised: Chapter author name in this chapter has been corrected. The correction to this chapter is available at https://doi.org/10.1007/978-3-030-99704-5_9

A. Ortmann and B. Walraevens, *Adam Smith's System*, Palgrave Studies in the History of Economic Thought,
https://doi.org/10.1007/978-3-030-99704-5_5

theory of self-command. We showed in particular that the acquisition of self-command can be understood as a one-sided (asymmetric) prisoner's dilemma, or principal–agent, or reputation, game between Man Today and Man Tomorrow. This conceptualization was important because elsewhere (Ortmann & Walraevens 2018 and chapter 2; Ortmann, Walraevens, & Baranowski 2019) we have argued that Smith used it as early as in his *LRBL* in his presentation of the strategic interests that speaker (writer) and listener (reader) might have. We also have argued that the understanding of the asymmetric information inherent in principal–agent interactions was instrumental in Smith's conceptualization of similar interactions discussed in *Wealth of Nations* (*WN*) (Ortmann 1999) and in the way he presented the material in *WN* in light of the interests of a commercial class that he knew would not take kindly to his ideas (Ortmann & Walraevens 2018 and chapter 2; Ortmann, Walraevens, & Baranowski 2019).

In the present chapter, we provide evidence of a related class of games, broadly of two-sided (symmetric) prisoners' dilemma or—generalizing from there to more players—social-dilemma games in *WN*, but not exclusively. For those having a good grasp on what Smith said, and/or those who have a good grasp on public economics, this will not come as a surprise: *WN*, and in particular Book V, showcases numerous cases of public-good provision and externalities problems. Kennedy (2010, pp. 182–3), following Viner (1927), enumerated—on top of "the accepted roles for government (defence, justice, public works and institutions, and the 'dignity of the sovereigns')"—no less than 27 instances where Smith saw a legitimate role for government intervention. Kennedy (2017) re-iterates his case and challenges (as he already did in Kennedy, 2010) the very questionable notion that Smith was a champion of laissez-faire and unregulated markets, as did West (1990) and Sandmo (2016) and Sen (2016), among many others. Kennedy (2017, pp. 105–7), apart from re-iterating this case, lists 17 examples of entrepreneurial actions that detrimentally affected the public good.

Both the principal–agent and the social-dilemma games are members of a rich class of models that we called in Ortmann and Meardon (1995) the "Smith-game" that represents phenomena as varied as (asymmetrically structured) seller-buyer transactions of goods of adjustable quality or employee-employer relations ("principal–agent"), or (symmetrically structured) attempts at collusion and public goods provision and externalities ("social-dilemma").

Uncovering from the very beginning the recurring appearance of such strategic thinking leads us to claim that Smith—while he did not use these terms—understood well and dealt with the pervasive nature of inter- and externalities, as well as the related issue of reputational enforcement. These issues, brought into sharp focus through the conceptual lenses of game theory and growing evidence supplied by experimental economics, have become the major concerns of practitioners of a wide variety of economic sub-disciplines: from modern micro-economic theory (Holmstroem and Tirole 1989, Tirole 1988, 1996, Kreps 1988, 1990a, 1990b, 2020) to modern macro-economic policy (Barro 1990, Romer 2018) and the political economy of institutions and decisions (Ostrom 1990).

Moreover, by showing once more how game theory can be fruitfully applied to Smith's oeuvre, we suggest a methodology that allows a novel answer to the often-asked question: "What would Smith say if he were alive today?" Game-theoretic models like the Smith Game can be (and are) applied to model a number of social and economic problems that did not exist in his day. One need only frame a current problem in game-theoretic terms and compare it to a problem isomorph in *WN* to infer what advice Smith would give if he were alive today. Such applications of his Game, though, lie for the most part outside the scope of the present paper. It is also difficult because today we find ourselves, surely in what is often called the developed world, in circumstances that are very different from what Smith observed, a point repeatedly driven home in Kennedy (2010).

The chapter is organized as follows: In Sect. 2, we briefly present the Smith Game. In Sect. 3, we apply the Smith Game to three prominent examples from the *WN*, with the first being an example of public good provision, and the second and third dealing with positive and negative externalities respectively. Section 4 is devoted to other examples of application of the Smith Game taken from the *WN* and *LJ*. A conclusion follows.

2 Presentation of the Smith Game

Before beginning the game-theoretic analysis, we will briefly explain the basic game form. Much of the present exhibition goes back to Ortmann and Meardon (1995; an interesting discussion and extension of that contribution can be found on the Dickinson College Wiki, no date). Most problems will be modeled as social-dilemma games or variants thereof in 2×2 strategic or normal form where the players are assumed to choose actions simultaneously. This is the key step necessary for our exercise here, as extensions such as the sequential choices, or repeated interactions, or interactions of this kind involving more than two players have been exhaustively analyzed and/or can easily fitted into this framework.[1]

The Row (Column) player receives their name since their options are shown as rows (columns) in a payoff matrix, in the standard normal form game format. Each player has two options (hence 2 × 2 strategic or normal form), and though the particular options will vary between problems, they will always fit the general form of "cooperate" or "defect".

Standard social-dilemma games have two distinguishing features: first, the game is typically modeled symmetrically—i.e., as mentioned above, players face identical strategies and payoffs—although extensions to asymmetric situations are straightforward. Second, the payoffs are structured such that the choice leading each player to the Pareto-optimal payoff is not the choice that maximizes her individual payoff. Given either decision by the other player, each player would prefer to defect. However, if both defect, they would be better off had they both cooperated. Technically, "dominance" induces a Nash equilibrium that does not coincide with the welfare-improving ("cooperative") outcome.

In our previous work (specifically, Ortmann & Meardon 1995, and there in particular the appendix; see also the Dickinson Wiki entry; Meardon and Ortmann 1996a, 1996b), we used an asymmetric version of social-dilemma games to show how Smith in *TMS* modeled the acquisition of self-command. In the asymmetric version, too, one of the players might have an individually rational choice that might undermine the choice that could induce a Pareto-optimal payoff and it is for that reason that we refer to these classes of games as the "Smith Game", being aware that the first can be solved by dominance, while the second cannot or only conditional on one player's specific choice of action, or iterative dominance.

We have found the Smith Game to be applicable to many problems noted by Smith, mostly, but not exclusively, in Book V of *WN*. Some of these problems, for instance, the first and second "duties of the sovereign", provision of public goods like defense (*WN*, Book V, Part

[1] Interactions involving more than two players can be presented in the 2 × 2 paradigm as follows: The players are one person in a population versus all other people in the population: since all players are assumed identical and face the same payoffs, the "Row" player is one person and the other ("Column") player is taken to be a representative of all the other people. This reduces the game to the 2 × 2 game that we analyze here.

I) and justice (*WN*, Book V, Part II), have been analyzed extensively by others both theoretically and experimentally[2]; their structure is well-known to be isomorph to social-dilemma games. We will include them informally in our discussion to emphasize Smith's views on the following matters: the expenditures of government under particular circumstances of time and space, the importance of incentive compatibility, and the implicit ideal of society which determines the severity of externality problems.

In his *Lectures on Jurisprudence*, Smith explained his stadial theory of societal evolution, saying that in each stage the responsibilities of government grow as the size of communities and the primary forms of property change. Thus, the proper roles of government vary with the particular circumstance of the time and place where the government is instituted. In *WN*, Smith expresses essentially the same idea in a different manner. He says that the expense of the sovereign in fulfilling certain roles will be larger or smaller in different periods of time, when the problems facing society differ in degree and nature. This is true for all duties of the sovereign: the first, defense (*WN*, p. 689); the second, justice (*WN*, p. 708); and the third and last duty, provision of public works and public institutions (*WN*, p. 723).

By recognizing a need for different levels of expenditure on the roles of government as society passes through stages of evolution, Smith provides notice that his prescription for government intervention is not written in stone. The analytical tools he uses implicitly to arrive at his recommendations may remain the same, and yet the recommendations might change over time. The type of problem Smith would solve by government intervention also remains the same: it is a problem where the incentives of individual actors are not compatible with achievement of their common optimal outcome, or the optimal outcome for the larger population to which they belong.

For Smith, "optimal" implies a standard which is set by the Deity and is embodied in the grand design. Smith's idea of the grand design, and society's natural convergence toward it, can be seen as his "Newtonian view" of the world (see Ortmann and Walraevens 2021; chapter 7 this book). His Newtonian view was often frustrated by his observance of ill-aligned incentives in the marketplace and of the influence of vested

[2] Fehr and Gächter (2000) and the more than 2,000 online references attached to the original article in the AEA website.

interests and "factions" in the legislature. Over time, Smith seems to have found more and more examples of the type of problem government intervention could help solve, which would put society back on track and move toward the grand design (see Kennedy 2010, pp. 182–3). He also found many examples of problems *caused* by government under the prevalence of the Mercantile system (Kennedy 2017 , pp. 105–7). It is important to note that the nature of government interventions advocated by Smith, insofar as it was intended to combat vested interests, was antithetical to the interventions witnessed in the Mercantile system (Ortmann & Walraevens 2018 and chapter 2; see also Ortmann, Walraevens, & Baranowski 2019; Sagar 2021).

Our approach strengthens our previous argument that identified Smith as an early (and perhaps the first) analyst of incentive compatible state intervention (e.g., Ortmann 1999; Ortmann & Walraevens 2018 and chapter 2; see also Ortmann, Walraevens, & Baranowski 2019).

By showing, once more, how game theory can be fruitfully applied to Smiths oeuvre, we suggest a methodology that allows an answer to the question: "What would Smith say if he were alive today?" Such an answer is important in determining Smith's stance regarding the proper role of government which is, as Smith never tired to emphasize, very different in the different states of society.

The game-theoretic framework allows us to better understand when Smith allows exceptions to his ideal system of natural liberty (for a list of these exceptions see Viner 1927, Kennedy 2017). Is there any (well-defined) general theory of state intervention in Smith? (Not that we know but game-theoretic formulation seems a good way toward some such goal.)

As mentioned before, the third duty of the sovereign according to Smith is the provision of public works and public institutions:

> The third and last duty of the sovereign or commonwealth is that of erecting and maintaining those public institutions and those public works, which, though they may be in the highest degree advantageous to a great society, are, however, of such a nature, that the profit could never repay the expense to any individual or small number of individuals, and which it therefore cannot be expected that any individual or small number of individuals should erect or maintain. The performance of this duty requires too very different degrees of expense in the different periods of society. After the public institutions and public works necessary for the defense of the

society, and for the administration of justice, both of which have already been mentioned, the other works and institutions of this kind are chiefly those for facilitating the commerce of the society, and those for promoting the instruction of the people. (*WN*, V.i.c.1, p. 723)

One can easily recognize his train of thought: in Book V Smith is concerned first with protecting the people from foreign enemies, second from domestic enemies, and third from other domestic problems which could amount to "enemies" in a broader sense. One of these problems is an insufficiency of ***physical*** capital "facilitating the commerce of society" (*WN*, V.i.c.2, p. 723). The other is an insufficiency of ***human*** capital, i.e., "education of the youth" and "education of the people of all ages" (ibid). We will see now how the Smith Game can be fruitfully applied to these issues.

3 The Smith Game and the Proper Role of Government in the WN

The aim of this part is to analyze in detail, applying our Smith Game, several problems that Smith discusses in the context of maintenance of public institutions and public works.

Among the detailed analyses are problems of: street-lights (an example of non-excludable public works) that overcome a public good provision problem; protection of infant industries and innovation (an application involving the realization of positive externalities); and negative externalities arising from the division of labor (and what to do about them). This brings us back to the provision of (excludable) public goods. That an excludable public good should be provided by (some level of) government is due to the important input education brings to the social fabric.

3.1 Provision of Non-Excludable Public Works: Street-Lights

Acknowledging Edwin West's objection that some of the "public works" on Smith's list (such as roads, canals, bridges, harbors) are excludable, and the role Smith envisioned for government to play in provision of these works in many cases extends no farther than granting a corporate charter[3]; we will not apply the Smith Game to such works. Instead, we focus on

[3] See West (1990), Chapter 7. See also West (1976), on canal building near Montpellier.

the non-excludable works: street-lights, for example. Or light-houses for that matter.

The example of street-lights is mentioned by Smith only in passing. Smith brings the issue of their provision up to make a broader point: those public works that can't be expected to be provided by private individuals would better be paid by government at the local level than by government at the national level—an early application of the benefit principle. Nevertheless, since government pays for them at some level, they qualify as an example of government intervention.

Says Smith,

> Even those public works which are of such a nature that they cannot afford any revenue for maintaining themselves, but of which the conveniency is nearly confined to some particular place or district, are always better maintained by a local or provincial revenue, under the management of a local and provincial administration, than by the general revenue of the state, of which the executive power must always have the management. Were the streets of London to be lighted and paved at the expense of the treasury, is there any probability that they would be so well lighted and paved as they are at present, or even at so small an expense? The expense, besides, instead of being raised by a local tax upon the inhabitants of each particular street, parish, or district in London, would, in this case, be defrayed out of the general revenue of the state, and would consequently be raised by a tax upon all the inhabitants of the kingdom, of whom the greater part derive no sort of benefit from the lighting and paving of the streets of London. (*WN*, V.i.d.18, pp. 730–1)

As a version of the Smith Game, the players in the street-lighting problem are each resident of the neighborhood versus n-1 other residents, which can be abstracted to be a 2 × 2 two-player game with the second player be representative of the n-1 residents in the neighborhood. Street-lights are non-excludable, of course, so a person or company cannot purchase them and then charge the neighborhood residents already living there for their provision and maintenance. Without government intervention, provision of street-lights must be worked out voluntarily between the residents.

Assume that each resident wants the security of street-lights on his street; he would be better off having the street-lights and not having to pay for them. He may "not pay" and try to free-ride on his neighbors, having them pay while he does not. This would be ideal for him—but

Table 1 Smith Game of non-excludable public works (street-light provision)

		Representative of n-i other residents	
		Pay	Not Pay
Resident i	Pay	0, 0	-1, 2
	Not Pay	2, -1	0, 0

then they may try to free-ride on him as well. If enough people try to free-ride, there will be no "ride" at all—a sub-optimal outcome. With that in mind he could instead "pay" a portion of the cost of the street-light. Of course, the resultant game is a standard public good provision problem. With cell entries denoting utility, a typical street-light game appears as follows (Table 1).

Each resident knows that regardless of the decisions of n-1 other residents, his utility maximizing choice is to not pay. Other residents know this as well; and each resident knows other residents know it, and so on and so forth. The standard game-theoretic analysis applies with force: in a one-shot game, the residents are unlikely to pay. In such a case, local government may step in and levy a tax on each resident for the street-lights. In effect, people are forced to pay, changing the game's outcome to the Pareto-optimal upper-left corner. This is precisely the solution Smith suggests in the quote preceding the game matrix.

3.2 *Addressing Positive Externalities: Incentivizing Innovation*

Though Smith was no friend of monopolists, or market power for that matter (e.g., *WN*, I.x.c.27, p. 145), he recognized the necessity of monopolies in some instances. For example, he thought some monopoly privileges should be granted by the government to innovating companies or individuals in order to compensate them for their ground-breaking investments. Patents and copyrights are two obvious examples (*LJ(A)*, ii. 31–33, p. 83; *WN*, V.i.e.,30, p. 754). Another example, which is less compatible with the view of Smith as a laissez-faire economist, is the protection of infant industries.

Indeed, Smith believed that if a new trade is beneficial to the public, requires high fixed costs for the first entrant, and yet requires much lower fixed costs for later entrants, it is a legitimate area for government intervention.

> When a company of merchants undertake, at their own risk and expense, to establish a new trade with some remote and barbarous nation, it may not be unreasonable to incorporate them into a joint stock company, and to grant them, in case of their success, a monopoly of the trade for a certain number of years. It is the easiest and most natural way in which the state can recompense them for hazarding a dangerous and expensive experiment, of which the public is afterwards to reap the benefit. A temporary monopoly of this kind may be vindicated upon the same principles upon which a like monopoly of a new machine is granted to its inventor, and that of a new book to its author. (*WN,* V.i.e., 30, p. 754)

The essence of Smith's argument in this case is that there are positive externalities involved in "blazing the trail". People or firms who have had nothing to do with the risk-taking, research and development involved in innovating a new trade may derive benefits from the risk and expense of others. Without a guarantee to the first entrant that he will not be immediately under-cut by competition from later entrants operating at lower average costs *because of his innovation*, no firm will want to be the first to enter the trade. The firms, as well as the general public, will then suffer a sub-optimal outcome: the trade will not exist.

This problem can be modeled as a Smith Game similar to the preceding one. The players are potential entrants to the trade. Their choices are to "enter first" or to "wait". Each firmwould prefer to wait while another firm enters the trade first, but all other firms have the same preference. Knowing the fate that almost certainly awaits the first entrant—to be driven out of business by one's future lower-cost competitors—no firm will be likely to take the plunge. Again, the game's set-up and solution fit the previous model and do not require further elaboration.

Smith says that in cases such as these government may intervene to ensure a first entrant a reasonable return on his investment. This would be done by granting him monopoly rights for a limited time.[4]

[4] Smith was adamant that monopoly privileges granted by government be strictly temporary, not perpetual. The former "may be vindicated upon the same principles upon which a like monopoly of a new machine is granted to its inventor ..." (*WN,* V.i.e.,30, p. 754). The latter, however, will "merely enable the company to support the negligence, profusion, and malversation of their own servants ..." (*WN*, ibid.).

3.3 *Addressing Negative Externalities: The Division of Labor Revisited*

Perhaps the most dramatic example Smith provides of free markets' failure to induce optimal outcomes is the division of labor. This might strike many as an outlandish statement; some of the most memorable and well-known passages of *WN* Book I illustrate how the division of labor is the most important cause of productivity increases. Smith's famous pin factory nicely illustrates the general principle:

> The division of labor ... so far as it can be introduced, occasions, in every art, a proportionable increase in the productive powers of labor. (*WN*, I.i.4, p. 15)

Smith does not change his mind or deny this in Book V. The division of labor does indeed have all the productive power he ascribed to it in Book I, but in addition it produces severe negative externalities on the human "character". While most people are educated in the course of their jobs, the division of labor limits their work to increasingly fragmented tasks, and therefore increasingly limits their understanding of the world, and of others. Smith does not mince words here:

> In the progress of the division of labour, the employment of the far greater part of those who live by labour, that is, of the great body of the people, comes to be confined to a few very simple operation, frequently to one or two. But the understandings of the greater part of men are necessarily formed by their ordinary employments. The man whose whole life is spent in performing a few simple operations ... becomes as stupid and ignorant as it is possible for a human creature to become. The torpor of his mind renders him, not only incapable of relishing or bearing a part in any rational conversation, but of conceiving any generous, noble, or tender sentiment, and consequently of forming any just judgment concerning many even of the ordinary duties of private life. (*WN*, V.i.f.50, pp. 781–2)

In Meardon and Ortmann (1996a, 1996b) we explained how in Smith's system, people's understandings of the standards of propriety are learned over time. We also showed how the standards themselves evolve through social interaction. Each result is highly dependent upon the mindsets of the people involved. The less educated they are, the longer it will take them to understand and adhere to standards of propriety, and the longer and less adequate will be the evolution of the standards of propriety. "Propriety" will not be as morally stringent as it was before the division of labor, and people will be less likely to act properly even by the new standards. Along the same lines, Walraevens (2011) argues that workers' capacity for sympathy is altered. Their inability to take part in a conversation and their isolation in anonymous cities will limit their social interactions and, as a consequence, will exclude them of the formation and sharing of social and moral values. Smith believed that, if left unaddressed, these external effects of the division of labor, representing internal enemies of sorts, could tear the social fabric to pieces. The "corruption" of workers' minds is also a political issue for Smith. It is vital for the peace, stability, and order of commercial societies to possess well educated people, Smith argues (WN, V.i.f.61, p. 788). For all these reasons he thought government *must* address them:

> In some cases the state of the society necessarily places the greater part of individuals in such situations as naturally form in them, without any attention of government, almost all the abilities and virtues which that state requires, or perhaps can admit of. In other cases the state of the society does not place the greater part of individuals in such situations, and some attention of government is necessary in order to prevent the almost entire corruption and degeneracy of the great body of the people. (*WN*, V.i.f.50, p. 781)

> Though the state was to derive no advantage from the instruction of the inferior ranks of people, it would still deserve its attention that they should not be altogether uninstructed. The state, however, derives no inconsiderable advantage from their instruction. The more they are instructed, the less liable they are to the delusions of enthusiasm and superstition, which, among ignorant nations, frequently occasion the most dreadful disorders. An instructed and intelligent people besides, are always more decent and orderly than an ignorant and stupid one. They feel themselves, each individually more respectable, and more likely to obtain the respect of their lawful superiors, and they are therefore more disposed to respect those superiors. They are more disposed to examine, and more capable of seeing through, the interested complaints of faction and sedition, and they are, upon that account, less apt to be misled into any wanton or unnecessary opposition to the measures of government. (*WN*, V.i.f.61, p. 788)

The problem described by Smith is not only thoroughly modern; it is also in its underlying structure isomorph to a Bertrand game, with introduction of technology as the decision variable instead of price. As technology progresses, each firm in an industry must decide whether or not to incorporate the new technology into their production process. To do so will allow the firm to gain an edge on its competitor—or at least to keep up, if the competitor chooses to do the same. Introduction of new technology also implies the further division of labor, however, and to that extent it will worsen the "mental mutilation" of employees. This effect in turn leads to a tearing of the social fabric, a sub-optimal outcome for all parties.

In game-theoretic terms, then, the choices of the firms are to "do without" new technology or to "introduce" it. If both firms make the same choice, whatever that choice may be, they end up at the same place they were before: on an even playing field where economic profits are competed away. However, if one firm introduces new technology while the other does not, the firm that introduces it will be at a competitive advantage that translates into greater profits. Though the firm may incur a high fixed cost for the technology, the productivity gains will be such that the firm's average cost will decline and it will be able to undercut its competitor—at the expense of its employees' understandings of the world. The firm that does not introduce the new technology will spare its employees' minds while suffering losses that will ultimately lead to bankruptcy. Given these choices and outcomes, there can be little doubt what firms will choose to do: they will "introduce" the technology. In strategic form this game may appear as follows (Table 2).

Note that the game is totally symmetric, hence each firm has an incentive to introduce the new technology. Once everyone does so, economic profits will be zero for every firm, as they were before. Thus the payoffs in the upper-left and lower-right (diagonal) cells are (0,0), and the payoffs in the lower-left and upper-right (off-diagonal) cells are (2,-1) and (-1,2), respectively. The likely outcome of this game, whether repeated or not, is

Table 2 Smith Game of division of labor externalities

		Representative of n-i other firms	
		Do without	Introduce
Firm i	Do without	0, 0	-1, 2
	Introduce	2, -1	0, 0

in the lower-right corner. The problem is that while firms will be indifferent between the upper-left and lower-right corners, workers and society may not be. In the upper-left corner, the pros and cons not introducing new technology have to be taken into account; in the lower-right corner, the impact of the division of labor and hence the social fabric have to be factored in. It has been argued that Smith, once confronted with the empirical evidence that he faced in London, was increasingly concerned about the impact of the division of labor on the mindsets of workers and consequently on the social fabric (see Evensky 1989). Yet, in his *LJ*, Smith had already pointed out the deleterious effects of the division of labor on workers' mind and behavior. But he had no solution to provide at that time and conceded that "To remedy these defects would be an object worthy of serious attention" (*LJ(B)*, 333, p. 541). The lengthy passages in Book V of the *WN* that deal with education for the youth and instruction of people of all ages are substantial evidence of his concern

The role for government that Smith advocated is to force all people to educate themselves:

> The public can impose upon almost the whole body of the people the necessity of acquiring those most essential parts of education, by obliging every man to undergo an examination or probation in them before he can obtain the freedom in any corporation, or be allowed to set up any trade either in a village or town corporate. (*WN*, V.i.f.57, p. 786)

He thought this role would not be very difficult to fulfill, particularly in educating the common youth:

> ... if, instead of a little smattering of Latin, which the children of the common people are sometimes taught [in those little school books], and which can scarce ever be of any use to them; they were instructed in the elementary parts of geometry and mechanics, the literary education of this rank of people would perhaps be as complete as it can be. (*WN*, V.i.f.56, p. 785)

Though such intervention will not alter the game's outcome in terms of the players' optimal choices or their payoffs, it will change the outcome for those outside the game who suffer the consequences.

In completion of this section, it should be noted that while in the preceding division-of-labor externalities game it does not matter whether the game is played once, repeated finitely, or repeated infinitely, in the street-lights and innovation examples it might. Under certain circumstances, most importantly a stable group of agents and reasonable monitoring possibilities, cooperation can be motivated by the discipline that the potential loss of future payoffs imposes. Elinor Ostrom is among those who analyzed this evolution of institutional capacity for collective actions in her book *Governing The Commons* (Ostrom 1990).

4 Further Examples of Social Dilemmas in Smith's Works

In this part, we summarize a few more examples of social-dilemma games but sketch them only since at this point the basic idea of individual rationality undermining collective rationality should be reasonably well established. We conclude with an application of the asymmetric version of these games that Smith used from the very beginning in constructing his theories of rhetoric and self-command (and ultimately the theory of moral sentiments) which we discussed previously. It turns out that this is nothing but the game-theoretic model on which Smith hangs his model of efficiency wages, or what is now occasionally known as the labor discipline model (The CORE Team, no date).

But first things first: We start with a discussion of three examples (captains of industry, professors, religious sects) where the actors agitate against society's welfare and state (or third-party) intervention is required to regulate various forms of collusion and turn it to the advantage of society. Then we discuss examples (ambassadors, court fees, supporting the dignity of the chief of the state) where state intervention is desirable in order to facilitate desirable forms of cooperation. Finally, we discuss situations (e.g., merchants, employer/employee relationship) where state intervention is *not* necessary because the stage game gets repeated and reputation gets a chance to work its magic.

4.1 When State Intervention is Required to Rein in Collusion that is Counterproductive

4.1.1 Collusion by "Captains of Industry"

> People of the same trade seldom meet together, even for merriment and diversion, but the conversation ends in a conspiracy against the public, or in some contrivance to raise prices. (*WN*, I.x.c.27, p. 145)

In the *WN*, Smith underlines that masters-manufactures are always in a natural, "tacit" but "constant and uniform" state of collusion against workers not to raise wages (*WN*, I.viii.13, p. 84) and that they try to persuade legislators to make laws to protect them from (foreign) competition. Interestingly, Smith underlines the issue of reputation for those who would act uncooperatively, noting that "To violate this combination is every where a most unpopular action, and a sort of reproach to a master among his neighbours and equals" (ibid.). He makes clear, though, that the interest of the capitalist class "is always in some respects different from, and even opposite to, that of the publick" (*WN*, I.xi.p.10, p. 267).

What then could be done to avoid the pernicious effects of such combinations on the public interest? Smith believes that preventing the "assemblies" or "meeting" of "people of the same trade" by the law would be inconsistent with "justice and liberty", as it is for workers (*WN*, I.viii.12, p. 84). But if the law can't hinder masters/ manufacturers to meet and break their tacit collusion, it should do nothing to facilitate such meetings or to make them necessary, Smith argues (ibid). Hence his plea for dismantling corporations: "An incorporation not only renders them necessary, but makes the act of the majority binding upon the whole. In a free trade an effectual combination cannot be established but by the unanimous consent of every single trader, and it cannot last longer than every single trader continues of the same mind" (*WN*, I.x.c.30, p. 145).

Smith also recommends that every proposition of law coming from the "masters" be studied with the most "scrupulous", "suspicious attention" by legislators and statesmen (*WN*, I.xi.p.10, p. 267).

4.1.2 Collusion by Professors

Here is a case where an authority is needed to dismantle a game that is being played cooperatively, rather than to provide an enforcement mechanism that forces non-cooperative players to be cooperative (*WN*, V.i.f.5–8, pp. 760–1). In Smith's time and earlier, honoraria made up a great part of the income of university professors, but the increasing endowments of colleges and universities made it possible for those institutions to pay their professors by salary and in some cases prohibit honoraria (*WN*, V.i.f.5–7, p. 760). Salaries, combined with such rules, create an incentive problem for the professors; the common good is best served if they apply themselves to teach and work hard, but they are paid the same regardless of how hard they work. They may collude in being lazy so that all of them can slack off and yet none will look bad relative to the others (*WN*, V.i.f.8, p. 761; see Ortmann 1999). Again, Smith didn't mince words:

> Have those public endowments contributed in general to promote the end of their institution? Have they contributed to encourage the diligence, and to improve the abilities of the teachers? ... The endowments of schools and colleges have necessarily diminished more or less the necessity of application in the teachers. Their subsistence, so far as it arises from their salaries, is evidently derived from a fund altogether independent of their success and reputation in their particular professions. (*WN*, V.i.f.5, p. 760)

Salaries and prohibition of honoraria thus create a situation where a repeated game can be played cooperatively among professors to reach their Pareto-optimal outcome, but this outcome is by no means optimal for everybody else. Students' education and the reputation of the university are likely to suffer.

In this game, professors play against each other (or against n-1 others), and they can choose to work hard or to slack off. The game is a standard prisoners' dilemma which has evolved to the cooperative "slack off" outcome through repetition. Smith believes some authority (preferably the university trustees) must step in to change the method of payment and thereby alter the incentives and change the game. He seems to be in favor of the system in place in Scottish Universities in which the salary makes "a small part of the emoluments of the teacher, of which the greater part arises from the honoraries or fees of his pupils" (*WN*, V.i.f.6, p. 760).

Strictly speaking, this is not an example calling for *government* intervention, but we think it is an interesting example along the same lines, calling for third-party intervention.

4.1.3 Collusion by Religious Sects

Here is another game, similar to the previous one (e.g., Ortmann 1999), in which the state must intervene to dismantle a game that is working all too cooperatively (*WN*, V.i.g.12, pp. 795–6). Smith says that when poor people move to cities for finding jobs, they feel lost in a big impersonal crowd—quite unlike the environment in their villages. Hence their willingness to become members of small sects in which their presence is felt and makes a difference. These sects are often religious ones, and the members, sheltering themselves from outside society, hype themselves into an anti-social religious zeal. Nobody deviates from this behavior because to do so would risk expulsion from the group; in the repeated game each member knows this is not in his interest.

The players are members of the sect playing against each other (or n-1 other sect members). Their choices are to act fanatically or moderately. The game fits the prisoner's dilemma, which in repetition has induced mutual fanaticism—here the equivalent of the "cooperate" strategy. Smith feels the resultant behavior of the sect members is "disagreeably rigorous and unsocial", implying that external costs are imposed on others (ibid., p. 796).

Government may intervene in much the same way as in the division of labor game. By enforcing an education in the sciences, he believes the state can make people skeptical of the religious beliefs underlying the fanaticism of these groups. Smith also provides a "market argument" on this issue. He claims that government should encourage the prolifera-tion of small sects because their competition will lead to a moderation of beliefs and practices, in the same way it lowers prices (*WN*, V.i.g.8, p. 793). This is an illustration of the "moral discipline" of the market brought about through reputation effects; as below also illustrated by the merchant-customer example.

4.2 When State Intervention is Desirable in that it Facilitates Desirable Forms of Cooperation (and the Provision of Public Goods)

4.2.1 Ambassadors Defending the Interests of the Country's Merchants

Ambassadors fall under the category of public works facilitating a partic-ular branch of commerce (*WN*, V.i.e., 1–3, pp. 731–2). For a particular branch of trade dealing in "barbarous and uncivilized nations", the traders may need protection of their lives and property. The game is played between independent traders (the game may not apply when the trading is done by companies with monopolies) or between a trader and n-1 traders. Especially when there are many traders, the services of an ambassador are non-excludable or not easily excludable. Each trader wants the protection of an ambassador, and all are better off with one, but each wants everyone else to pay for it. The choices are to pay or not to pay, and government may step in to ensure the optimal outcome by taxing the particular goods traded by the traders in this country (ibid., p. 732). This game also fits the standard prisoners' dilemma.

4.2.2 Court Fees

Smith's views on court fees (*WN*, V.i.b.13–17, pp. 715–8) can be considered an issue independent of the provision of justice as a public good. Before court fees were standardized, the system of justice was paid for by voluntary gifts from the parties in a dispute. One often found that "justice" was bestowed upon the party offering the more impressive gift *(WN*, V.i.b.14, p. 716). Obviously, this was creating undesirable externalities such as a mistrust in the system of justice administration.

As a game, the players are two enemies who take their case to court, and their choices are to "cooperate" or "defect". Cooperation implies giving a gift agreed upon by both players in advance, and defection implies not agreeing or giving a gift of greater value than agreed upon. In the former case, justice goes to the more deserving party, while in the latter it goes to the highest bidder. Given either choice by the other player, each player is better off defecting. If both players defect justice again goes to the more deserving party, though it is more costly to them than if they both cooperated. The game fits the payoffs of the standard prisoner's dilemma (recall the street-light game). By standardizing court fees, government can intervene to pull the outcome of the game to the upper-left corner.

4.2.3 "Supporting the Dignity" of the Chief of State

Though Smith doesn't explain this in depth, he feels it is important for society to maintain the sovereign (today the ruler, president, prime-minister, etc.) at a certain level of dignity (*WN*, V.i.h.1–3, p. 814). Everybody benefits, but the benefits are not excludable, so everybody has an incentive not to pay the cost and to free-ride off of others. The players are a citizen vs. n-1 other citizens, and their choices are to pay or not to pay. This fits the model of other public goods problems. Government may intervene to enforce payment through taxation of some kind.

4.3 *Situations Where State Intervention is not Necessary Because the Stage Game Gets Repeated and Reputation gets a Chance to Work its Magic*

4.3.1 *The Trustworthiness of Merchants*

In his *LJ*, Smith explains why merchants, contrary to politicians, and especially ambassadors, usually are trustworthy.[5]

Smith's discussion could be studied as a game of seller-buyer transactions for goods of adjustable quality. The merchant can sell high or low quality products. The buyer can monitor or trust him. The solution of the game is similar to the precedent case. "A dealer", Smith writes, "is scrupulous in observing every engagement" because "he is anxious of losing his character" (*LJ(B),* 327, p. 538). Yet "when a person makes perhaps 20 contracts in a day, he cannot gain so much by endeavoring to impose on his neighbours, as the very appearance of a cheat would make him lose" (ibid.). By contrast, "where people seldom deal with one another, we find that they are somewhat disposed to cheat, because they can gain more by a smart trick than they can lose by the injury which it does their character" (ibid., p. 539). Ambassadors, for example, "may gain more by one piece of fraud than lose by having a bad character" because "nations treat with one another twice or thrice in a century" (ibid.). The frequency of interactions is crucial here. Politicians cheat because they are involved in a one-shot game. Consequently, they can gain in defecting. However,

[5] Sagar (2021) discusses the conspiracy of merchants, very much in line with what we discuss above under the heading of the collusion by "captains of industry". In fact, he motivates his study with the quote that we use as epigraph for that section. Sagar wants to understand why and how, in Smith's opinion, the merchants were able to exert such disproportionate influence in modern societies. He starts his argument with merchants' advocacy of a faulty economic theory—the balance of trade—which "enabled them to deceive political rulers into granting vast networks of monopolies, drawbacks, and bounties, that enriched the merchants whilst impoverishing the rest of the nation" (p. 465). Sagar's key argument is (p. 475) that the employees of the East India Company—i.e., private merchants—acted as just that, short-term profit maximizers when in fact they were de facto sovereigns that should have a long-term profit maximization perspective. "Yet because the merchants saw themselves as British, and India as simply a foreign place to extract profit before leaving for home, they never made this connection" (ibid.). The consequences were costly in that the entire colonial system could ultimately be sustained only by violent oppression that relied on military force. Pack (2010, in particular pp. 71 - 73), curiously not even referenced by Sagar, makes a very similar argument. He stresses that the questionable behavior of merchants, against which Smith railed, was designed by them and reflected their ability in the England of their time to extract more than their fair share.

merchants cooperate and are trustworthy (so that buyers cooperate too) because of the discipline that the potential loss of future payoffs imposes on them in the infinitely repeated game of commerce. Smith applies this reasoning about reputation effects in repeated games to workers/artisans too:

> The real and effectual discipline which is exercised over a workman, is not that of his corporation, but that of his customers. It is the fear of losing their employment which restrains his frauds and corrects his negligence. An exclusive corporation necessarily weakens the force of this discipline. A particular set of workmen must then be employed, let them behave well or ill. It is upon this account that in many large incorporated towns no tolerable workmen are to be found, even in some of the most necessary trades. If you would have your work tolerably executed, it must be done in the suburbs, where the workmen having no exclusive privilege, have nothing but their character to depend upon, and you must then smuggle it into the town as well as you can. (*WN*, I.x.c.31, p. 147)

4.3.2 "Efficiency Wages"

Another example taken from Smith's works in which mutual cooperation (in a social dilemma) is reached without state intervention can be found in Book I, Chapter VIII, "Of the Wages of Labour",. There, Smith's discussion could be treated in game-theoretic form as an "efficiency wage" game. He writes:

> The liberal reward of labour, as it encourages the propagation, so it increases the industry of the common people. The wages of labour are the encouragement of industry, which, like every other human quality, improves in proportion to the encouragement it receives...Where wages are high, accordingly, we shall always find the workmen more active, diligent, and expeditious, than where they are low; (*WN*, I.viii.44, p. 99)

Workers do an intertemporal calculus of utility. They know that work is a pain, a loss of time and liberty. Yet, they understand that working hard now can make them better off in the future when they are given a plentiful subsistence. In the worker's position "the comfortable hope of bettering his condition, and of ending his days perhaps in ease and plenty animates him to exert his strength to the utmost" (*WN*, I.viii.44, p. 99).

It should be noted that Smith was a pioneer in the defense of a positive correlation between wages and the level of effort. This is in sharp contrast with the dominant theory of his time, in which it was claimed that high wages led to indolence, so that workers had to be kept in poverty (see Mandeville for a typical case).

The game pits employers against employees. The employer can pay a premium for high-quality work or can pay the standard wage. The employee can work hard or slack off. In each case, the first choice is cooperative or proper and the second non-cooperative or improper. The resultant set-up is a standard principal–agent game which Meardon and Ortmann (1996a) to represent Smith's model of the acquisition of self-command. The solution of the game is straightforward. In a one-shot game, each party gains by making the proper choice, but each gains more by choosing improperly when the other chooses properly. In an infinitely repeated game, cooperation is again motivated by the discipline that the potential loss of future payoffs imposes.[6] Note the interesting parallels to merchants' incentive to care about their reputation. Workers and merchants play the same Smith game here, the former in the factor market, the latter in the product market. It is a telling example of Smith's remarkable analytic insights that he recognized the incentive issues here, yet did not advocate government intervention. In light of his understanding of the power of reputational enforcement, as exhibited in *TMS*, this should come as no surprise.

5 Conclusion

After having presented our general framework, the Smith Game, in Sect. 2, we have seen in Sects. 3 and 4 how this Smith Game can be applied to model a number of incentive problems as they are found in Smith's works, in particular in *WN*. We have used the Smith Game

[6] In this game, the optimal result is reached when both choose to cooperate. Yet, Smith underlines that when laborers work hard and capital owners pay them by the piece it can lead to a suboptimal outcome. The reason lies in the workers' tendency to overwork (*WN*, I.viii.44, p. 100). Doing so, they "ruin their health" and become less productive than people who make moderate but constant efforts (ibid.). Here, the workers' faculty to calculate has failed. Maybe it is an unfortunate consequence of the deleterious effects of the division of labor on workers' mind and understanding (see above), the latter being defined as an essential component of prudential behavior in *TMS*. But it is not Smith's first and foremost argument. According to him, this failure of the employer-employee relationship comes from capitalists' inability to "listen to the dictates of reason and humanity" (ibid.). Capital owners are blinded by the love of domination and the quest for profit (Dellemotte & Walraevens 2015).

to show formally that although Smith was indeed a market-oriented economist, he was not a laissez-faire economist. He understood that problems of externalities and public good provision, broadly construed, lead to undesirable outcomes from the society's point of view and undermine what Smith liked to call the natural system of liberty (Pack & Schliesser 2018), or what today is often referred to as the free-market system. He believed a role for government exists in attempting to reverse the consequences of such problems. We have exemplified in some detail Smith's views along these lines for some prominent examples.

By framing a variety of central problem isomorphs as social-dilemma games or variants thereof, we have suggested a novel way of looking at *WN* and especially at his views on the proper role of government in commercial societies. We have also indirectly made a case for the central importance in *WN* of Book V, "Of the Revenue of the sovereign or Commonwealth".

Our game-theoretic interpretation of *WN* is part and parcel of our attempt to re-orient the discourse about the significance and structure of *The Wealth of Nations*, *The Theory of Moral Sentiments*, and their relationship to each other. We have shown elsewhere in detailed studies how Smith modeled the acquisition of self-command *given general rules of morality* as game whose structure is identical to principal-agent models well-known in the game theory literature. We have also shown how Smith used the hawk-dove game to model the origin and evolution of general rules of morality. Both the principal-agent and the hawk-dove game are members of a rich class of models—which we call the summarily the Smith Game—representing phenomena as varied as (asymmetrically structured) seller-buyer transactions of goods of adjustable quality or employee-employer relations ("reputation games"), or (symmetrically structured) attempts at collusion and public goods provision and externalities problems.

Uncovering the pervasive existence of the Smith Game has led us to claim that Smith—while he did not use these terms—understood well and dealt with the pervasive nature of inter- and externalities, as well as the related issue of reputational enforcement. By framing Smith's work in game-theoretic terms, we have suggested that he was an early theoretician of incentive compatible state intervention. Thus, *contra* Schumpeter (and others), in our view there can be no doubt that Smith was a major theorist. His vigorous advocacy of economic freedom was a methodological device intended to set the stage for his ultimate purpose: the analysis of incentive compatible state intervention.

Finally, by showing how game theory can be fruitfully applied to Smith's oeuvre, we suggest a methodology that allows an answer to the question: "What would Smith say if he were alive today?" Such an answer is particularly important in determining Smith's stance regarding the proper role of government which is, as Smith never tired to emphasize, very different in the different states of society. In particular, the appropriate degree of third and last duty of the sovereign, provision of public works and institutions facilitating commerce (and particular branches of commerce), and institutions for the education of the youth (and of people of all ages), may have expanded over time. Smith himself justified this approach by saying in most instances where he saw a role for government that the role "requires ... very different degrees of expense in the different periods of society" (*WN*, V.i.b.1, p. 709). Though we do not intend in this paper to take this approach very far, we can provide a glimpse toward where it might lead. Just think about telecommunications. In the conclusion of Book V, Chapter 1, Smith discusses the possibility of a governmental role in facilitating communications[7] and urges application of the benefit principle wherever possible, but he understands that externalities have to be accounted for.[8]

In the late eighteenth century, "communications" were conducted over land and sea; today they are also conducted over telephone lines and via satellite. By Smith's rationale, government may have a role in helping to provide these modern "roads" of communication. The group of people who most often use public works facilitating telecommunications should pay for them as much as possible. There are positive externalities to these

[7] "The expense of maintaining good roads and communications is, no doubt, beneficial to the whole society, and may, therefore, without any injustice, be defrayed by the general contribution of the whole society. This expense, however, is most immediately and directly beneficial to those who travel or carry goods from one place to another, and to those who consume such goods. The turnpike tolls in England, and the duties called peages in other countries, lay it altogether upon those two different sets of people, and thereby discharge the general revenue of the society from a very considerable burden" (*WN*, V.i.i.4, p. 815).

[8] "When the institutions or publick works which are beneficial to the whole society, either cannot be maintained altogether, or are not maintained altogether by the contribution of such particular members of the society as are most immediately benefited by them, the deficiency must in most cases be made up by the general contribution of the whole society" (*WN*, V.i.i.6, p. 815).

works, however, and therefore a case can be made that the state may be justified in forcing others to pay, through taxation, for the works as well.

References

Barro RG (1990) Macroeconomic Policy. Harvard University Press, Cambridge

Bevilaqua C (1968) Adam Smith and some philosophical origins of eighteenth-century rhetorical theory. Mod Lang Rev 63:3

Brown V (1994) Adam Smith's Discourse: Canonicity, Commerce and Conscience. Routledge, New York

Browning EK, Browning JM (1987) Public Finance and the Price System. Palgrave Macmillan, New York

The CORE Team . The Economy. Economics for a changing world. https://www.core-econ.org/project/core-the-economy/. Accessed 10 Jan 2022

Davis DD, Holt CA (1993) Experimental Economics. Princeton University Press, Princeton

Dellemotte J, Walraevens B (2015) Adam Smith on the Subordination of Wage-Earners in Commercial Societies. Eur J Hist Econ 22(4):692–727

Dickinson College Wiki (no date) Group 4: Game Theory and Adam Smith. https://wiki.dickinson.edu/index.php/Group_4:_Game_Theory_and_Adam_Smith. Accessed 3 Jan 2022

Endres A (1991) Adam Smith's rhetoric of economics: an illustration using 'smithian' compositional rules. Scott J Polit Econ 38(1):76–95

Evensky J (1989) The Evolution of Adam Smith's Views on Political Economy. Hist Polit Econ 21:123–145

Fehr E, Gächter, S (2000) Cooperation and Punishment in Public Goods Experiments. American Economic Review 90(4):980–994

Holmstroem BR, Tirole J (1989) The Theory of the Firm. In: Schmalensee R, Willig, RD (eds) Handbook of Industrial Organization, vol 1. Elsevier Science Publishers, New York

Howell S (1975) Adam Smith's Lectures on Rhetoric: An Historical Assessment. In: Skinner A, Wilson T (eds) Essays in honour of Adam Smith. Oxford University Press, Oxford, p 11–43

Kennedy G (2010) Adam Smith: A Moral Philosopher and His Political Economy, 2nd edn. Palgrave Macmillan, Basingstoke

— (2017) An Authentic Account of Adam Smith. Palgrave Macmillan, London

Kreps DM (1988) Corporate Culture and Economic Theory in Alt J, Shepsle K (eds) Perspectives on Positive Political Economy. Cambridge University Press, Cambridge, p 90–143

— (1990a) Game Theory and Economic Modelling. Oxford University Press, Oxford

— (1990b) A Course in Microeconomic Theory. Princeton University Press, Princeton
— (2020) A Course in Microeconomic Theory (paperback). Princeton University Press, Princeton
McKenna S (2005) Adam Smith: the Rhetoric of Propriety. State University of New York Press, New York
Meardon SJ, Ortmann A (1996a) Self-Command in Adam Smith's Theory of Moral Sentiments: A Game-Theoretic Re-Interpretation. Ration Soc 8(1):57–80
— (1996b) Yes, Adam Smith was an Economist (A Very Modern One Indeed). Reply to Brown. Ration Soc 8(3):348–352
Muller J (1993) Adam Smith in his time and ours. Princeton University Press, Princeton
Ortmann, A, Colander, DC (1997). A Simple Principal-Agent Experiment for the Classroom. Econ Inq 35(2):445–450
Ortmann A (1999) The Nature and Causes of Corporate Negligence, Sham Lectures, and Ecclesiastical Indolence: Adam Smith on Joint-Stock Companies, Teachers, and Preachers. Hist Polit Econ 31(2):297–315
Ortmann A, Meardon SJ (1993) Adam Smith on the Origin and Evolution of Moral Sentiments. Working Paper, Bowdoin College, June 1993
— (1995) A game-theoretic re-evaluation of Adam Smith's Theory of Moral Sentiments and Wealth of Nations. In: Rima IH (ed) The Classical Tradition in Economic Thought. Perspectives on the History of Economic Thought Vol XI. Edward Elgar, Brookfield, p 43–61
Ortmann A, Walraevens B (2018) The Rhetorical Structure of Adam Smith's Wealth of Nations. Working Paper. Available via SSRN. https://papers.ssrn.com/sol3/papers.cfm?abstract_id=3300236
— (2021) Adam Smith's Reasoning Routines and the Deep Structure of his Oeuvre. Working Paper. Available via SSRN. https://papers.ssrn.com/sol3/papers.cfm?abstract_id=3992914
Ortmann A, Walraevens B, Baranowski D (2019) Schumpeter's Assessment of Adam Smith and 'The Wealth of Nations': Why He Got It Wrong. J Hist Econ Thought 41(4):531–551
Ostrom E (1990) Governing the Commons: The Evolution of Institutions for Collective Action. Cambridge University Press, Cambridge
Pack SJ (2010) Aristotle, Adam Smith and Karl Marx. On Some Foundational Issues in 21st Century Political Economy, Edward Elgar, Cheltenham & Northampton
Pack SJ, Schliesser E (2018) Adam Smith, Natural Movement and Physics. Camb J Econ 42(2):505–521
Pouchain T (2017) Adam Smith's Socio-Cultural Theory of Evolution. New insight from his 1749 lecture. Adam Smith Rev 9:49–74

Rasmusen E (1989) Games and Information: An Introduction to Game Theory. Basil Blackwell Inc., Cambridge

Rima IH (1972) Development of Economic Analysis. Richard D Irwin Inc., Homewood

Romer D (2018), Advanced Macroeconomics, fifth edition, McGraw Hill, New York

Rosen S (1987) Some Economics of Teaching. J Labor Econ 5:561–575

Sagar P (2021) Adam Smith and the conspiracy of the merchants. Global Intellectual History 6(4): 463–483

Salber Philips, M (2006) Adam Smith, Belletrist. In: Haakonssen K (ed) The Cambridge Companion to Adam Smith. Cambridge University Press, Cambridge, p 57–78

Sandmo A (2016) Adam Smith and Modern Economics. In: Hanley R (ed) Adam Smith. His Life, Thought, and Legacy. Princeton University Press, Princeton, p 231–246

Sen A (2016) Adam Smith and Economic Development. In: Hanley R (ed) Adam Smith. His Life, Thought, and Legacy. Princeton University Press, Princeton, p 281–302

Skinner A (1986) 'Introduction' to The Wealth of Nations: Books I-III. Penguin Classics, New York

Smith A (*LJ*), Lectures on Jurisprudence. Meek RL, Raphael DD, Stein PG (eds) (1982a). Liberty Classics, Indianapolis (Corresponding Glasgow edition: 1978)

— (TMS), The Theory of Moral Sentiments. Raphael DD, Macfie AL (eds) (1982b). Liberty Classics, Indianapolis (Corresponding Glasgow edition: 1976)

— (LRBL), Lectures on Rhetoric and Belles Lettres. Bryce JC, Skinner AS (eds) (1985) Liberty Classics, Indianapolis (Corresponding Glasgow edition: 1983)

— (WN), An Inquiry into the Nature and Causes of the Wealth of Nations. Campbell RH, Skinner AS (eds) (1981). Liberty Classics, Indianapolis (Corresponding Glasgow edition: 1976)

Tirole J (1988) The Theory of Industrial Organization. MIT Press, Cambridge

— (1996) A Theory of Collective Reputations (with Applications to the Persistence of Corruption and to Firm Quality). The Rev of Econ Stud 63(1):1–22

Viner J (1927) Adam Smith and Laissez Faire. J of Pol Econ 35(2):198–232

Walraevens B (2010) Croissance et progrès chez Adam Smith. These de doctorat en sciences economiques, Universite Paris 1 Panthéon Sorbonne

— (2011) Corruption des travailleurs et éducation dans les sociétés commerciales selon Adam Smith. Cahiers d'Economie Politique 60:11–44

Walraevens B (2014) Vertus et Justice du Marché chez Adam Smith. Revue Economique 65:419–438

West E (1976) Adam Smith. The Man and his Works. Liberty editions, Indianapolis
— (1990) Adam Smith and Modern Economics. Edward Elgar Publishing, Brookfield

CHAPTER 6

Adam Smith's Economics and the Lectures on Rhetoric and Belles Lettres: The Language of Commerce

Benoît Walraevens

1 Introduction

Under the light of Adam Smith's Lectures on Rhetoric and Belles Lettres (*LRBL*),[1] the aim of this paper will be to reinterpret some Smithian economic and moral issues. More precisely, it will try to highlight the relationship between discursive practice and economic reality in apparent simplicity, exchange. According to Smith, the essence and foundation of exchange and commerce lies in language. The departure point of this study will be to examine the dichotomy that he establishes between two main types of discourse: the rhetorical discourse and the didactic discourse. Didactic discourse is described as aiming at truth whereas

[1] *LRBL* after. See Howell 1975, Skinner 1979, Salber Phillips 2006 for the historical and theoretical relevance of *Smith's LRBL.* A significant exception is Brown 1994b whose conclusions, especially on the bartering of the market, are often similar to ours. Yet she does not provide a significant account of the relationship between Smith's moral philosophy and the persuasive side of exchange. In the first section, this is the point we will focus on.

A. Ortmann and B. Walraevens, *Adam Smith's System*, Palgrave Studies in the History of Economic Thought,
https://doi.org/10.1007/978-3-030-99704-5_6

rhetorical discourse obeys a strictly instrumental logic: it only aims at reaching an end and persuading by any mean. This distinction can be used to develop a new approach of exchange relations. The rhetorical discourse brings along to the social and human dimension concerning exchange relations to light. The exchange of goods requires an agreement obtained by «higgling and bargaining».[2] Economics is "political economy" in the sense that in parallel with the relations of men to things, it is a science which studies the relations between men themselves. The supply and demand embody the desires and wants of men. Therefore, this leads us to carry out a detailed study of exchange relationships as moral and persuasion relationships, revealing the «language of exchange ».

First of all, we will study the distinction that Smith established in the *LRBL* between rhetorical discourse and didactical discourse. That will enable us to define the rhetorical discourse as persuasion science, as compared with the didactical discourse which consists in truth seeking. As he wishes to persuade by all means to reach his ends, the rhetorician «moves away» from truth, hoodwinking and deceiving his audience. He doesn't impartially treat the topic he studies. He pleads a cause and manipulates his audience. Besides, some scholars[3] recently underlined that the famous «natural propensity to truck, barter, and exchange» comes from reason and language, and more particularly from the desire to persuade. It opens up the possibility to treat exchange relations as persuasion, domination, or power relationship and exchange as a bargaining process.[4] It is the «malevolent nature»[5] of exchange that we aim at revealing. To persuade someone that it is their interest to exchange at a certain price, every mean is justified, including slyness and cheating, lie and information dissimulation. The example of the butcher is clear: no benevolence brought during an exchange. But does it mean that we are immoral? The question of the morality of exchange relations comes into light. In this second point, we answer the Adam Smith Problem[6] thanks

[2] See *WN*, i.v.4.

[3] See Brown 1994a, Force 2003 and Dellemotte 2005.

[4] We follow here the way opened by Brown 1994a.

[5] See Young 1997.

[6] For the state of the debates, see Montes 2003.

to a brief examination of some passages of *The Theory of Moral Sentiments*.[7] There Smith explicitly mentions the wish to be believed and to be worthy of this trust, in the same way, he previously referred to the longing for praise and the desire to be praise-worthy. In other words, both the moral constraint coming from the impartial and internal spectator on one side, and the public constraint due to the external spectators on the other side, prevent us from using immoral practices in the exchange. We want to preserve our reputation and our consciousness. Economic behavior is neither immoral nor amoral. Following this, the third and last point of our study tries to identify an analogy between the exchange of feelings, opinions, and goods.

It is a reference to the pleasure of mutual sympathy which finds its corollary in the pleasure of persuading. It underlines the social and human (communicative) dimension of exchange. After being for so long forgotten by the neoclassical model, it was rediscovered by contemporary economists. This is essential to understand the key role of sympathy in the process of exchanging goods and it offers an answer to the question of the unity of the Smithian corpus. The virtuous character of economic behavior is shown through an examination of the way commerce fosters prudence, justice, and self-command, three of Smith's four cardinal virtues.

2 Rhetoric and Exchange

Our starting point is Smith's claim in the *LRBL* that there are only two main kinds of discourse. More precisely, «every discourse proposes either barely to relate some fact, or to prove some proposition» (*LRBL*, i.149). The first kind of discourse is called «narrative» and has to do with the work of the historian, while the second one is used by the orator. The latter is divided by the author into two sorts of discourse, characterized by their method and their aim: the didactic discourse and the rhetorical discourse. Within the didactic discourse «instruction is the main end» thus persuasion is only the «secondary design», whereas in the case of the rhetorical one the main design is persuasion. Rhetorical discourse stands for the individual who «endeavours to persuade us by all means» (ibid.). So, in that case instruction is neglected or considered «only so far as it is

[7] *TMS* after.

subservient to perswasion» (ibid.). In a word, instruction is subordinated to persuasion. Rhetoric is persuasive while didactic is convincing.

Moreover, a debate can be engaged about the impartiality of those different kinds of discourse. We know the importance of this word in Smith's moral philosophy. Indeed, what Smith underlines is the fact that the rhetorician, contrary to the man who uses a didactical discourse, is not an impartial "judge" of the topics he works on. In other words, the rhetorician presents a partial point of view about the question he is asked. He defends a cause, with no respect for truth:

> The former (the didactical discourse) proposes to put before us the arguments on both sides of the question giving each its proper degree of influence, and has it in view to perswade no farther than the arguments themselves appear *convincing*. The Rhetoricall again endeavours by all means to perswade us; and for this purpose it magnifies all the arguments on the one side and diminished or conceals those that might be brought on the side contrary to that which it is designed that we should favour.
> (*LRBL*, i.149; italics added)

Thus, the rhetorician pleads a cause. Ready to persuade by all means, he doesn't look for truth or for fairness anymore. He conceals or minimizes every fact and argument which contradicts his preconception while magnifying the ones which can legitimate his cause. Moreover, he "plays" with people's feelings, sentiments, and passions,[8] while the didactic thinker addresses their reason only. Being voluntarily unable of impartiality, the rhetorician seems morally condemnable or, at least, seems unworthy of praise. Didactic discourse attempts to give a fair representation of all sides of the issue rather than just the one-sided partial presentation of the rhetorical kind. This binary opposition is reminiscent of the one settled in Plato's Gorgias between philosophy and rhetoric where the latter is compared unfavorably with the former on the grounds that rhetoric aims at satisfying personal ends and at conquering power, while philosophy's quest is intended to reach wisdom and the Good. Rhetoric is seen as an art of pleasure and flattery whose end is persuasion. Philosophy's end, by contrast, is to find truth.[9]

[8] See *LRBL*, ii.38.

[9] For more details, see Brown 1994a, 70; 1994b, 16.

As a result, Smith's *LRBL* are mainly aimed at exploring the communication of ideas. It is to be seen as part of Smith's system and as a fruitful text for exploring moral and economic issues in particular. With an eye on the latter, it is possible to create a "bridge" between discourse and exchange, to cast a light on the «language of exchange ». Understanding the "chains" unifying rhetorical discourse and exchange relationships requires investigating the foundation of the division of labor and the «propensity to truck, barter and exchange». In the *WN*, Smith explains that the division of labor «is the necessary, though very slow and gradual consequence of a certain propensity in human nature...the propensity to truck, barter, and exchange one thing for another» (*WN*, i.ii.1). This natural propensity to exchange is a typically human attribute[10] because «nobody ever saw a dog make a fair and deliberate exchange of one bone for another with another dog» (*WN*, i.ii.2). What is interesting here is that Smith does not mention the origin of this natural propensity to exchange. He hardly suggests that it is probably «the consequence of the faculty of reason and speech» (ibid.). It is no surprise, for in *WN* Smith is not concerned with first principles. To him, reason and language are «intimately» linked. He sees language as «a natural expression of our thoughts»—*LJ(a)*, ii.54—, contrary to writing. Besides, the example of the two savages who invent the first words in order to make their desires and wants mutually intelligible[11] in the *Considerations concerning the first formation of languages* reveals how the beginning of commerce cannot be separated from the invention of language. More generally, in the *LRBL*, Smith adds that Prose is the language of commerce (whereas Poetry is the language of pleasure and entertainment).[12] As a consequence, the development of commerce allows and requires the improvement of language.[13] However, it is in the *LJ* that we will find the real explanation of the foundation of the exchange and the division of labor:

> If we should enquire into the principle in the human mind on which this disposition of trucking is founded, it is clearly the naturall inclination every

[10] For Smith, Man is by nature a social being. The inter-subjectivity is the foundation of his subjectivity.

[11] Here lies the difference between Man and the animal because Man needs to satisfy his desires but also to make them recognized by others.

[12] No pleasure and entertainment in commerce?

[13] Specifically Prose. See *LRBL*,ii.115.

> one has to persuade. The offering of a shilling, which to us appears to have so plain and simple a meaning, is in reality offering an argument to persuade one to do so and so as it is for his interest. Men always endeavour to persuade others to be of their opinion even when the matter is of no consequence to them. If one advances any thing concerning China or the more distant moon which contradicts what you imagine to be true, you im- mediately try to persuade him to alter his opinion. And in this manner every one is practising oratory on others thro the whole of his life. You are uneasy whenever one differs from you, and you endeavour to persuade him to be of your mind; or if you do not it is a certain degree of self command, and to this every one is breeding thro their whole lives. In this manner they acquire a certain dexterity and address in man- aging their affairs, or in other words in managing of men; and this is altogether the practise of every man in the most ordinary affairs. This being the constant employment or trade of every man, in the same manner as the artisans invent simple methods of doing their work, so will each one here endeavour to do this work in the simplest manner. That is bartering, by which they address themselves to the self interest of the person and seldom fail immediately to gain their end.
>
> (*LJ(a)*, vi.57)

So, exchange is founded on this «desire of persuading, of leading and directing other people», which «seems to be one of the strongest of all our natural desires. It is, perhaps, the instinct upon which is founded the faculty of speech, the characteristical faculty of human nature» (*TMS*, vii.iv.25). The individuals who carry out an exchange may now be conceived as rhetoricians, and the exchange as a bargaining process. We are able to explain why the natural propensity to truck, barter, and exchange is a human characteristic. It is founded on the desire to persuade which is itself a desire of approbation, more precisely a desire of approbation in relation to our opinions and ideas. Rhetoric is the foundation of human life. We have a strong desire to persuade because we need others if we want to satisfy our desires and our needs.

Unlike animals, human beings are fundamentally dependent on others' assistance for their survival.[14] That's why they are endowed with the faculty of speech in order to persuade them to do what they need. For it is

[14] «In almost every other race of animals each individual, when it is grown up to maturity, is intirely independent, and in its natural state has occasion for the assistance of no other living creature. But man has almost constant occasion for the help of his brethren» (*WN*, i.ii.2).

«by treaty, by barter, and by purchase, that we obtain from one another the greater part of those mutual good offices which we stand in need of» (*WN*, i.ii.3). We practice oratory through all of our lives, and «the offering of a shilling, which to us appears to have so plain and simple a meaning, is in reality offering an argument to persuade one to do so»: *LJ(a)*, vi.57. Furthering this point, we approve of others' opinions in the same way we approve of their moral sentiments, by sympathizing. The desire of approbation comes from the pleasure of mutual sympathy.[15] And sympathy is typically a human attribute and the key to the social nature of Man. A second explanation is explicitly given by Smith in the passage mentioned below. The propensity to truck is founded on the desire to persuade and «this is the instinct upon which is founded the faculty of speech, a characteristical faculty of human nature». The use of the expressions «faculty of speech» and «reason and speech» leads us to believe that what Smith has in mind here is not language in a narrow sense but rather the Aristotelian logos, the power of reasoning and expressing one's ideas. So, persuasion, language, and exchange are inseparable. Men possess an innate desire to persuade; so they spend their whole life exercising their power of persuasion. In the eighteenth century, the word "commerce" had a broader sense than today. It meant diffusion, communication, propagation.[16] It was not restricted to economic relationships. That's why we can say that throughout his works, Smith describes Man as a «commercial» or an «exchanging animal». He exchanges words and ideas in the *LRBL* and the Considerations concerning the first formation of languages, feelings, and moral sentiments in the *TMS*, and goods in the *WN*. Moreover, there is a pleasure in persuading in the same manner, there is a pleasure in mutual sympathy.[17] Finally, persuasion is an end in itself for Smith. We exchange goods not only for the goods themselves but in order to persuade others and obtain this pleasure of persuading, even if we know we are mistaking.[18]

[15] I develop this point in i.iii.

[16] For instance, Smith's use of the term in its broader sense is explicit in *LJ(a)*, iv.13 and *TMS*, iii.3.7.

[17] See Dellemotte 2005 for the relationship between sympathy and the desire to persuade.

[18] This is true for most people but not, Smith adds, for the man of virtue who has enough self-command not to be corrupted.

3 The Morality of Exchange

Defining people engaged in the exchange of goods as rhetoricians provide us with significant clues to understand their behavior in the marketplace. A rhetorician is one who pleads a cause and whose primary design is to persuade by every means. Economic agents plead their cause too. They try to satisfy their personal interest. If we compare them with rhetoricians, does it mean that they will endeavor to satisfy their own interest by every means? The "selfish" character of the economic man seems to find some textual support.[19] Rhetorical discourse and power are intrinsically linked, the rhetorical discourse being at the beginning the science of men aspiring to political power,[20] Smith explicitly defines the faculty of speech and the desire of persuading as useful instruments for governing men.[21] As a consequence, exchange relationships become power and domination relationships. It is interesting to notice that Smith describes a «learning process». In other words, the individuals who are often persuaded, led, and directed because of their lack of rhetorical ability will not remain infinitely dominated by others since «from being led and directed by other people we learn to wish to become ourselves leaders and directors» (*TMS*, vii.iv.24). The traditional presentation of exchange as a mutually beneficial process is called into question. This malevolent side of exchange is concealed by the fact that exchange is built on an agreement and based on this principle: «Give me that which I want, and you shall have this which you want» (*WN*, i.ii.2). The most important point is that the individual who dominates does not let his (or her) superiority appear and that he manages to give the other one the impression he is not dominated. It

[19] A close look at Smith' moral theory reveals how deceptive this interpretation can be. See below, pp. 13–15.

[20] See Plato's *Gorgias* for example.

[21] «No other animal possesses this faculty, and we cannot discover in any other animal any desire to lead and direct the judgment and conduct of its fellows. Great ambition, the desire of real superiority, of leading and directing, seems to be altogether peculiar to man, and speech is the great instrument of ambition, of real superiority, of leading and directing the judgments and conduct of other people» (*TMS*, vii.iv.24).

mainly consists of ***making believe***[22] the other one that it is his interest to exchange, without knowing if it is really the case.

What matters is only to persuade[23] in order to reach one's ends. Rhetorical discourse aims at persuading by all means. This being so, to cheat, to lie, to mislead, or to hide information become means to persuade someone, creating what we call today asymmetric information. The language of exchange is not a language of truth.[24] Rhetoric is a source of power: the power of directing, manipulating others' minds. It reveals the absolute power of language to govern Men.

As a consequence, the question of the morality of exchange relationships is asked. In a "scholastic" perspective, when someone hoodwinks and deceives or "hides" any fundamental information, the exchange resulting from the bargaining is morally condemnable.[25] Along the same line, it seems possible to point out a moral condemnation of exchange relationships inside a strictly Smithian body of theory. Indeed, in the manner of the rhetorician, the individual performing an exchange, aiming solely at his personal gain, adopts a partial point of view on the exchange situation. He will naturally defend his cause, leaving aside any information which could be unfavorable to him while highlighting and magnifying every argument which serves him. Contrary to the historian, he is not «an impartial narrator of facts»,[26] he pleads a cause. Being unable of impartiality, the individual who exchanges using lie and cheat may be morally condemnable for he or she would not get the approbation of the impartial spectator. In other words, he would not be worthy of being believed. Here comes the spectrum of the Adam Smith Problem[27]: Do we have

[22] «Man continually standing in need of the assistance of others, must fall upon some means to procure their help. This he does not merely by coaxing and courting; he does not expect it unless he can turn it to your advantage or make it appear to be so»: *LJ(a)*, vi.45.

[23] «But man has almost constant occasion for the help of his brethren, and it is in vain for him to expect it from benevolence only. He will be more likely to prevail if he can interest their self-love in his favour, and shew them that it is for their own advantage to do for him what he requires of them» (*WN*, i.ii.2).

[24] See Brown 1994a.

[25] See Young 1986 for a just price interpretation of Smith's theory of value.

[26] *LRBL*, ii.40, i.83.

[27] For a very rich and historical account of the Adam Smith Problem, see Montes 2003. Paganelli 2008 tries a reversal of the asp by arguing that *TMS* presents a more favorable account of self-interest than *WN* does.

in Smith's economic treatise people who are immoral? Do they keep a proper, respectable, and virtuous degree of self-love or is human nature essentially selfish? To answer this question, we have to keep in mind that for Smith, man is a social being who wants nothing else than being looked at, loved and admired by his fellow citizens.[28] But he does not only look for praise contrary to what Mandeville or La Rochefoucauld asserted in their «licentious systems» (*TMS*, vii.ii.4.7). They are condemned for being pernicious because they destroy the distinction between vice and virtue (*TMS*, vii.ii.4.6).

In opposition with them, Smith claims that men would be mortified if they were praised without being praise-worthy. According to Smith, the desire of approbation is one of the strongest of our desires. Two different tribunals will judge our conduct: the external spectators and the internal one. The actual spectators may be misleading because they can be manipulated (by rhetoricians) in their passions and sentiments. The role of the impartial spectator is precisely to correct the imperfection of their judgments[29] by looking at ourselves as if we were an external observer of the scene. The judgment on our own conduct is based on the same principle that when we judge the conduct of another man. We approve of our own conduct when, placing ourselves in the situation of another and view it «with his eyes and from his station», we can enter into and sympathize with the sentiments and motives which influenced it. This is the voice of reason, of man's conscience. Two modes of approbation are presented to us. On one side, there is the social approbation, or the approbation of others. On the other hand, we find our own, inner approbation, or the approbation of the impartial spectator. The latter constitutes a higher tribunal, representing the ethical standard. When we get the approbation of the impartial spectator, we can be «more indifferent about the applause, and, in some measure, despise the censure of the world; secure that, however misunderstood or misrepresented, we are the natural and proper objects of approbation» (*TMS*,

[28] We agree with Kalyvas and Katznelson 2001, 553, who write that for Smith «markets are not simply, or exclusively arenas for the instrumental quest by competitive and strategic individuals to secure their material preferences… they are a central mechanism for social integration derived not from strategic self-interest but rather from the inexorable struggle by human agents for moral approbation and social recognition».

[29] See a paragraph from edition 1 where Smith states that «common looking glasses are extremely deceitful» (*TMS*, 112).

iii.i.5). The social standard is explicitly associated with misrepresentations and misunderstanding while that of the impartial spectator comes along with virtue and deserves love and reward (*TMS*, iii.i.6). Working from this point, he develops the seminal role of conscience in our lives by asserting that man has a natural desire, not only to be praised, but to be praise-worthy. The consciousness of being praise-worthy compensates for the lack of actual praise. The approbation of the inner tribunal is a consolation for men's erroneous judgments. Very generally, Smith's point is that we must discern actual from deserved praise, the latter. For «the most sincere praise can give little pleasure when it can- not be considered as some sort of proof of praise-worthiness» (*TMS*, iii.2.4) being much superior to the former as it is the nearest approximation of the truth of moral judgment.[30] Is there a correspondence between the two modes of discourse and the two modes of moral judgment? We come close of the answer when he explains that in the same way as we desire to be praised and to be praise-worthy, we crave to be believed and to be worthy of being so:

> so we cannot always be satisfied merely with being believed, unless we are at the same time conscious that we are really worthy of belief... It is always mortifying not to be believed, and it is doubly so when we suspect that it is because we are supposed to be unworthy of belief and capable of seriously and wilfully deceiving. To tell a man that he lies, is of all affronts the most mortal.
>
> (*TMS*, vii.iv.24–26)

The duality of moral judgments is reflected in the realm of intellectual judgments. There is a striking analogy between the exchange of sentiments and the exchange of opinions. Being believed means nothing else than being approved in our ideas by real spectators. On the other hand, following Smith's concept of praiseworthiness we argue that being worthy of belief has to do with the approbation of the impartial spectator. Smith's theory of the communication of ideas is to be found in his *LRBL*. That's why, we claim, his dichotomy of the two kinds of discourse can be used to understand these lines. Opinions and ideas are believed when they are approved by actual spectators. While they are worthy of belief as far as the

[30] The man within the breast is only a semi-god. The perfection of moral judgment is the privilege of God.

imaginary and ideal spectator approves them. Persuasion is opposed to conviction, the rhetoric to the didactic discourse. The end of the rhetorician is to be believed, even though he is wrong, to get the pleasure of persuading. For «if a person asserts anything about the moon, tho'it should not be true, he will find a kind of uneasiness in being contradicted, and would be very glad that the person he is endeavouring to perswade should be of the same of thinking with himself»: *LJ(b)*, 222–223.

His aesthetical pleasure, as will be shown below, lies in the beauty of the harmony of minds. His language is partial and deceitful. The didactic thinker, by contrast, strives for truth. He is worthy of belief because his opinions are the nearest approximation of the truth of intellectual judgments. His language is just and impartial. He displays arguments on both sides of the issue, giving each of them its proper weight.

He is an impartial spectator of his topic and represents the figure of the judge, as opposed to the rhetorician which personifies that of the advocate. The didactic discourse is that of the virtuous man whose tranquility of mind reflects the pleasure of inner approbation. He is endowed with enough self-command to resist the natural temptation of desiring to persuade in every circumstances.[31]

With this in mind, what can be said about the morality of people involved in exchanging goods? How can we transpose these considerations to the market? Reputation (the external, public constraint) and merit (the internal, personal constraint) are central features of social and economic lives within which confidence arises from «frankness and openness» (*TMS*, vii.iv.28). These two kinds of constraints (sociality and consciousness) explain why probity[32] is a distinctive virtue of commercial societies and why the economic exchange is globally "immunized" against immoral practices. In other words, the individuals carrying out exchange are not selfish but self-interested: they respect the rules of justice because they respect each other and themselves. It makes them trusted and trustworthy. While trust is to be considered as the result of the approbation of our ideas, that is, of rhetorical discourses, trustworthiness is to be seen as

[31] «Man always endeavours to persuade others to be of their opinion even when the matter is of no consequence to them...You are uneasy when one differs from you, and you endeavour to persuade him to be of your mind; or if you do not do it is a certain degree of self-command »: *LJ(a)*, vi.57.

[32] «Whenever commerce is introduced into any country, probity and punctuality always ac- company it.»: *LJ(b)*, 327.

the consequence of men's use of didactic discourses. For someone trustworthy is, to use our analogy, worthy of belief and praise. Consequently, the probity of men in commercial societies is a consequence of their use of didactic discourses in social intercourse. They are deeply concerned with their honor (the internal spectator) and their reputation (the external spectators). People want to be approved, and to be worthy of approval. They are naturally led from the use of rhetorical discourses to the use of didactic discourses. What does it mean for market process?

Both free competition and consumer's satisfaction will compel merchants to use didactic discourses, that is, to sell commodities at their "true" price. For if one of them deceives the buyers (the goods are of much inferior quality that was claimed, or they are cheaper elsewhere while it had been refuted) in order to persuade them to buy his products, he will immediately be "sanctioned" by the market. Disappointed consumers will choose another seller.

Probity, Smith underlines, comes from the merchant's regard for his own interest. Anxious of «losing his character», he is «scrupulous in observing every engagement». For «when a person makes perhaps 20 contracts in a day, he cannot gain so much by endeavouring to impose on his neighbours, as the very appearance of a cheat would make him lose»: *LJ(b)*, 327.

The frequency of dealings is crucial here. When people seldom deal with one another, their reputation is not threatened. There Smith contrasts public with private life. Politician are said to be «somewhat disposed to cheat, because they can gain more by a smart trick than they can lose by the injury which it does their character» (ibidem). In opposition with them, «a prudent dealer, who is sensible of his real interest, would rather chuse to lose what he has a right to than give any ground for suspicion.»: *LJ(b)*, 328. If merchants want to be approved, they need to be honest. The fairness in exchange is the natural consequence of man's sociability, consciousness, and independence in commercial societies.[33]

[33] The importance of independence will be furthered in part ii.

Animated by a moderate self-love, people are prudent[34] and hence, praise-worthy (*TMS*, vii.ii.3.16).

For prudence[35] is entirely approved by the impartial spectator.[36] That's why commerce is among men as among nations mutually beneficial:

> A *free commerce* on a *fair* consideration must appear to be *advantageous* on *both sides*. We see that it must be so betwixt individualls, unless one of them be fool and makes a *bargain* plainly ruinous; but betwixt *prudent* men it must always be advantageous. For the very cause of the exchange must be that you need my goods more than I need them, and that I need yours more than you do yourself; and if the bargain be man- aged with ordinary *prudence* it must be profitable on both. It is the same thing with regard to nations.
>
> (*LJ(a)*, vi.160; my emphasis)

[34] In the *TMS* Smith explains that in the race for wealth, the one who will not be «fair play» will be blamed by his fellows. As a consequence, he is naturally led, thanks to the impartial spectator, to lower his self-love and to be self-interested rather than selfish: «Though it may be true, therefore, that that every individual, in his own breast, naturally prefers himself to all mankind, yet he dares not look mankind in the face, and avow that he acts according to this principle. He feels that in this preference they can never go along with him, and that how natural soever it may be to him, it must always appear excessive and extravagant to them. When he views himself in the light in which he is conscious that others will view him, he sees that to them he is but one of the multitude in no respect better than any other in it. If he would act so as that the impartial spectator may enter into the principles of his conduct, which is of all things he has the greatest desire to do, he must, upon this, as upon all other occasions, humble the arrogance of his self-love, and bring it down to something which other men can go along with. They will indulge it so far as to allow him to be more anxious about, and to pursue with more earnest assiduity, his own happiness than that of any other person. Thus far, whenever they place themselves in his situation, they will readily go along with him. In the race for wealth, and honours, and preferments, he may run as hard as he can, and strain every nerve and every muscle, in order to outstrip all his competitors. But if he should justle, or throw down any of them, the indulgence of the spectators is entirely at an end. It is a violation of fair play, which they cannot admit of. This man is to them, in every respect, as good as he: they do not enter into that self-love by which he prefers himself so much to this other, and cannot go along with the motive for which he hurt him. They readily, therefore, sympathize with the natural resentment of the injured, and the offender becomes the object of this hatred and indignation. He is sensible that he becomes so, and feels that those sentiments are ready to burst out from all sides against them» (*TMS*, ii.ii.2.1).

See also *TMS*, iii.3.4 on the role of conscience in lowering self-love.

[35] The sincerity of the prudent man is underlined in *TMS*, vi.i.8.

[36] *TMS*, vi.i.11.

This quote makes an explicit link between commerce and virtue. For people must be prudent for trades to be mutually beneficial. Dogs never make «fair and deliberate»[37] exchanges but humans do. To conclude, we don't face the Adam Smith Problem. The man of the *TMS* and the man of the *WN* are a one and only person. Economic behavior is deeply rooted in human nature and fosters cardinal virtues such as prudence and justice.

4 Sympathy and Exchange

Going further, as Young[38] rightly argued we can think that Smith believes economics fits within a broad moral social science. Indeed, his three major works are hierarchically connected and the most important for him is the *TMS* as it «provides the general theory of human nature and morality which informs the more particular inquiries into law, government and economics... In moving from morality to jurisprudence to political economy he is moving from the general to the particular; from the higher levels of abstraction to the lower. Moral philosophy shades into jurisprudence, which in turn shades into economics».[39] Since the last quarter of the twentieth century, many works[40]have dealt with the idea that the *TMS* and the *WN* are consistent and, furthermore, parts of an incomplete system. At the end of the *TMS* and again in a letter to La Rochefoucauld,[41] Smith himself confessed he intended to provide such a system, including a history of jurisprudence.[42] Our attempt to recover the unity of Smith's thought in this work focuses on the compatibility of the *TMS* and the *WN* with the *LRBL*. To this purpose, we study the links between sympathy and exchange. This analysis allows us to shed light on the various, seminal features of exchange. First, it is a process: time matters, we are in a dynamic approach. More precisely, it is a communication process: debating is essential and founded on a common language. Moreover it is a bargaining process: each one is urged by the desire to persuade and uses his (her) rhetorical abilities to reach his (her) ends by

[37] *WN*, i.ii.2.

[38] See also Winch 1978.

[39] Young 1997.

[40] See Skinner 1979, Young 1997, Otteson 2002, Fitzgibbons 1995 to name a few.

[41] *TMS*, vii.iv.37; Smith 1987, 237.

[42] The *LJ* certainly are the material on which he would have built such a history.

putting himself in the place of others and by playing with their feelings and sentiments. More generally, it is fundamentally a human and social process: man is a passion being, he strives to get the approbation of his fellows. Persuasion is the end of communication. Sympathy, we argue, is needed to be successful in communicating our sentiments as well as our opinions. The "commerce of sympathy" pervades economic relationships.

We asserted that exchange relationships are persuasion relationships because the individuals who are in the process of exchanging are rhetoricians. And rhetoric is a kind of discourse.

As a consequence, the exchange involves a discussion process and according to Smith discussion is the very place par excellence to practice sympathy.[43]

In the *TMS* discussion is almost synonymous with social life. He explains that we approve the feelings of others in the same way as we approve of their opinions, by an imaginary change in position, namely sympathy: «The great pleasure of conversation and society, besides, arises from a certain correspondence of sentiments and opinions, from a certain harmony of minds» (*TMS*, vii.iv.27; my emphasis). When doing so, we judge of the propriety or impropriety of the affections or opinions of other men by estimating their concord or dissonance with our own. Passions will appear suitable and proper to their objects if the sympathetic passions of the spectator are keeping with the original passions of the principally concerned person. I will approve of your opinions if I sympathize with them, which is to say if I endorse them because your arguments convinced me.[44] Man's social nature naturally leads him to look out for the other's agreement, for their approbation of his opinions or passions, for the sake of the pleasure residing in harmony. To look for an agreement when

[43] «But if you have either no fellow feeling for the misfortunes I have met with, or none that bears any proportion to the grief which distracts me; or if you have either no indignation at the injuries I have suffered, or none that bears any proportion to the resentment which transports me, we can no longer converse upon these subjects. We become intolerable to one another» (*TMS*, i.i.4.5).

[44] «To approve of another man's opinions is to adopt those opinions, and to adopt them is to approve of them. If the same arguments which convince you convince me likewise, I necessarily approve of your conviction; and if they do not, I necessarily disapprove of it: neither can I possibly conceive that I should do the one without the other. To approve or disapprove, therefore, of the opinions of others is acknowledged, by every body, to mean no more than to observe their agreement or disagreement with our own. But this is equally the case with regard to our approbation or disapprobation of the sentiments or passions of others» (*TMS*, i.i.3.2).

exchanging goods is a way to get the approbation of my ideas on the goods (its characteristics and price) and above all to test my power of directing men. As Dellemotte[45] rightly noticed, we are likely to imagine a strategic use of sympathy within the exchange process.[46]

In the *LRBL*, Smith explains how the rhetorician, and as a consequence the exchanging individual, plays with people's feelings, sentiments, and passions to persuade his audience. The diffusion and communication of feelings, passions, and sentiments is achieved through the capacity of sympathy. The idea is to get some information about the person you exchange with. In other words, this is a way to discover his preferences. The more you figure out people's character and temper, the better you will reach your own ends. In modern, commercial societies, it is paradoxically by "plunging" myself into you that I achieve "my self."[47] The repetition of exchanges (social interactions) with the same person (customer, buyer, or seller), or a group of persons you identify thanks to your experience, should allow you to reach more easily agreements (sympathy and approbation) afterwards.

Nonetheless, sympathy is not only an essential component but it is also a prerequisite to the exchange process. Indeed, if people want to discuss, they have to share a common language. This common language allows a mutual comprehension which is fundamental in every coordination issue. Those people have to share common values and knowledge.

[45] See Dellemotte 2005.

[46] We follow Danner's interpretation who convincingly argued that the mutual and reciprocal coordination needed in economic interactions arises from the phenomenon of sympathy. This interpretation is rejected by Werhane because «Smith does not use the term 'sympathy' in the *WN* ... and sympathy is not a principle of motivation». Yet she misses the point. Heavily influenced by Turgot and Cantillon, Smith understood the market process at a macro-economic level in which aggregate supply and aggregate demand are the key factors and the bargaining process vanishes. He did not provide a comprehensive analysis of the «higgling of the market» because its influence on the final result is supposed to be inexistent. The market price tends to be equal to the natural price, or to reveal the objective characteristics of the goods. Language is therefore a transparent medium as it does not affect the final values (see Brown 1994a, 73–74 for more details). Maybe that's why the word is absent from the *WN*. Moreover, in this paper we argue that sympathy is essential to reach an agreed valuation as an efficient cause of exchange and not as its final cause. Self-interest is my end and this end is achieved by means of sympathy. See Werhane 1989 and Danner 1976.

[47] Our social interactions, including here the exchange of goods, foster our own consciousness.

Thanks to his concepts of sympathy and impartial spectator Smith explains in the *TMS* this organic or spontaneous genesis of common beliefs and values. Communication is at the core of the emergence of moral values and norms. In this scheme, the impartial spectator may be represented as an internalization of social interactions. He will "memorize" the episodes of approbation and disapprobation. If people sympathized with my affection in a given situation or if they approved of my opinions, I will tend to reproduce this behavior and opinions. If my opinions (my arguments about the qualities of the goods and its price) didn't convince many spectators (buyers), I will correct it (to cut price) in order to get their approbation (to sell). This is a «self-strengthened» mechanism, a natural, spontaneous, or organic emergence of common values[48] and knowledge. Moral norms emerge as a result of an unconscious evolutionary process. Commerce is an important not to say fundamental element of social life in modern societies.[49] The norms prevailing in this sphere are some way the result of the internalization of sympathetic experiences by the impartial spectator. The market is to be seen as the "agora" of modern, commercial societies. There people exchange sentiments and opinions on goods and debate on prices and quantities.

Therefore, we would like to underline the great similarity between the exchange of goods and the exchange of sentiments and passions by briefly defining a model of bilateral exchange of goods. When two individuals try

[48] The emergence of economic (prices) and moral values (norms of behavior) seems to be founded on a similar "evolutionary" process of trials and errors. This perspective was adopted by Otteson 2002 who brilliantly explained Smith's marketplace of morality. He shows that the standards of moral judgments arise unintentionally from the moral judgments and actions of individuals and that the standards that develop in this way constitute a self-regulating order. This market model of unintended order is then extended to explain the formation of economic and linguistic norms as well. Otteson claims that the market model is Smith's overall representation of human institutions. I agree with him on this point. Yet, even if he points out the analogy between the three models, they are presented in separate ways. It is as if the emergence of economic rules (prices) was independent of the emergence of moral rules. My argument in this article is that moral and linguistic norms are essential to the working of the «economic» market. The process that leads to the formation of economic values is not merely analogous to the one giving rise to the formation of moral values, it is built upon it. The mutual benefits of exchange relationships are founded on the ethical character of economic agents. Probity, prudence, and fairness are successful qualities in both economic and social life. Fair practices give rise to fair exchanges at fair prices.

[49] Griswold 1999, 297 rightly argued that for Smith «life in a market society is an ongoing exercise in rhetoric ».

to exchange affections, there is an agent who feels the original passion, and a spectator who tries to sympathize with him and who feels a sympathetic passion. What is important here is the fact that the intensity of the original passion is necessarily higher than the one of the sympathetic passion because sympathy is an imaginary change in positions and an imperfect mechanism. The spectator will never be able to plainly enter in the agent's character or to exactly know the objects of his passion. However, even if the spectator will never feel the passion of the agent with the same intensity, a "harmony," a "concord" may be attained thanks to the pleasure of mutual sympathy. By his self-command, the agent will lower the intensity of his passion for the spectator to sympathize with him, while the spectator will increase his own by trying to enter into every circumstance which may have caused the passion. By doing so, they will reach a "propriety point." Mutual sympathy will then arise. In this "model," the convergence of feelings is attained through the pleasure of mutual sympathy. That underlines the innate tendency of men to look for the approbation of others. We are convinced that there is here a striking parallel with a bilateral exchange of goods. On the one side, the agent would be a seller who wants to sell at the highest price. On the other side, the spectator would be a buyer, who wants to buy at the lowest price. Once again, a convergence may be attained because there is pleasure in persuading in the same way, there is pleasure in mutual sympathy.[50] The desire to be believed is a desire of approbation, and to approve of someone's feelings or opinions means nothing else than sympathizing with them. The buyer and the seller will strive for an agreement in order to get this pleasure and will exchange at what we call a "propriety price." To reach an agreed valuation, each one has to go beyond his partial and selfish position.

As Kennedy rightly argued, «bargainers must be other-centred, not self-centred».[51] They have to satisfy the other's self-love if they want to satisfy their own. To reach an outcome agreeable to both, they must contain their self-love, tending toward a position of impartiality. Once more, the market can be seen as a public place in which we are educated to self-command and to impartiality. Let me now briefly describe the process

[50] Furthering this point, we add that man's willingness to be approved and, therefore, to persuade, is also the result of the "pain" associated with disapprobation which finds its corollary in the "uneasiness" of being contradicted. See *TMS*, i.ii.1 and *LJ(b)*, 222.

[51] See Kennedy 2008.

leading to the "propriety price." Our market is composed of one seller and one buyer. The final outcome will depend on each one's negotiation or communication power. The price range is defined by a high bound (the buyer's highest price he wants to pay) and by a low bound (the seller's minimum price to cover his production costs). Every acceptable price (propriety prices) for both is included into this price range. The buyer will try to take the seller's place to discover his minimum price. Sympathy is also to be used by the individuals involved in the bargaining process to play with each other's passions. As a result, if the agreed valuation is nearer from the low bound, it means that the buyer's communication and negotiation power is stronger than the seller's one. The buyer will get a greater part of the surplus. From this point, it is possible to imagine a "just" price, distinct from "propriety" prices. Smith is clear that we exchange if and only if our well-being is increased. For «the very cause of the exchange must be that you need my goods more than I need them and that I need yours more than you do yourself»: *LJ(a)*, vi.160. The ideal and just result of the bargaining process is reached, we claim, when the gains are equally divided among the participants, that is, when their respective outcomes are equal. This "just" price is perfectly in the middle of the price range, where every change in price leads to a fall of one's well-being. In analytical terms, some assumptions are needed to reach that optimal result. One of them was implicit in our reasoning. People involved in the exchange must have equal rhetorical power; otherwise one of them will naturally use his superiority to get the greatest part of the surplus. Doing so, he will come nearer of his "maximizing point," considered here, if he is the seller (respectively the buyer), as the high (low) bound of the price range. We add that symmetry of positions, or social status, is needed. For people engaged in a subordination relationship will not be prompt to contradict their superiors.[52] To conclude on this point, the pleasure to exchange is a pleasure to persuade and to get the approbation of someone on our own valuation of the goods. The exchange of goods seems similar to the exchange of sentiments.

[52] See part ii, where it is shown that the employment relationship exhibits none of these assumptions. Consequently, the distribution of the surplus between capital owners and workers is unjust and suboptimal. The growth rate is then, too, suboptimal.

An "equilibrium" is reached through a (dynamic) process, restoring order and tranquility thanks to the harmony[53] of minds it creates. Going further, we agree with Griswold to claim that the exchange process «is not merely analogous to the process of sympathy described in the *TMS*: it is built upon it».[54]

However, the link between sympathy and exchange is more complex than it appears at first sight. Indeed, sympathy requires social proximity. It is very difficult to sympathize with someone we don't know.[55] With this background in mind, it becomes interesting to reread the famous passage of the butcher, the brewer, and the backer in the *WN*. Commercial society is defined as one in which every man is a merchant. It means he lives by exchanging the surplus part of the produce of his labor against that of other men. Men become entirely dependent on others for the satisfaction of their needs. What art will they use to get what they want from their fellows? Man, it is said, must work «on the selflove of his fellows, by setting before them a sufficient temptation to get what he wants»: *LJ(b)*, 220. Smith says that the individuals in economic interactions have in mind their own advantage. Why aren't they assumed to be benevolent? A commonplace argument is that we cannot be benevolent in the marketplace because we are facing strangers. The supposed impersonality of the market is seen as allowing little room for spectator mechanisms to work in this arena. Therefore, this lack of social proximity could lower the importance of sympathy and benevolence in the exchange of goods. Indeed, the more you know people, the better you sympathize with them and the more benevolent you are toward them. Benevolence can be seen as the result of repeated sympathy.[56] So that we could nonetheless imagine the gradual appearance of benevolence in economic intercourses by the repetition of interactions as the individuals involved would know each other better and better. Besides, Young convincingly argued that sympathy's effectiveness is more closely tied to physical distance than social

[53] This is an aesthetical and disinterested pleasure. There is an aesthetical pleasure for the man of system too, coming from his observation of the harmony and the order of society in which many people «act in concert». See *TMS*, iv.1.11.

[54] See Griswold 1999, 297–298.

[55] See *TMS*, i.i.3.4.

[56] See Nieli 1986.

distance.[57] What is seminal to sympathize is to see and to be seen. We are able to sympathize with strangers if we meet face to face.[58]

However, Smith's plea for self-love in economic interactions is founded on a plain argument. Human nature is much more self-interested than benevolent. Nature has endowed man with a strong love of himself for him to survive. Smith is not weary to repeat that man's satisfaction of his basic needs would be threatened if it was not so.[59] When people «address themselves to the self-interest of the person», they «seldom fail immediately to gain their end»: *LJ(a)*, vi.57. Man expects anything from self-love, since it is a much more powerful spring than benevolence.[60] That's why he is said to be more successful if he addresses to their self-love. It is no more than the best strategy to persuade them.[61]

Our second argument lowering the importance of sympathy in exchange has to do with the "essence" of sympathy. This is a more fundamental objection. We can easily think of a seller trying to make an imaginary, strategic change of position in order to discover what the buyer's personal interest is. But the specificity of this imaginary change of position comes from the fact that it is the seller's self-love which motivates him to «take the buyer's position». It is not, contrary to sympathy, a spontaneous and disinterested change of position.[62] In the exchange of goods, a distinctive form of sympathy appears: what we call an "interested sympathy." Using Aristotle's words, we can say that self-interest undoubtedly is the exchange's final cause, while its efficient cause is sympathy. In order to satisfy my self-love, I need to know yours. That's why I have to look at the situation from your point of view. Sympathy and self-interest

[57] See *TMS*, iii.3.4.

[58] See Young 1986, 371.

[59] «No man but a beggar depends on benevolence, and even they would die in a week were their entire dependence upon it»: *LJ(b)*, 220.

[60] «It is not the soft power of humanity, it is not that feeble spark of benevolence which Nature has lighted up in the human heart, that is thus capable of counteracting the strongest impulses of self-love»: *TMS*, iii.3.4.

[61] See Force 2003, 132. Note that benevolence is to be found in *WN*, v.iii.31 with people making «family settlements» and providing for «remote futurity».

[62] Remember the first lines of the *TMS*: «However selfish man may be supposed, there are evidently some principles in his nature, which interest him in the fortune of others, and renders their happiness necessary to him, though he derives nothing from it except the pleasure of seeing it».

are not contradictory human motives. By looking at us with the eyes of others, sympathy allows us to understand our interest in a true light. Self-love is a reflexive modality of sympathy.[63] We know ourselves only insofar as we can look at ourselves with the eyes of others. Man's consciousness is deeply rooted in social, sympathetic interactions.

5 Conclusion

The aim of this chapter is to further our understanding of Smith's conception of economic exchange.

To that end, we decided to identify the language of commerce. Three significant conclusions may be drawn from this analysis. First, the coherence of Smith's system is emphasized. We went far beyond the traditional combination of his moral and economic treatises to include his lectures on rhetoric, a youth writing whose importance has so far been neglected by historian of economic thought. Together with his later lectures on jurisprudence, they exhibit Smith's continuity of thought and the fecundity of a great but unfinished intellectual system. As was redundantly shown, the Adam Smith Problem vanishes once we accept to cross the texts. From this point, an analogy between the exchange of sentiments, opinions, and goods was developed so that man may be seen as a "commercial" animal. Smith provides us with a unified conception of human nature which cannot be reduced to the «selfish hypothesis». Here comes our second point. Far from the vision of the Chicago School, where Smith is considered as the founding father of economic science for having identified human nature with self-interest,[64] we argued that what was seminal in exchange relationships is not man's autonomy and selfishness. Rather we should look at the passage of the brewer, the baker, and the butcher as one in which people's concern for others is put into light.[65] We cannot satisfy ourselves if we do not satisfy others too. Consequently,

[63] For a similar idea, see Dupuy 1992, 80.

[64] Force 2003 has wonderfully showed how mistaken it was to identify Smith with a selfish interpretation of human nature. Many eighteenth-century philosophers, predominantly French, such as D'Holbach, La Rochefoucauld, or Helvétius, were explicitly adopting such a narrow and pessimistic concept of human nature. This view is the result of a lack of knowledge of *tms* where selfish systems, as we underlined, were harshly criticized.

[65] See Fleischacker 1999, 155; 2004, 21; and Vivenza 2005, 43.

we have to imagine and to see us as if we were at their place. Only through this process of changing places can we get our true self interest. Self-love is appealed to because it is much more persuasive than benevolence. For we «are not ready to suspect any person of being defective in selfishness» while the same could not be said of benevolence (*TMS*, vii.ii.3.16). Yet, it is not to say that people in exchange are immoral or even amoral. The virtuous character of the "economic man," not different from man in general, was underlined through the workings of the duality of moral judgments. Both the social and the ethical constraints create the conditions for a virtuous commerce. Three of Smith's four cardinal virtues (prudence, justice, and self-command) are met. Impartiality and consciousness are fostered. For Smith, commerce is founded on cooperation, not on conflict.[66] That's why commerce «ought to be, among men as among individuals, a bond of union and friendship» (*WN*, iv.iii.c.9).

Acknowledgements I am indebted to Jean Dellemotte, André Hervier, and Saul Hughes and to the two anonymous referees for their helpful comments on previous drafts of this paper. Remaining errors are mine.

References

Biziou M (2003) Adam Smith et l'origine du libéralisme. PUF, Paris

Brown V (1994a) Higgling: the language of markets in economic discourse. In: de Marchi N, Morgan MS (eds) Higgling: transactors and their markets in the history of economics, History of Political Economy, Duke University Press, Duke (Annual Supplement) p 26

——— (1994b) Adam Smith's Discourse: Canonicity, Commerce and Conscience. Routledge, New York

Calkins MJ, Werhane PH (1998) Adam Smith, Aristotle, and the Virtues of Commerce. J Value Inq 32:43–60

Danner PL 1976) Sympathy and Exchangeable Value: Keys to Adam Smith's Social Philosophy. Rev Soc Econ 34(3):317–331

Dellemotte J (2005) Sympathie, désir d'améliorer sa condition et penchant à l'échange. Cahiers d'Économie Politique 48:51–78

Dickey L (1986) Historicizing the "Adam Smith Problem": Conceptual, Historiographical and Textual Issues. J Mod Hist 58(3): 579–609

66 See Cropsey's comment in Griswold 1999, 298.

Duboeuf F (1985) Adam Smith: Mesure et Socialité. Economies et Sociétés Série pe 3:73–107

Dupuy JP (1992) Le sacrifice et l'envie. Le libéralisme aux prises avec la justice sociale. Calmann-Lévy, Paris

Fitzgibbons A (1995) Adam Smith's System of Liberty, Wealth and Virtue: The Moral and Political Foundations of "The Wealth of Nations". Clarendon Press, Oxford

Fleischacker S (1999) A Third Concept of Liberty: Judgment and Freedom in Kant and Smith. Princeton University Press, Princeton

——— (2004) Adam Smith's Wealth Of Nations. A Philosophical Companion. Princeton University Press, Princeton

Force P (2003) Self-Interest Before Adam Smith. A Genealogy of Economic Science. Cambridge University Press, Cambridge

Griswold C (1999) Adam Smith and the Virtues of Enlightenment. Cambridge University Press, Cambridge

Howell S (1975) Adam Smith's Lectures on Rhetoric: an Historical Assessment. In: Skinner A, Wilson T (eds) Essays in honour of Adam Smith. Clarendon Press, Oxford, pp 11–43

Kalyvas SN, Katznelson I (2001) The Rhetoric of the Market: Adam Smith on Recognition, Speech, and Exchange. Rev Polit 63(3):549–579

Kennedy G (2008) Adam Smith on bargaining. Paper presented at the hes 35th annual Conference, Toronto

Khalil E (2005) An Anatomy of Authority: Adam Smith as Political Theorist. Camb J Econ 29(1):57–71

Mathiot J (1990) Adam Smith, philosophie et économie. PUF, Paris

Montes L (2003) Das Adam Smith Problem: Its Origins, the Stages of the Current Debate and One Implication for Our Understanding of Sympathy. J Hist Econ Thought 25(1):63–90

Nieli R (1986) Spheres of Intimacy and the Adam Smith Problem. J Hist Ideas 47(4):611–624

Otteson J (2002) Adam Smith's Marketplace of Life. Cambridge University Press, Cambridge

Pack S J (1991) Capitalism as a Moral System. Adam Smith's Critique of the Free Market economy. Edward Elgar Publishing, Aldershot

Paganelli M (2008) The Adam Smith Problem in Reverse: Self Interest in the Wealth of Nations and The Theory of Moral Sentiments. Hist Political Econ 40(2):365–382

Raphael DD, Macfie AL (1982) [1974] Introduction to the tms. In: Glasgow Edition of the Works and Correspondence of Adam Smith. Liberty Fund, Indianapolis

Salber Phillips M (2006) Adam Smith, Belletrist. In: Haakonssen K (ed) The Cambridge Companion to Adam Smith. Cambridge University Press, Cambridge, pp 57–78

Skinner AS (1979) Language, Rhetoric and the Communication of Ideas. In: A System of Social Science, Papers Relating to Adam Smith. Oxford University Press, Oxford

Smith A (1999) [1759–1790a] Théorie des sentiments moraux, transl. by Biziou M, Gautier C, Pradeau JF. PUF, Paris

——— (1976) [1759–1790b] The Theory of Moral Sentiments (tms). Oxford University Press, Oxford

——— (1991) [1776a] Recherche sur la nature et les causes de la richesse des nations, transl. by Garnier G. Garnier-Flammarion, Paris

——— (1976) [1776b] An Inquiry into the Nature and Causes of the Wealth of Nations (wn). Oxford University Press, Oxford

——— (1980) [1795] Essays on Philosophical Subjects (eps). Oxford University Press, Oxford

——— (1978) [1978] Lectures on Jurisprudence (lj). Oxford University Press, Oxford

——— (1983) Lectures on Rhetoric and Belles Lettres (lrbl) Oxford University Press, Oxford

——— (1987) The Correspondence of Adam Smith. Clarendon Press, Oxford

Vivenza G (2001) Adam Smith and the Classics. The Classical Heritage in Adam Smith's Thought. Oxford University Press, Oxford

——— (2005) The agent, the actor, and the spectator. Adam Smith's metaphors in recent literature. Hist Econ Ideas 13(1): 37–56

Werhane P (1989) Self Interest in Adam Smith's Wealth of Nations. J Philos 86(11):669–680

Winch D (1978) Adam Smith's politics. An essay in historiographic revision. Cambridge University Press, Cambridge

Young JT (1986) The Impartial Spectator and Natural Jurisprudence: An Interpretation of Adam Smith's Theory of the Natural Price. Hist Political Econ 18(3):365–382

——— (1995) Natural Jurisprudence and The Theory of Value in Adam Smith. Hist Political Econ 27(4):755–773

——— (1997) Economics as a Moral Science: The Political Economy of Adam Smith. Edward Elgar Publishing, Cheltenham

CHAPTER 7

Adam Smith's Reasoning Routines and the Deep Structure of His Oeuvre

> In the Professorship of Logic [at Glasgow] ... [Smith] dedicated [most] of his time to the delivery of a system of rhetoric and belles lettres. The best method of explaining and illustrating the various powers of the human mind, ... arises from the examination of the several ways of communicating our thoughts by speech, and from an attention to the principles of those literary compositions which contribute to persuasion or entertainment.
>
> (Stewart 1795 in Smith 1982, pp. 274–275)

1 Introduction

Over time we develop stable motoric, cognitive, and behavioral processes/algorithms. We develop, for example, fairly stable ways to produce manuscripts, to play chess, to deal with our children, spouses, friends, and colleagues, to select goods and services of desirable quality, or to conceptualize the ways the world around us works (e.g., Allison 1969; Cohen and Bacdayn 1994; Cohen et al. 1995; Cosmides 1989; Cosmides and Tooby 1996 [1997] ; Goldberg 2005, 2010; March and Simon 1993; Ortmann 2008; Pentland and Rueter 1994; Weick 1979; Hohwy 2013; Clark 2016). We shall call cognitive processes/algorithms "reasoning routines," and sets of reasoning routines "conceptual lenses."

We argue that Smith, very early in his life and career, developed reasoning routines that he employed as moral philosopher, in *The Theory*

A. Ortmann and B. Walraevens, *Adam Smith's System*, Palgrave Studies in the History of Economic Thought,
https://doi.org/10.1007/978-3-030-99704-5_7

of Moral Sentiments (TMS), and as economist, in *An Inquiry into the Nature and Causes of the Wealth of Nations (WN)*. Key exhibits for his early thinking are that "pearl of the collection" (Schumpeter 1954, p. 182)[1] titled "The History of Astronomy" [*HA*] (in Smith 1982 pp. 33–105),[2] his "Considerations Concerning the First Formation of Languages" [from here on *Considerations*] (in Smith 1985, pp. 203–226), and the lectures on rhetoric and belles lettres that Smith started teaching soon after his return from Oxford in 1746. It is well-documented that he taught these lectures for almost two decades (e.g., Buchan 2016) and we now have a set of elaborate and reasonably congruent student notes on Smith's lectures on rhetoric and literature (*LRBL*, in Smith 1985) which embed as lecture 3 a short version of the *Considerations* article. It is important to note that this essay on the origin and evolution of language, a much debated topic in the Age of Enlightenment,[3] was first published separately in 1761 in a short-lived review called the *Philological Miscellany* and then was added, from 1767, to the third and subsequent editions of *TMS* on Smith's demand. It is thus very clear

[1] Schumpeter was much less enthusiastic about the *WN*, probably because he did not understand—and arguably, since he had no access to the *LRBL*, could not understand—the rhetorical structure of that book (Ortmann and Walraevens 2018; Ortmann et al. 2019; see also Dow 1987).

[2] While the importance of this work is documented by Smith exempting it explicitly from the bonfire that he wanted much of his other unpublished works to contribute to, there is some dispute about how early it was written. Phillipson (2010, pp. 283–234; see also Kennedy 2013, 2017 for further references pointing in the same direction), for example, argues that it was written in the 1740s and hence while Smith was still at Oxford. Kennedy (2013) has made an interesting case for the likely reason that led Smith to have his juvenile essay published posthumously. It was a work essential to Smith's fledgling intellectual development since it reflects his thinking about "the origins of philosophical thought, the creation of philosophical systems, and the appeal which philosophy has to its public. Philosophy's roots, Smith suggested, lay in the psychological need to explain the unexpected, to soothe the imagination and to restore the mind to a state of cognitive order and tranquility" (Smith 1982; see also Montes 2013). The editor of the relevant passages of the Glasgow edition of the *EPS*, Wightman—drawing in his Introduction heavily on Smith's first biographer, Dugald Stewart—argues that "it has been fairly generally assumed that he at least laid the foundation of the *History of Astronomy* at Oxford; but from further internal evidence it may be inferred that he did not finish it there" (Smith 1982, p. 7).

[3] Condillac, Rousseau, and Turgot, three French philosophers that Smith held in high esteem, also contributed to this debate, Smith mentioning and criticizing Rousseau's views on the origin of languages in his essay (see Smith 1985, pp. 9, 205).

that Smith thought his theories of language and morality to be highly complementary, as we shall see later.[4]

Identifying the *History of Astronomy* (*HA*), the *Lectures on Rhetoric and Belles Lettres (LRBL)*, and *TMS* and *WN* as key products of his personal and academic life,[5] one of our central contentions is that Smith's thinking was throughout his work informed by his early insights into the strategic nature of all things rhetorical, moral, and economic. Importantly, Smith understood well that strategic interactions often were afflicted by information asymmetries, an insight prominently on display in *LRBL* (Smith 1985) where he pays particular attention to the principal-agent nature of some forms of communication, namely acts of persuasion, but also in *TMS* and *WN*. While moving from rhetoric to moral philosophy, we believe that Smith looked at the latter through the conceptual lens of the former. While moving from moral philosophy to economics, he looked at the latter through the conceptual lens of the former. By the chain rule then, he looked at economics through the conceptual lens of rhetoric, broadly construed.

Toward the identification of Smith's conceptual lenses and of the "deep structure" of his work, we identify three key components of his conceptual lenses or "reasoning routines," that are triggered by Smith's Wonder–Surprise–Admiration "meta-routine" (*WSA* routine from here on) that, at an early stage of his career, in juvenile works such as *HA* and early lectures such as those on languages and rhetoric (*LRBL*), Smith

[4] Says Phillipson (2010, pp. 165–166): "In 1761 he [Smith] had published an extended version of his lecture on the origins of language in a little known and short-lived review called the *Philological Miscellany* under the title '*Considerations Concerning the Fist Formation of Languages*'. One can see why he wanted to do so. His theory of morals and the elaborate discussion of the process of sympathetic exchange on which it was based had presupposed the theory of language on which his theory of rhetoric was based. The theory of language he had presented to his Edinburgh and Glasgow students had been designed to show that language was essentially a vehicle for communication which had a history that was probably as old as civilization. Not only was this a subject of obvious relevance to an understanding of the workings of sympathy...Stewart commented, it was an essay 'on which the author himself set a high value'." Stewart also hailed it as a "very beautiful specimen" of "theoretical or conjectural history," which "may be traced in all his different works" (Stewart 1982, pp. 33, 36, 37).

[5] We do not deny the importance of the *Lectures on Jurisprudence (LJ)* but we believe that of the (un)published works, this is the least relevant for the key arguments that we make here. This will not prevent us from using them whenever necessary for our argumentation.

developed and later put to good use as moral philosopher, in *TMS*, and as economist, in *WN*.[6]

We think of the three reasoning routines, and the *WSA* routine that triggers them, together as a conceptual lens (Allison 1969; Ortmann 2008), or a set of particular ways of thinking about the world or about particular domains such as ethics or economics.

In *HA*, Smith identified a basic way of thinking about the world—both the natural and the social world—that he conceptualized as a machine following certain invisible laws of motion (such as gravity) that it was the philosopher's mind to discover and to distill, preferably in a minimal set of principles.

> The beauty of a systematical arrangement of different observations connected by a few common principles, was first seen in the rude essays of those ancient times towards a system of natural philosophy. Something of the same kind was afterwards attempted in morals. The maxims of common life were arranged in some methodical order, and connected together by a few common principles, in the same manner as they had attempted to arrange and connect the phenomena of nature. The science which pretends to investigate and explain those connecting principles, is what is properly called moral *philosophy*.
>
> (*WN*, Smith 1981 p. 724)

Whenever observations were in conflict with established principles, they had the potential to cause "wonder," "surprise," and "admiration" which triggered the search of our imagination for new explanations and a revision of the few common principles explaining the natural and the social world.

This first reasoning routine—Smith's conceptualization of the world as a machine that followed certain invisible laws of motion that philosophers

[6] Smith considered himself first and foremost a moral philosopher, as attested by his willingness to sign the *WN* as "Adam Smith, Formerly Professor of Moral Philosophy at the University of Glasgow" (*WN*, 1). And it bears repeating that Smith saw himself, maybe even more, from the very beginning as a philosopher: As Stewart reported famously (after Smith had died), Smith thought that "[t]he best method of explaining and illustrating the various powers of the human mind, the most useful parts of metaphysics, arises from an examination of the several ways of communicating our thoughts by speech, and from an attention to the principles of those literary compositions which contribute to persuasion or entertainment" (*EPS*, p. 274).

had to imagine and discover—reflects Smith's well-documented infatuation with the Newtonian, or deductive, view of the world, and his attempt to do for moral philosophy what Newton had done for natural philosophy. "The History of Astronomy" (in Smith 1982) is exhibit A for this claim. The Newtonian perspective is widely perceived to be about the equilibrium of a system.

The second reasoning routine we identify in Smith's works is reflected in his understanding of the strategic nature of all things rhetorical, moral, political, and economic. The conceptualization of life as being beset with strategic interactions featured prominently first in Smith's papers on rhetoric and the emergence of languages and then, as discussed above, also in *TMS*. In fact, the acquisition of "self-command" in Smith's *TMS* is our exhibit A for this claim. Game theory is a self-suggesting means of modeling strategic interactions because it has shown its usefulness in many other contexts. It is useful because once a problem has been framed game-theoretically, we have identified its substrate (which can be used for understanding similar situations in different contexts or domains like rhetoric and economics) and we also can access the whole machinery that game theory provides (e.g., in particular the distinction between one-shot and indefinitely repeated games which, when ignored, leads to considerable confusion.).

The third reasoning routine[7] reflects Smith's belief in the evolutionary, or inductive, nature of many systems, be they social or other. *Considerations Concerning the First Formation of Languages* (Smith 1985, pp. 203–226) is exhibit A for this claim. The evolutionary view is essentially about the process toward equilibrium, if it exists. Smith, who modeled the origin and evolution of languages and moral sentiments as a bottom-up process driven by repeated interactions of self-interested, but "empathetic" agents (Ortmann and Meardon 1995; Otteson 2002a, 2002b, 2002c), realized *peu a peu* that some such program might be path-dependent and not necessarily, like the laws of motion of the natural

[7] To avoid misunderstandings, we note here and make clear in the chapter in detail that we see these three reasoning routines, in particular the first and third, to be on the same level. The first is the discovery of the laws of motion of the machine called natural and social world. This discovery—for the social world in particular—requires evolutionary processes whose beginnings can only be reconstructed through historical theorizing. The second reasoning routine or, maybe better, set of reasoning routines, rides on the first in that it highlights the interactive nature of the interactions that we consider. The numbering of the reasoning routines is therefore just a convention without deep meaning.

world, be immutable. There is indeed evidence that Smith originally assumed that evolutionary processes would uncover the optimal design of the social machine, which he saw as going through distinct stages[8] and moving toward some divine or providential design. Later, Smith seems to have become increasingly aware that outcomes in social systems were much less pre-determined than those in nature and that multiple equilibria might exist (Evensky 1989; Phillipson 2010).

Our central argument is that Smith understood exceptionally well the strategic interactions between speakers (writers) and listeners (readers), Man Today and Man Tomorrow, and the principals and agents engaged in various commercial interactions including those involving adjustable quality and/or effort, as can be demonstrated by extracting the common underlying normal-form "games" (as we did in previous work, see Meardon and Ortmann 1996a, 1996b). Smith used interactive scenarios over and over again, mainly focusing on what we now call symmetric and asymmetric prisoner's dilemma games (the latter nowadays typically called "principal-agent" games). In this respect the second reasoning routine is actually a set of reasoning sub-routines, or problem isomorphs, that are bound together by their similar strategic nature. They ride on the first and third reasoning routine in that they are the building blocks for the story of the evolution of languages and moral sentiments but also for other concepts such as efficiency wages and the internal organization of the types of organizations being successively discussed in Book V of *WN* (Ortmann 1999).

The reasoning routines that we present here are Adam Smith's reasoning routines as identified by us, and to some extent by others. Smith himself, in his *HA*, identified a specific algorithm, or meta-routine, that philosophers employed when they became aware of the world and its underlying connecting principles and that actually triggered the reasoning routines that we identified (see Fig. 1 below, Sect. 2.2). This was the already mentioned Wonder–Surprise–Admiration mechanism. One can think of this algorithm as a meta-principle (or meta-reasoning routine)[9] which is triggered when our worldview is disrupted by unknown phenomena that unsettle our imagination. It triggers an

[8] See Berry (2001) for a general presentation of Smith's four-stage theory.

[9] Smith noted that, while in principle this algorithm was accessible to all, it was not equally accessible even to those of philosophical pretensions; but the difference was owed to habit, custom, and education rather than natural abilities (Smith 1982, p. 45).

attempt at understanding the coherence or order of the world which might involve different ways of going about it.

We thus argue that Smith's interest in various subject matters was a derived one, and that as such he was, initially, an experimental philosopher as well as a cognitive and social psychologist *avant la lettre*. His well-documented "conjectural-history" strategy (Stewart 1795 in Smith 1982, pp. 292–293; see also Phillipson 2016, pp. 113–115) was a key methodological ingredient in his exploration, and the source of his experimentation in matters rhetoric, moral, and economic.

The examination of the ways our thoughts on the natural and social world come about and how we communicate them, for entertainment and/or persuasion, was in Smith's view the best method for explaining and illustrating the various powers of the human mind. Even though he never published a specific work on this issue, as his buddy (Rasmussen 2017) David Hume did in book 1 of his *Treatise of Human Nature* and later in his *Enquiry Concerning Human Understanding*, a close reading of Smith's early essays on philosophical subjects and of his works on rhetoric and the origin of language clearly reveals that his overriding interest was to understand how people reasoned and tried to make sense of the natural and social world around them—a point made before (e.g., Raphael and Skinner, drawing heavily on Smith's first biographer, Dugald Stewart, in their General Introduction to the *EPS*). We thus also offer a reconstruction of Smith's ideas concerning man's principles of knowledge which, most importantly, provide the necessary micro-foundations of his analysis of social interactions and of man's understanding of the natural world. In other words, Smith was deeply involved in the Scottish Enlightenment's project of founding a new "science of man" based on the "experimental method" borrowed from natural sciences and inherited from Bacon.[10]

Later in his life, Smith's focus seems to have switched: he became obsessed with "the American question" (Fleischacker 2002, 2021; Ortmann et al. 2019) which is now generally blamed for the delay in the publication of his *WN* (see Phillipson 2010, 2013). But Smith's

[10] As Phillipson notes, "In 1759, one of Smith's former students, a young Presbyterian minister, wrote enthusiastically and perceptively about Smith's use of the 'experimental method' in moral philosophy, noting the 'wonderful profusion of Examples to illustrate the different parts of the theory which seem like so many facts and experiments in Natural Philosophy & seem to confirm & support the author's principles in the most satisfying manner" (Phillipson 2016, p. 113).

continued work on the *TMS*, and there especially the new part 6 on "the character of virtue" in the 1790 edition, demonstrates that he remained throughout an experimental philosopher as well as a cognitive and social psychologist.

Moreover, even after he became "very zealous in American Affairs" (Hume, according to Smith *Corr.* 149, p.185), the conceptual lenses Smith had acquired early in his life, and especially his rhetorical insights, served him well throughout (e.g., Ortmann and Walraevens 2018 and chapter 2).

The current chapter is organized as follows. Section 2 details our understanding of reasoning routines and defines the origin of the reasoning routines that we identify as important for an understanding of Smith's oeuvre. It also presents how over time the first and third reasoning routine came increasingly into conflict with each other, inducing an inherent tension in Smith's work and leading him increasingly to think about incentive compatible ways of intervention in rhetorical, moral, political, and economic affairs.

In Sect. 3, we use the known facts about Smith's life to provide a "conjectural history" of his reasoning routines. We take the opportunity to identify five stylized facts that speak to the nature, causes, and persistence, of Smith's conceptual lenses.

In Sects. 4 and 5, we show how Smith's reasoning routines are omnipresent in his works on rhetoric and morality, respectively, and prepare the discussion of the parallels between rhetoric and moral philosophy in Sect. 6. In Sect. 7, we focus on Smith's work on economics, and prepare the discussion of the parallels between his economic theories and those concerning morality and rhetoric in Sects. 8 and 9, respectively. We conclude with a short summary of our main arguments and an identification of our contribution.

2 Adam Smith's Reasoning Routines

2.1 Reasoning Routines: What They Are, What They Are Not

Routines mean a lot of things to a lot of people, as evidenced by Cohen et al. (1995). Here, the meaning attached to the label is that of cognitive processes/algorithms. In the words of Cohen and his collaborators, reasoning routines are neither routines in the narrow sense, i.e., "complex, highly automatic behaviors that 'function as a unit' and typically involve high levels of information processing that is largely repetitive over separate invocations of the routine" (p. 10) nor rules of thumb, i.e., "quantitative, relatively simple decision rules that are consciously invoked and require low levels of information processing" (p. 10). Rather, they can be understood as heuristics, strategies, or cognitive algorithms/frameworks. It is the sense in which the word is used in the present context to characterize Smith's way of thinking about the social and natural world.

A frequently encountered situation in daily life, and one that will play a central role in the following sections, may illustrate the meaning of a reasoning routine. Imagine you want to buy a good or service of unknown, adjustable quality. Say, you want to buy a cello, or an organic banana, childcare, or car repairs. Do you trust the seller's utterance that she will provide you with a good and/or service of high quality? You know (or at the minimum, might have an inkling) that the seller has an incentive to promise you the world and deliver a pittance. In fact, it is very likely that you have been in numerous situations like that before. You have learned, undoubtedly in some cases from your own experience, and from your discussions with others, that some sellers can be trusted more than others. You are likely to have learned that trusting a seller has little to do with his blue eyes, nice clothes, and slick talk, but with his incentives to care about repeated business, i.e., his reputation, as Smith explained to his students (*LJ*(B), p. 327, pp. 538–539; see also *WN*, I.xi.c.31, p. 146).

Mental warning signs will automatically flicker whenever you encounter a good or service of unknown quality and you will try to assess the likelihood of being cheated. The reasoning process with which you will react to the situation will be fairly routinized (but may not be automatic). You may, for example, try to figure out what the worst case scenario could be, or, what the seller stands to gain, imagining yourself in her shoes. Depending on your assessment of the situation, you will buy the good or service in question, insist on certain guarantees, or determine that you are better off buying elsewhere. Your decision will be based on canonical representations of the situations and on a matching process that identifies them (see Ortmann 2008 and references therein; see also Hohwy 2013, 2017; Clark 2016, 2017, about which more below).

Translated into modern economic language, you understand that you are engaged in a principal-agent reputational game, with you—the buyer—being the principal and the seller being the agent, and with each of you having essentially two options which are for the seller to deliver on her promises and for the buyer gauging the situation and either trusting the seller's utterances, or not, given the circumstances (e.g., Ortmann and Colander 1997; Meardon and Ortmann 1996a, 1996b).

Hopefully, your course on game theory and modern industrial organization helped you to better understand the incentive structure of the particular problem that you face and to what extent it is isomorph to other problems that you have previously encountered. If you also have taken a course in cognitive psychology, you may have learned that—being the intuitive statistician that you are—you have just activated a cheating detection module (Cosmides 1989; Cosmides and Tooby 1996 [1997]; Gigerenzer and Hug 1992). Whatever label you attach to it, you will recognize the situation as one involving a good of unknown adjustable quality (Tirole 1988), and you will react to the situation in a routinized manner.

So did Smith. For instance, he understood remarkably well that the same incentive structure typically known as principal-agent game underlies such diverse problems as speaker/listener or writer/reader interaction (e.g., Collings and Ortmann 1997), self-command (e.g., Meardon and Ortmann 1996a, 1996b), efficiency wages, teaching and preaching (Ortmann 1999), and seller-buyer transactions of goods and services of adjustable quality (Ortmann et al. 2022; chapter 5 this book).

Whenever Smith came across a problem of that kind, we argue, he intuitively understood the nature of the problem, and took it through a consistent reasoning pattern/routine/algorithm: This is the (empirically observable) problem, here are the particular circumstances that create it, these are scenarios and institutional arrangements or incentive structures that could overcome the "moral hazard" aspects of the situation.

Showing that Smith thought in these (game-theoretic) terms is important because it was exactly these patterns/routines/algorithms, once understood, that Smith used to understand new problems. We call the different games that he employed (see also Chap. 5) his second set of reasoning routines or reasoning sub-routines, as we shall see presently.

Recently, considerable evidence has accumulated in favor of the conceptualization of the brain as "Bayesian" (Editorial 2017; Clark 2016, 2017; Hohwy 2013, 2017); in this conceptualization the brain deals with the "barrage" (Clark 2017, 728) of incoming sensory stimuli by creating, and importantly continuously updating, a statistical top-down generative model. This updating process is driven by "prediction errors" (Clark

2017; Hohwy 2013); it seems that this part of the argument has considerable theoretical and empirical support and it makes, in our view, intuitive sense. Somewhat more controversial is the idea of "prediction error minimization" (Clark 2017 and Hohwy 2017, drawing on Clark 2016 and Hohwy 2013) which motivates the use of the term Bayesian. But, again, to the extent that humans are conceptualized as prediction machines that continuously test hypotheses about the world it seems eminently sensible a proposition.

Engstroem et al. (2018) have illustrated the idea of "predictive processing" and "prediction error minimization" in the context of driving. Suppose you drive on an empty highway and follow another car. Your "generative model" predicts that there should be no visual expansion (looming) of the car that you follow, indicating that you keep a fixed distance. If looming happens (either because the car you follow slowed down, or because you sped up), then your visual sensory system will register a mismatch between predicted and actual visual expansion and this prediction error will lead to a revision of the model. The brain, through its relevant sensors, thus processes the incoming data and matches them with predictions that it continuously makes and it does so for lower-level sensory signals such as looming, as well as for higher-level sensory signals of a more abstract nature (e.g., principal-agent games about which more below).

As we shall see below (Sect. 2.2), Smith's conceptualization of the formation and evolution of beliefs, and for that matter, of understanding of the world around us, anticipates some such mechanism in what Smith sees as a three-step process, leading from wonder and surprise (in response to evidence contradicting a prior) to admiration once the model of the world had been adjusted.

2.2 *What Are Smith's Reasoning Routines?*

Figure 1 below provides a summary of the reasoning routines and a sketch of their relations to each other.

We now elaborate in more detail on what we identify as Smith's reasoning routines. Reasoning routines (RR) 1–3 and the meta-reasoning routine are discussed here in detail. Then in Sect. 2.3, we address what we identify as possible conflicts between the reasoning routines (specifically between RR1 and RR3) and how Smith dealt with this.

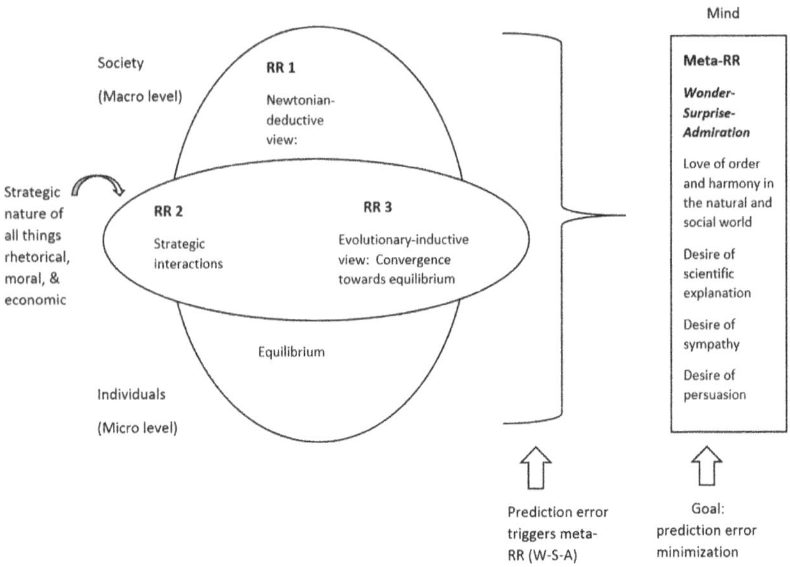

Fig. 1 The reasoning routines and their relations to each other

We call RR1 Smith's "Newtonian view" of the world. It is well-known that Newton's work had a major influence on Smith (Smith 1985, *LRBL* pp. 145–146; see also Evensky 1989, 1993; Lindgren 1967; Hetherington 1983; Skinner 1986; Redman 1993; Dellemotte 2002; Montes 2004, 2008, 2013; Schliesser 2005, 2017; Diemer and Guillemin 2011). In fact, Smith explicitly praised Newton's system (*HA*, pp. 99–105). Following the latter, Smith visualizes the Universe as "a complete machine, as a coherent system, governed by general laws, and directed to general ends ..." (*History of Ancient Physics*, in *EPS*, p. 112). The director is the Deity, "the Author of Nature" (*TMS*, II.i.5.10, p. 77; II.iii.3.2, p. 105; III.ii.31, p. 129),[11] or the universal mind responsible for the

[11] Smith's true belief in God, and the place of religion in his thinking, remains a controversial issue among scholars writing on Smith (see Pack 1995; Fleischacker 2021). For a general overview of these debates, see Kennedy (2013, 2017) and Graham (2016). Rasmussen (2017), like us, seems to find Kennedy's case persuasive. Kennedy argues that Smith was an agnostic who was kept from revealing the fact by what he saw happened to Hume but also to not hurt his beloved mother who was deeply religious. Fleischacker (2021), somewhat surprisingly, does not mention Kennedy's work. He does concede that

design of the machine; and since the Deity communicates his grand design not directly, but through external sensations and ideas only, "it was the business of Physics, or Natural Philosophy to determine wherein consisted the Nature and Essence of every particular Species of things, in order to connect together all the different events that occur in the material world; ..." ("History of Ancient Logics and Metaphysics," *EPS,* p. 119), Smith's treatise of moral philosophy is an explicit attempt to model the social world in the same vein.[12] In other words, Smith's Newtonian view of the world was very much informed by notions of (general) equilibrium although he did not use that word.[13] It is a very ***deductive*** view of the world.

Smith's infatuation with the Newtonian approach, by which "we may lay down certain principles known or proved in the beginning, from whence we account for the severall Phenomena, connecting all together by the same Chain" is reflected in a passage from lecture 24 in *LRBL* in which Smith compares it with Aristotle's approach of science, which consists in "giving a principle commonly a new one for every phenomenon" (*LRBL,* p. 146). For Smith "the Newtonian method is undoubtedly the most Philosophical, and every science whether of Morals or Naturall philosophy etc., is vastly more ingenious and for that reason more engaging than the other" (*ibid.*).

To be more precise, the Newtonian method of exposition is praised by Smith for its persuasiveness based on the use of very few and familiar philosophical principles to bind together phenomena which seemed initially unconnected to each other, hence satisfying the imagination by presenting nature and social life as a coherent and beautiful

"What Smith believed, privately, about religion can therefore play a significant role in how we interpret his work" (Fleischacker 2021, p.19).

[12] "The beauty of a systematical arrangement of different observations connected by a few common principles, was first seen in the rude essays of those ancient times towards a system of natural philosophy. Something of the same kind was afterwards attempted in morals. The maxims of common life were arranged in some methodical order, and connected together by a few common principles, in the same manner as they had attempted to arrange and connect the phenomena of nature. The science which pretends to investigate and explain those connecting principles, is what is properly called moral philosophy" (*WN*, V.i.f.25, p. 724).

[13] Liu and Weingast (2021) also underline the importance of the notion of equilibrium (and of the comparative statics which draws on it) in Smith's system of thought. Their reading is very much what we identify as the Newtonian deductive view, i.e., RR1.

order.[14] Therefore, it is no surprise that Smith both in *TMS* and *WN* applied the Newtonian method. He sought to uncover the Deity's grand design for human society—to discover the connecting principles, such as the principle of sympathy which he identified as underlying the set of moral sentiments that would ultimately implement this grand design for human society, to the advantage and happiness of mankind (*TMS*, III.5.7, p. 166).

Moreover, Smith claimed that actions guided by moral faculties generally promote the Deity's design ("the scheme which the Author of nature has established").[15] Smith's tendency to think in terms of comprehensive systems and design is thus what we call his first reasoning routine, his "Newtonian-deductive view" of both the natural and the social world. Smith's stated belief that the "Author of Nature," "the Deity," had a vision for the happiness and perfection of the world, and that men are endowed by him with "natural" principles, faculties, and propensities leading them to realize, though unconsciously, the "plan of Providence," is what we call his "providential view."

Turning to RR2 in Fig. 1, this reasoning routine is best thought of as a set of reasoning sub-routines, whose common denominator is Smith's deep understanding of the strategic nature of all things rhetorical, moral, and economic. Life is being beset with strategic interactions—something that Smith is likely to have picked up as a boy traversing the local market while on his way to school (Phillipson 2010, p. 17) and that was featured prominently first in Smith's lectures on the emergence of languages and rhetoric. It is here where he starts to think about symmetric and asymmetric strategic interactions (which beget different rhetorical strategies especially when the parties involved have conflicting interests), with the latter including linguistic acts of agents engaged toward their principals. In fact, Smith's understanding of the information asymmetry of

[14] Smith thus defends parsimony in science and underlines the importance of relying on principles of which we have an everyday experience. For more details on the main characteristics of good, persuasive "systems" in Smith, see Biziou (2003).

[15] "By acting according to the dictates of our moral faculties, we necessarily pursue the most effectual means for promoting the happiness of mankind, and may therefore be said, in some sense, to co-operate with the Deity, and to advance as far as in our power the plan of Providence. By acting otherways, on the contrary, we seem to obstruct, in some measure, the scheme which the Author of nature has established for the happiness and perfection of the world, and to declare ourselves, if I may say so, in some measure the enemies of God" (*TMS*, III.5.7, p. 166).

principal-agent situations is very early on display and up until the rhetorical strategies that he himself applied in *WN* in order to persuade a presumably hostile audience, the powerful representatives of the mercantile system of Great Britain of his day that he chose to attack (see Ortmann et al. 2019, Ortmann and Walraevens 2018). Hill (2020) recently argued that Smith's stated preferred solution for the Empire's trouble with the American colonies was likewise motivated by his being convinced that his truly preferred solution for the situation could not possibly carry the way in the England of his day. Note that this parallels Smith's stated beliefs about the reality of the "Author of Nature" and his alleged "providential plan," which might be seen also as a rhetorical device (hypothesis) to soothe the imagination of his readers and persuade them of the (meaning and) coherence of the world.[16]

Game theory, apart from forcing the researcher to be explicit about players, available actions, payoffs to those actions, and information conditions, provides a suitable language and a rich set of useful concepts to frame these interactions, such as the distinction between finitely and indefinitely repeated games of which Smith had a firm grasp (e.g., Ortmann and Meardon 1995; Meardon and Ortmann 1996a, 1996b; Ortmann and Colander 1997; Ortmann 1999; Ortmann et al. 2019; Ortmann and Walraevens 2020). Our central argument is that Smith understood the strategic interaction between speakers (writers) and listeners (readers), Man Today and Man Tomorrow, and the principals and agents engaged in various commercial interactions including those involving adjustable quality and/or effort exceptionally well, as can be demonstrated by extracting the common underlying normal-form games.[17] Smith used interactive scenarios over and over again—mainly focusing on symmetric and asymmetric prisoner's dilemma games (asymmetric "principal-agent" games). This second reasoning routine is actually a set of reasoning sub-routines, or problem isomorphs, that have similar structures (see Ortmann et al. 2022; chapter 5 this book).

Turning to RR3 in Fig. 1, we identify it as Smith's belief in the evolutionary, or *inductive*, nature of many systems, be they social or other.

[16] Pack (1995) interestingly claims that Smith's religious beliefs were certainly more influenced by his philosophical and epistemological views than the other way round.

[17] A technical term that, for the two-player case, describes a bi-matrix with rows and columns that intersect and each cell featuring the payoffs for the two players, Row and Column.

While RR1, the Newtonian perspective, is widely perceived to be about the *equilibrium* of a system, Smith's belief in the evolutionary nature of many systems is essentially about the *process* toward equilibrium, if it exists, and if it exists *uniquely*. "Considerations Concerning the First Formation of Languages" (Smith 1985, pp. 203–226) best exemplify our claim. Indeed, Smith represents languages, standards of moral conduct, and economic values as conventions, that is, as equilibrium outcomes of repeated interactions of self-interested but "empathetic" agents (see Otteson 2002a, 2002b, 2002c; see also Meardon and Ortmann 1996a, 1996b; Ortmann and Meardon 1995). Smith's evolutionary beliefs implied that the purpose of systems had to be explained bottom-up, by means of the principles of motion of the system's constituent parts: the principles of human nature for the social world, the principles of matter for the natural world.

Smith believed that human capacities like languages or moral sentiments, as well as institutions like property rights, cultures, governments, philosophical systems, etc., evolve over time. He demonstrated this evolutionary mode of thinking in most, if not all, of his major published and unpublished works. Indeed, works as seemingly diverse as his *History of Astronomy* (*EPS*, Smith 1982) and *Lectures on Jurisprudence* (Smith 1982a) rely upon a method of theorizing that Stewart famously called "conjectural history" (Stewart 1795 in Smith 1982, p. 293); in what are now called his *Essays on Philosophical Subjects*, he applies it to the history of astronomical science, logics, and ancient metaphysics, while the *Lectures on Jurisprudence* and *WN* apply it to the history of civil society. His *Considerations Concerning the First Formation of Languages* and *TMS* apply it to the origin and formation of languages and moral sentiments. Conjectural or theoretical history is based on conjectures about processes that cannot be derived from data. That is, we do not know how exactly languages originally evolved but we can have reasonable guesses about their likely development from previously identified principles of human nature (RR1).[18] And this method of philosophizing helps to soothe the

[18] " … in a general review of his publications, it deserves our attention less, on account of the opinions it contains, than as a specimen of a particular sort of inquiry, which, so far as I know, is entirely of modern origin, and which seems, in a peculiar degree, to have interested Mr Smith's curiosity. Something very similar to it may be traced in all his different works, whether moral, political, or literary; and on all these subjects he has exemplified it with the happiest success […] When, in such a period of society as that in which we live, we compare our intellectual acquirements, our opinions, manners, and

imagination, to restore the tranquility of the mind by filling gaps when data are missing (meta-RR). Smith used this technique quite often and successfully.

Notwithstanding the labeling of the reasoning routines as 1 through 3, and while there is some chronological rhyme and reason to the labeling, we think of them as three complementary sets of routines. Smith started out thinking about the Newtonian method of exhibition while thinking about natural philosophy (in his history of "astronomy" in particular, but not exclusively) and it is here where RR1 featured prominently and dominantly. But as soon as Smith moved into the social sphere and became occupied with understanding rhetoric, languages, and ultimately moral sentiments, RR2 and RR3 kicked in with a vengeance. That's because the information asymmetry of principal-agent situations was something that he first struggled with in the evolution of languages and rhetoric but whose strategic nature he realized about the same time. RR2 simply acknowledges his insights into the interactive nature of things ethical, moral, and economic, which is the essence of game theory (Binmore 1994, 1997).

We finally turn to the meta-heuristic: Wonder–Surprise–Admiration, or the aesthetic love of order and coherence. Smith, we argued, was infatuated by the Newtonian method which he considered "the most Philosophical" because "It gives us a pleasure to see the phaenomena which we reckoned the most unaccountable all deduced from some principle (commonly a well-known one) and all united in one chain, ..." (Smith 1982, p. 146). This pleasure is the aesthetic love of order and systems.

It was first underlined by Smith in his *HA* in which he identified a specific algorithm, or reasoning routine, that—he argued—philosophers

institutions, with those which prevail among rude tribes, it cannot fail to occur to us as an interesting question, by what gradual steps the transition has been made from the first simple efforts of uncultivated nature, to a state of things so wonderfully artificial and complicated. [...] On most of these subjects very little information is to be expected from history [...] Thus, in the instance which has suggested these remarks, although it is impossible to determine with certainty what the steps were by which any particular language was formed, yet if we can shew, *from the known principles of human nature*, how all its various parts might gradually have arisen, *the mind is not only to a certain degree satisfied, but a check is given to that indolent philosophy, which refers to a miracle, whatever appearances, both in the natural and moral worlds, it is unable to explain...*" (Stewart 1795 in Smith 1982, pp. 292–293, our italics).

of all kinds (natural and moral philosophers alike) employed when they became aware of the world and of its underlying connecting principles. This algorithm was the Wonder–Surprise–Admiration triad, representing what we could call the "passions of scientific inquiry." Smith's story runs like this. Given the philosopher's current understanding of the world, some unexpected observation in conflict with that understanding, or in terms of emerging theories about the "Bayesian brain" (Editorial 2017; Clark 2016, 2017; Hohwy 2013, 2017) the "prediction error" in Fig. 1, would cause him to be surprised. This surprise would lead him to wonder, which would trigger a process of philosophizing (and attempts to better calibrate the complex process that led to the prediction error), and then—possibly—lead to admiration of a new insight that explains what was surprising, creating (thanks to our imagination and understanding) a new chain of reasoning and order, i.e., a new association of ideas in our mind.

The process of philosophizing always begins with wonder and surprise, which subsequently leads to attempts to understand what "we have before been either little or not at all acquainted." This process leads to a new understanding and admiration because "These sentiments, like all others when inspired by one and the same object, mutually support and enliven one another" (*HA*, intro. 6, p. 34).

We note the striking analogy between this process of scientific discovery, as Smith presents it here, and his concept of gravitation of the market price around the natural price in *WN* (I.vii),[19] which has also been tied to "market models" of languages and morals (e.g., Otteson 2002a, 2002b, 2002c; see also Ortmann and Meardon 1995 and Meardon and Ortmann 1996a, 1996b). Indeed, Smith describes the process of scientific inquiry as a ***natural*** and ***stable*** equilibrium process of the imagination in three steps:

i. First, we are in a state of (psychological) equilibrium. Smith underlines the existence of a "natural" state of "tranquility and composure" of the imagination when everything we observe happens as expected, when our world is in order (*HA*, II.12, p. 46).
ii. Then, the observation of unknown, unexpected events create an exogenous shock which create feelings of "wonder" and "surprise,"

[19] Along the same lines, Breban (2014) shows that in *TMS* Smith presents a "gravitational" theory of happiness in which unexpected events create only momentary changes and deviations from our natural state of happiness.

i.e., the prediction error. The methodical order, connected together by a few common principles, is disrupted, and the cognitive routine, the association of ideas is interrupted because our chain of explanation is broken. The imagination faces an unpleasant "gap" in sense-making, which triggers attempts to regain an enjoyable equilibrium state of "tranquility and composure" of the imagination by finding a new cause or common causal chain to the different events we observe, leading to step 3.

iii. Lastly, our imagination engages in sense-making exercises that allow us to regain the equilibrium state of "tranquility and composure" when everything we observe happens as expected, when similar causes produce the same effects. We desire to relieve the pain associated with our inability to understand and to anticipate the events of the natural world. When our explanation of the external, natural world is again in order, our mind is at peace.[20]

This W—S—A routine thus triggers an attempt at understanding the world and as such it provides the foundation not only of Smith's Newtonian view of the world, but also of the other two reasoning routines. Hence our qualification of a "meta" reasoning routine.

Indeed, as we shall see later (and as we already pre-shadowed), Smith does not confine men's love of order and harmony to the observation and understanding of the natural world. Observing order and harmony in the social world is also a source of pleasure, and the foundation of human sociability. There is as much pleasure in mutual sympathy as there is pleasure in persuading, Smith argues. Sharing and observing similar sentiments, opinions, or thoughts is a source of joy for people while, by contrast, disagreements are painful to them.

2.3 Reasoning Routines 1 and 3, Conflicting

Smith's simultaneous infatuation with the Newtonian view of the world and his (the Scottish Historians') belief in the evolutionary nature of civil society, systems, and what not—identified here as Smith's first and third reasoning routines—created a natural tension in Smith's work.

[20] Following the Stoics on this point, Smith thinks that happiness is due to a state of tranquility of our mind. See *TMS*, III.iii.30, p. 149.

Smith started out believing that human society, by going through stages, would eventually realize the design of the Deity (whatever that meant for him) for the happiness and perfection of the world to a reasonable approximation; the evolutionary process would inevitably lead to the implementation of the grand design, the very plan of Providence.[21] Later in his life, Smith was still a believer in the providential view (whatever that means for him, see fn 11), but he increasingly had doubts about it. (See Evensky 1989: 125–126, for a similar argument; see also Hanley 2006 on Smith's increasing worries about the virtues of the commercial era and his remedies for it.)

This tension has often confounded his readers and critics (e.g., Otteson 2002a, 2002b, 2002c who seems to argue that there is a natural convergence in languages as well as sentiments of the Impartial Spectator) but it seems to have been instrumental, or so we argue, in making Smith think about incentive-compatible arrangements in matters ethical, political, and economic.

As we shall see, Smith derives social behavior or conventions from a theory of strategic interaction, very much in the spirit of Hume.[22] He distances conceptions of society from both the old theories of the divine, or sovereign constitution of the state, and from Enlightenment theories of the origin of societies as "social contracts"; he emphasizes instead the self-constructed, historical nature of society, and its fallible and possibly fragile forms of operation.

Importantly, in this view of the world, the location of the equilibrium was not pre-determined and Smith was indeed increasingly convinced that it was socially constructed (e.g., Phillipson 2010, chapter 10) and that quite possibly societies faced equilibrium selection problems. A prime example of this changed belief can be found in Book 3 of the *WN* where Smith explains how Europe did *not* follow the "natural progress of opulence" (*WN*, III.1), beginning with the development of agriculture, then of manufactures, and finally of foreign trade. Rather, European

[21] Detailed arguments along these lines can be found in Evensky (1989, 2005), Meek (1976), Skinner and Wilson (1975), and (1986, section II).

[22] In two important volumes, Binmore (1994, 1997) has argued for a bottom-up approach to ethical issues that draws heavily on David Hume's approach. To what extent Smith's "evolutionary" approach was inspired by Hume, and deviated from him, is an intriguing question that we do not address here because it is tangential to our argument. See though Meardon and Ortmann (1996a, 1996b).

countries followed an "unnatural and retrograde order" (*WN*, III.1.9, p. 380) and yet some progressed for Europe to become the richest region of the world at that point. The North American colonies, however, Smith noted, were rapidly catching up with them because they ***did*** follow a more natural path toward opulence and had institutions closer to the ideal system of natural liberty.

In other words, Smith believed that there are times when human behavior can interfere with the divine or providential plan and prevent it from being realized, as was prominently the case with the mercantile system. (See for similar arguments, Ortmann and Meardon 1995; Evensky 1989, p. 135; West 1996, pp. 21–23.)

In terms of the machine metaphor, founded on the Newtonian view of the world, this process could be viewed as a breakdown or malfunction of the machine.[23] Thus, Smith's emphasis shifted from the Newtonian to the evolutionary view, or from RR1 to RR3. Understanding that maybe society would not automatically realize the plan of Providence, Smith increasingly started to ponder the existence of, and possible solutions to, incentive problems regarding all things moral, political, and economic.

Evensky's argument regarding the evolution of Smith's views traces this change back to the fact that Smith in 1773 found himself confronted with a dramatically different set of evidence about the trajectory that commercial society was moving along. It became clear to Smith that mercantilism could no longer be considered a historical artifact. Smith developed "growing frustration that the incentives in commerce lead merchants to behavior that is inconsistent with the social welfare" (Evensky 1989, p. 135; for related takes see Pack 2010 and Sagar 2021). Smith's "new awareness" explains also, as Evensky argues, why it took Smith about three years (instead of the anticipated few months) to finish *WN*. According to Evensky, during those years Smith found, in addition to his first voice as moral philosopher, his second voice as "social critic,"

[23] "Human society, when we contemplate it in a certain abstract and philosophical light, appears like a great, an immense machine, whose regular and harmonious movements produce a thousand agreeable effects. As in any other beautiful and noble machine that was the production of human art, whatever tended to render its movements more smooth and easy, would derive a beauty from this effect, and, on the contrary, whatever tended to obstruct them would displease upon that account: so virtue, which is, as it were, the fine polish to the wheels of society, necessarily pleases; while vice, like the vile rust, which makes them jar and grate upon one another, is as necessarily offensive" (*TMS*, VII.iii.1.2, p. 316).

highlighting in the last edition of *TMS* the corruption of men's moral sentiments (the natural admiration of the rich and the despise of the poor) and the need for wise, virtuous legislators (Evensky 2005). Along similar lines, Hanley (2006) highlighted Smith's growing concern for the ethical ills of commercial societies and at the same time his willingness to offer some remedies to the corruption of men in advanced societies, as illustrated by the addition of part six on the "Character of Virtue" in the 1790 edition of *TMS*. Phillipson (2010) follows broadly the arguments proposed by Evensky and Hanley. The second voice as social critic informed Smith's concerns, as reflected especially in Book V of the *WN*, about a variety of public goods provision and externalities problems but also in Smith's deep interest in the American Question and his related plan for a new British Empire and Constitution (Ortmann and Walraevens 2018 and chapter 2; Ortmann et al. 2019; Hill 2020; Fleischacker 2004, 2021; Paganelli 2010).

In any case, Smith's thinking was firmly grounded in the insight that the particular circumstances of space and time, of nations and ages as he puts it, require different plans and institutions for regulating the social world (*WN*, p. 689). Smith himself stresses the fundamental importance of this aspect at every instance (See, for example, *WN*, pp. 707, 709, 724).

3 A Conjectural History of Smith's Reasoning Routines

We propose now to relate Smith's reasoning routines to important events of his personal and intellectual life. In other words, we try to provide a "conjectural history" of the emergence of what we identify as Smith's reasoning routines.

Smith was born in 1723 in Kirkcaldy, a Scottish harbor town with about 1500 inhabitants. Rae suggested that it was "not an unfavourable observatory for beginning one's knowledge of the world. It has more sorts and conditions of men to exhibit than a rural district can furnish, and it exhibits each more completely in all their ways, pursuits, troubles, characters, than can possibly done in a city" (Rae 1895, p. 7).

Rae also notes the excellent education that Smith got at the Burgh School of Kirkcaldy, on which are based some of his proposals on education in *WN*, and his "studious disposition, his love of reading, and his power of memory" (Rae 1895, p. 8). From 1737 to 1740, young Adam studied at the University of Glasgow, attending lectures on Mathematics, Natural and Moral Philosophy, Greek and Latin (Stewart 1795, p. 270). It was there that the "never to be forgotten" Professor Hutcheson opened his mind to the study of human nature in all its branches (Stewart 1795, p. 271). Smith then transferred to Balliol College (Oxford) for three years where he carefully studied languages, was involved in translation works,[24] and discovered for himself Hume's *Treatise of Human Nature*. Indeed, Smith was caught and chastised for reading the book alone in his room (Stewart 1795, p. 272; Kennedy 2017, p. 20). Interestingly, Stewart underlines that Smith's "study of languages" at that time "was subservient, not to a vain parade of tasteless erudition, but to a familiar acquaintance with every thing that could illustrate the institutions, the manners, and the ideas of different ages and nations" (Stewart 1795, p. 270). A quick look at what is left of Smith's library illustrates the point. It consisted of numerous books, especially in French, on political economy, morality, rhetoric, philosophy, literature, politics, history, and natural sciences (See Phillipson et al. 2019 and references therein).

Smith's stay at Balliol College was not a happy time for him but he learned important lessons. We know that he suffered from anxiety[25] and did not like his academic experience there, criticizing the poor quality of teaching and the minimal and useless contacts with professors. Later, in *WN*, Smith claimed that it was due, at least in part, to teachers being poorly incentivized to meet the needs of their students (see also Ortmann 1999, 1997). Kennedy argues that Smith learned in Oxford also to bargain, and quite efficiently so. First, he did so in order to change his courses, switching from the Ordination path to graduation in civil law without having to personally fund his university fees. He also negotiated a "temporary" compassionate leave which prepared the ground for him to eventually withdraw from Balliol College without penalty.[26] So, following Kennedy's narrative, Smith's time in Oxford led him to think about strategic interactions and incentives.

After having wisely negotiated his early departure from Oxford (see Weingast 2018 for a game-theoretic reconstruction of Smith's bargaining,

[24] His juvenile *Letter to the Edinburgh Review* bears testimony of his early interest in translation (Smith 1982).

[25] On the possible reasons of Smith's stress, see Kennedy (2017, pp. 13–19).

[26] For more details on this, see Kennedy (2017, pp. 25–29).

as laid out in Kennedy 2017), Smith spent the years 1746–1748 again in Kirkcaldy, and it was there that he seems to have refined his *History of Astronomy* (Wightman 1982, p. 7), a text he most likely started at Oxford, and in which displayed his first reasoning routine, his "Newtonian" view of the world, but also the "meta" reasoning routine. This work was praised by someone eminently skeptical of Smith as "the pearl of the (*EPS*) collection" (Schumpeter 1954, p. 182) and it is one of the few works that Smith did not want burned after his death, in case it could shed light on his whole project. Between 1748 and 1751, Smith offered successful public lectures on jurisprudence and rhetoric and literature at Edinburgh (Phillipson 2010, chap 5) which included, according to Pauchant (2017), the first version of the four-stage theory of human history. Smith's very first job was thus to teach how to efficiently communicate ideas, passions, facts, and opinions. We know from the student notes on Smith's lectures on rhetoric and belles letters that he had thought hard about how languages emerged between savages (Smith 1985, pp. 203–226, see specifically *Considerations*) and was also very much aware of the strategic situation in which persuasion often happened, as illustrated by his deep analysis of orators and of the different forms of eloquence (Smith 1985, pp. 129–200). Therefore, we find in his early lectures, even before he properly began his academic career, the rudiments of Smith's second and third reasoning routines.

In late 1750, he was appointed Professor of Logic at Glasgow University. It is noteworthy that his course included materials on rhetoric and belles lettres.[27] About a year later, and apparently thanks to the success of his previously mentioned public lectures on rhetoric and jurisprudence in Edinburgh (Buchan 2016, p. 6), he was elected to the prestigious chair of Moral Philosophy and remained in this position for thirteen years, a part of his life he referred to as the happiest of all (Stewart 1795 in Smith 1982, p. 273).

The changes in Smith's official job description apparently did not dramatically affect what he taught. According to Bryce, the editor of the

[27] "In the Professorship of Logic [at Glasgow] ... [Smith] dedicated [most] of his time to the delivery of a system of rhetoric and belles lettres. The best method of explaining and illustrating the various powers of the human mind, ... arises from the examination of the several ways of communicating our thoughts by speech, and from an attention to the principles of those literary compositions which contribute to persuasion or entertainment" (Stewart 1795 in Smith 1982, pp. 274–275).

Glasgow edition of *LRBL*, Smith continued for instance to teach rhetoric for years in private classes (Bryce 1985, p. 7, reported in Stewart 1795, p. 274, and based on conversations he had with Millar) and, importantly, "although they were never published in his own day, Smith's rhetoric lectures were widely circulating and had the effect of a book" (Bevilacqua 1965, p. 6). It was during that time that Smith developed the rudiments of his thoughts on the subject matters that he later published in *TMS* and *WN*.[28]

The course of lectures that Smith gave at Glasgow University shows that he conceived of his rudimentary ideas on the subject matters of *TMS*, *LJ*, and *WN* as part of a single or consistent overall project whose publication he had very early planned, but could never accomplish (see *TMS*, VII.iv.37, p. 341 and Advertisement to the 6th edition; see Young 1997), as is well-known now.

What is less well-known is that Smith's set of lectures on moral philosophy at Glasgow University was also conceived during a time when Smith was still very much concerned with rhetoric. And we know from a letter he sent to the Duke of La Rochefoucauld his willingness to publish also a book in which rhetoric would have been a major topic (*Corr.* 248, p. 296).

Hence, while Smith engaged qua teaching demands with rhetoric, then moral philosophy, then economics, in that order, it is well-documented that Smith thought about these issues in parallel from the late forties and fifties onwards (the 1750's that is), as also reflected later in his interleafing of the various editions of *TMS* and *WN*.

Toward the end of 1763, Smith received an invitation to accompany, as a tutor, the Duke of Buccleuch on his travels. Smith accepted the invitation and set out for the continent in March 1764. During the following

[28] "About a year after his appointment to the Professorship of Logic, Mr. Smith was elected to the chair of Moral Philosophy. His course of lectures on this subject was divided into four parts. The first contained Natural Theology; in which he considered the proofs of the being and attributes of God, and those principles of the human mind on which religion is founded. The second comprehended Ethics, strictly so called, and consisted chiefly of the doctrines which he afterwards published in his *TMS*. In the third part, he treated at more length that branch of morality which relates to *justice*, ... In the last part of his lectures, he examined those political regulations which are founded, not upon the principle of *justice*, but that of *expediency*, and which are calculated to increase the riches, the power, and prosperity of a State. ... What he delivered on these subjects contained the substance of the work he afterwards published under the title of *WN*" (Stewart 1795, pp. 274–275).

two and a half years, he stayed for nearly a year in Paris and frequented there the most famous *salons*. There he met Turgot, Mirabeau, Quesnay, Helvetius, D'Holbach, Diderot, and Morellet, among others[29] (Stewart 1795, p. 302).[30] Smith returned in October 1766 and, with the Duke of Buccleuch providing a generous stipend, he went into semi-retirement for the next ten years. Stewart, the typically reliable and widely used source (last but not least because he was the one closest to events; see Buchan 2016, p. 10 on the constraints that he faced and seems to have taken into account; see also Leser 1881), argued: "During the whole of this period, (with the exception of a few visits to Edinburgh and London) he remained with his mother at Kirkcaldy; occupied habitually in intense study" (Stewart 1795, p. 307).

Phillipson (2010, chaps. 10, 11) has written persuasively about the importance of Smith's stays in London during eight months in 1766–1767 and even more in the three between 1773–1776, i.e., during the run-up to the printing of *WN*. He makes it clear that Smith "was able to move in political circles at a time when the future of Anglo-American relations, the role of the East India Company in the government of India and public finance and taxation were under discussion, all matters of importance to the WN," and especially to its Book V (2010, p. 201).[31] It was, in Phillipson's view (who draws among other sources on well-known expressions of anxiety and relief by David Hume), Smith's increasing obsession with "the American question" (Fleischacker 2002; Ortmann and Walraevens 2018 and chapter 2) that led to ever new postponements of the publication of the *WN*.

That Smith spent three years in London before publishing *WN* is the key; there he could be an uninvolved and impartial spectator of the dangerous collusion between the political elite and the economic powers, and exchange ideas with both groups in intellectual clubs and

[29] Smith also met Voltaire during his stay on the Continent, in the latter's house in Ferney.

[30] Smith spent most of his time in the south of France. For more details on this, see Alcouffe and Massot-Bordenave (2020); see also West (1996).

[31] In Smith's *LJ* (1762 and 1766), we find no mention of the "mercantile system," nor of the "agricultural system" or the "system of natural liberty," while hindrances to the freedom of internal and foreign commerce and the false belief in the monetary foundation of wealth are repeatedly denounced. Smith's enemy in *WN*, the pernicious system of merchants and manufacturers persuading legislators to make laws favoring them at the expense of the interest of society, was not clearly "conceptualized" yet.

salons of which he was a well-known member.[32] In a letter to Smith dated 04/01/1776, Hume writes him that "it [*WN*] is probably much improved by your last Abode in London" (Smith *Corr.* 150, pp. 186–187). We argue that while Smith undoubtedly had the premises of the "system of natural liberty" sorted out in his mind early (Stewart 1795 in Smith 1982, p. 322), only later he started its theoretical ***conceptualization*** and that of its antagonistic counterpart, the mercantile system, because what happened in the North American colonies was key to understanding both.[33] The result of this extended retreat was published in April 1776 as *WN,* just three months before the American Declaration of Independence and it was indeed "a very 'American' book" (Fleischacker 2002: 903; Ortmann and Walraevens 2018; Ortmann et al. 2019; Hill 2020).

The conceptual lenses Smith had acquired early in his life served him well, even after he became "very zealous in American Affairs" (Hume, according to Smith *Corr.* 149, p. 185) and increasingly concerned about the politics of the day, the long-term consequences for the Empire of the American question and related questions of how to deal with the increasing debt the colonies brought about.

For the greater part of the following two years, Smith lived in London. He was then appointed as one of the Commissioners of his Majesty's Customs in Scotland and spent the last twelve years of his life in Edinburgh, spending apparently a significant amount of time on his new obligations as Commissioner, to the detriment of his academic pursuits, although he published a new and significantly revised version of *TMS* a few months before his death[34] (Stewart 1795, p. 326).

Five aspects of Smith's life deserve highlighting in the current context.

[32] See Phillipson (2010, p. 209) on the sociable time he had in London.

[33] It is Smith who first developed the concept of the mercantile system in the *WN* (Spector 2003). Completing his system of political economy required a conceptualization of the different discourses prevailing at that time and of their influence on economic and political reality, a task still to be accomplished and for which the colonies of North America, his later example of the natural progress of opulence, seemed a useful reference point that had the advantage of being policy relevant as well as far removed from the very violent attack Smith set out to launch. Right in the center of both the commercial system of Great Britain and the British Empire, London was for Smith the proper place for observing the mercantile system, which threatened the survival of the Empire, and for being informed about the tumultuous relations between the mother country and the American colonies.

[34] On Smith's life and work as a commissioner of customs, see Anderson et al. (1985).

First, Smith spent more than 40% of his life in a small harbor town in Scotland, allowing him to experience the origin and evolution of social fabric in an ideal observatory. In other words, he was at Kirkcaldy in the perfect place to become a (social and moral) philosopher whose job, as we are reminded in *WN*, is "to observe everything" (*WN*, I.i.9, p. 21). More specifically, Phillipson (2010, p. 17) noted that as a child, Smith had to travel through the local market to go to school, thus daily observing the "higgling and bargaining of the market." This allowed him to understand the strategic interaction of self-interested citizens in repeated-game contexts, the source from which RR2 and RR3, in particular, spring (see Meardon and Ortmann 1996a, 1996b).

Secondly, the time he spent in Glasgow, as student and professor for about 20% of his life, was the perfect place to become an economist. Not only was Glasgow growing dramatically during these years—Phillipson called it a "boomtown" (Phillipson 2010, p. 25, see also pp. 25–27)—because of its size it also offered Smith a contrasting experience of the origin and evolution of social fabric in another laboratory that was decidedly more urban. These experiences, as well as those in Edinburgh, must have re-enforced his understanding of the strategic interaction of self-interested citizens in repeated-game contexts albeit contexts that surely must have relied less on reputational enforcement, a theme that has prominence in both *TMS* and *WN*.

Thirdly, and against this backdrop of the years spent in the laboratories that were Kirkcaldy, Glasgow, and Edinburgh, and benefitting from both his understanding of the strategic nature of social interactions and from the time of learning about rhetoric, literature, and languages that his stay in Oxford as Snell Exhibitioner afforded him, Smith went through further reinforcement of RR2 and RR3 by transferring many of the interactions among (im)morally acting agents engaged in repeated games to languages, their formation, evolution, and use. It is not coincidental that Smith wanted his *Considerations Concerning the Formation of Language* to be published with *TMS*. Note that Smith saw very clearly the interaction of RR2 and RR3 in this context and that in particular, he had learned enough about human nature to understand that readers–listeners' and writers–speakers' preferences are not always aligned in the same way, just as the preferences of Man Today and Man Tomorrow may not always be properly aligned.

Fourth, we documented that RR1 goes back to his early interest in history of astronomy and his infatuation with Newtonian approach.

While, as documented, RR2 emerged early on, RR3 developed later, probably when he prepared his lectures in Edinburgh (1746–1748, as we argued at the beginning of this section) and on the bedrock of Smith's attempt to do for social sciences what Newton had done for natural sciences (a rather common enterprise for eighteenth century moral philosophers).

Fifth, Smith had a phenomenal *memory*,[35] a faculty of the mind which is crucial for scientific inquiry (together with a strong imagination), i.e., for finding a few connecting principles binding together a great variety of phenomena and for updating associations of ideas when new data are observed. Ortmann (2021) looked into Vernon L. Smith's conjecture that Adam Smith was afflicted by Asperger's Syndrome, a condition that is known to often come with the ability to hyper-focus and extraordinary powers of memory, and found suggestive evidence in favor of the conjecture (see also Fleischacker 2021, p. 15).

4 Smith on Language and Rhetoric

All three reasoning routines, as well as the meta-RR, were on display already in Smith's lectures on languages and rhetoric. The Newtonian-deductive view (RR1) was on display in Smith's conceptualization of the natural desire (and need) to persuade as the driver of human development. RR2 was present in the acknowledgment that interaction could be strategic and that interests between interacting parties could be in conflict and information asymmetric. We see here the first time in appearance the principal-agent game that later also prominently featured in Smith's *TMS* and *WN*. The evolutionary-inductive approach (RR3) was on display in Smith's conceptualization of languages and their development as sets of conventions similar to moral sentiments. Propriety of style contributed to persuasion succeeding or failing, as did the substance of the argument.

[35] See Rae (1895, p. 8) and Stewart 1795, pp. 270, 271, and 330:

"Mr Smith attracted notice, by his passion for books, and by the extraordinary powers of his memory" (Stewart 1795, p. 270).

" ... he still retained, and retained even in advanced years, a recollection of his early acquisitions, which not only added to the splendor of his conversation, but enabled him to exemplify some of his favourite theories concerning the natural progress of the mind in the investigation of truth, ..." (Stewart 1795, p. 271).

"I have often, however, been struck at the distance of years, with his accurate memory of the most trifling particulars; ..." (Stewart 1795, p. 330).

When persuasion failed, the prediction error was addressed by adjustments in the means of persuasion that would ultimately bring about the pleasure of persuasion and the tranquility of mind that Smith saw as the equilibrium (meta-RR). We elaborate on this brief summary next.

RR1: The faculty of language, and the desire (and need) to persuade

Smith's manuscripts on rhetoric were among those he wanted destroyed in the week before his death (Bryce , p. 1; Stewart 1795). However, notes that two students had taken during the academic year 1762–1763 (now available as *LRBL*), were found in 1958, and they became an official part of the Glasgow edition of his work. The student notes were taken in the fifteenth winter in which Smith lectured on rhetoric; it is therefore difficult to ascertain to what extent they reflect Smith's initial thoughts on the subject matter although there seems to be consensus that these lectures did not change much since Smith taught them initially.[36]

An additional important document, also now reprinted in *LRBL*[37] is Smith's *Considerations* (Smith 1985, pp. 201–26); it is an expanded version of lecture 3 of the *LRBL* (Smith 1985, pp. 9–13). This essay, of which Smith was quite proud, was also lauded by his first major biographer, Stewart, "(who) saw that its value lies, not in the possible accuracy of the opinions, but in its being a specimen of ... 'Theoretical or Conjectural History'" (Bryce 1985, p. 24), a general method of inquiry Smith used in almost all of his work, as we noted earlier. There, Smith speculates first on the conditions of emergence of languages, that is, on the origin of men's use of their natural "faculty of speech." It is interesting to

[36] In Bryce's opinion, there are "few datable post 1748 references" (p. 12, see also his reference to Millar and Dougall). As was noted by McKenna (2006, p. 73) "on the basis of a range of evidence, scholars have come to regard the students notes as being very close to Smith's words" because "it can be said that they did capture Smith's prose style well, and that the notes are consistent with Smith's other published work." He adds, "What revisions the rhetoric lectures underwent cannot be known, though Smith's most recent biographer [Ross] argues that the Glasgow version of the lectures reproduces the Edinburgh material without much alteration" (2006, p. 74).

[37] The decision of the editors of the Glasgow edition of Smith's complete works not to include the *Considerations* with his *TMS*, as Smith had wanted, strikes us as questionable and might explain why this essay was until recently neglected in the scholarship on Smith's oeuvre.

note that for Smith, language emerges first when savages meet and want "to make their mutual wants intelligible to each other." This foreshadows what Smith identified in *WN* as the natural propensity to truck, barter, and exchange.

Language is man's gift of Nature for successful and pleasurable social interactions, provided he adopts the "proper" language and style for communicating his thoughts and ideas to them. For Smith, "The desire of being believed, the desire of persuading [...] seems to be one of the strongest of all our natural desires" and is "the instinct upon which is founded the faculty of speech, the characteristical faculty of human nature" (*TMS*, VII.iv.25, p. 336).

As we shall see, the faculty of language is what allows men to persuade their fellow citizens to cooperate with them to satisfy their mutual needs.

RR2: Persuasion as strategic interaction, possibly in the form of conflicting interests/informational asymmetries, and hence as principal-agent games

In the "Considerations," we find in full bloom already the second and the third reasoning routines. To wit, Smith proposes that "[t]wo savages, who had never been taught to speak, but had been bred up remote from the societies of men, would naturally begin to form that language by which they would endeavor to make their mutual wants intelligible to each other by uttering certain sounds, whenever they meant to denote certain objects" (Smith 1985, p. 201). He goes on to conjecture how nouns, adjectives, prepositions, verbs, and pronouns emerged as conventions[38] and, most importantly, how men's faculties of the mind concomitantly refined to allow for the creation of these ever more abstract and complex forms of language (Smith 1985, pp. 9–11).[39] Languages emerge naturally

[38] "Two Savages who met together and took up their dwelling in the same place would very soon endeavour to get signs to denote those objects which most frequently occurred and with which they were most concerned. The cave they lodged in, the tree from whence they got their food, or the fountain from whence they drank, would all soon be distinguished by particular names, I as they would have frequent occasion to make their thoughts about these known to one another, and ***would by mutual consent agree on certain signs*** whereby this might be accomplished" (Smith 1985, p. 9, our italics).

[39] We insist on this crucial link between the evolution of language and the evolution of the human mind in the conclusion. See below, p. 50. For an excellent summary of the *Considerations* ... see Bryce (1985, pp. 23–26).

in people's interactions (Smith 1985, p. 9); as we shall see, they serve a definite purpose. And they are adapted toward the purpose of persuasion often in situations of asymmetric information.

Smith understood that communication is not necessarily a cooperative game. The speaker or writer may be guided by an agenda, and may employ rhetorical strategies to deflect from his or her true intentions. The orator or writer, in other terms, may be an agent facing a moral hazard problem, and the listener or reader, i.e., the principal, may have to discern to what extent the logic of the argument is contaminated by the speaker's or writer's agenda.[40] Along these lines, Smith distinguishes between the impartial, instructive, and convincing "didactic" discourse on the one hand, and the partial, persuasive, and interested "rhetorical" discourse on the other hand.[41] Both of these discourses assume some degree of information asymmetry.

RR3: Social interactions and language rules as conventions, as driven by propriety of style

In addition to the analysis of the emergence and evolution of languages, Smith discussed at length in *LRBL* the issue of the propriety and perfection of style. Around that time, language overloaded with figures of speech, tropes, metaphors, and other ornaments was widely considered *de rigueur*. While Smith readily admitted that figures of speech had their place if used judiciously, his overriding concern was of language that was

[40] "(T)he perfection of stile consists in Express < ing > in the most concise, proper and precise manner the thought of the author, and that in the manner which best conveys the sentiment, passion or affection with which it affects or *he pretends* it does affect him and which he designs to communicate to his reader" (Smith 1985, pp. 55–56).

[41] "Every discourse proposes either barely to relate some fact, or to prove some proposition. ... The latter is the foundation of two Sorts of Discourse: The Didactick and the Rhetoricall. The former proposes to put before us the arguments on both sides of the question in their true light, giving each of its proper degree of influence, and has it in view to perswade us no farther than the arguments themselves appear convincing. The Rhetoricall again endeavors by all means to perswade us; and for this purpose it magnifies all the arguments on the one side conterary to that which is designed that we should favour. Persuasion which is the primary design in the Rhetoricall is but the secondary design in the Didactick. It endeavours to persuade us only so far as the strength of the arguments is convincing, instruction is the main End. In the other Persuasion is the main design and Instruction is considered only so far as it is subservient to perswasion, and no farther" (Smith 1985, p. 62). See also Smith (1985, p. 89).

neat, clear, plain, and clever—language as a means of communication and persuasion, fit for life in commercial societies in which "everyone becomes in some measure a merchant" (*WN*, I.iv.1, p. 37). Language, in other words, that would persuade others to cooperate to satisfy one's own needs. Metaphors often create friction, or "obscurity" in the process of communication. They may act as impediments to the clarity of the expression of feelings and opinions (Smith 1985, p. 8), that is, as barriers to the enjoyable open commerce of our sentiments (*TMS,* VII.iv.28, p. 337). Effective and mutually pleasant communication is reached when readers (listeners) can easily and freely enter into the writer (speaker)'s mind, heart, and thoughts, that is, when they can identify or sympathize with her. This analysis of the "propriety of style" is the key concept of Smith's *LRBL* (Bryce 1985; McKenna 2006) and his application to rhetoric, or the exchange of ideas, of his third reasoning routine:

> When the sentiment of the speaker is expressed in a neat, clear, plain and clever manner, and the passion or affection he is possessed of and intends, *by sympathy*, to communicate to his hearer, is plainly and cleverly hit off, then and then only the expression has all the force and beauty that language can give it. It matters not the least whether the figures of speech are introduced or not. (Smith 1985, pp. 25–26)

To sum up, Smith's attack on figures of speech used excessively, his emphasis on language not for its own sake but rather for its communicative purposes, and his emphasis on using speech in order to persuade, shows that he conceptualized language as an instrument, a function, a means of communication, persuasion, and cooperation. This foreshadows major themes of Smith's work on economics, starting with the natural propensity to truck, barter, and exchange.

His second and third reasoning routines—his implicit conceptualization of the principal-agent games played between speakers/writers and listeners/readers as well as his functionalist view of language and his opposition to artificial constraints on language—are already discernible in full bloom in his *LRBL* and *Considerations.* The one aspect that is missing in theses texts (though certainly not in Smith's mind), and which was to play a key role in his moral philosophy, is the role of reputation, or how the repeated play of social life influences our individual behavior toward greater morality and social cooperation.

Meta-RR: Pleasure of persuading = pleasure of the harmony of minds which restores its tranquility (disturbed by disapprobation or misunderstanding, by the [unpleasant] gap between people's ideas/opinions or language)

His meta-RR, driven by the same error prediction minimization that leads to the adjustment of our model of the world to the sight of rare phenomena of nature, also applies to the social sphere as Smith makes clear when talking about the sudden appearance of a friend, whom we have seen a thousand times, but did not expect to see then and there. The desire to persuade, with its potential to restore the tranquility of our mind which was perturbed by the "gap" between our own ideas and opinions and those of our companions, is just another way of saying prediction error minimization.

5 Smith on Moral Philosophy

All three reasoning routines, as well as the meta-RR, are on display in Smith's work on moral sentiments too. The Newtonian-deductive view (RR1) is on display in Smith's conceptualization of the natural desire (and need) to be praised and be praise-(rather than blame-)worthy as the driver of ethical behavior. RR2 is present in the acknowledgment that the interaction between Man Today and Man Tomorrow could be strategic and that interests between interacting parties could be in conflict (and information asymmetric). We see here once again in action the principal-agent game that will also prominently feature in Smith's work on *WN*. The evolutionary-inductive approach (RR3) is on display in Smith's conceptualization of the development of moral sentiments as set of conventions similar to languages. Praise- and blame-worthiness moderate, via empathy (sympathy in Smith's words), moral sentiments (and behavior), and whenever a sentiment (or action) is considered blame-worthy, the prediction error is addressed by adjustments in behavior that would ultimately bring about the pleasure of being in harmony with others' sense of moral behavior and the tranquility of mind that Smith saw as the equilibrium.

RR1: The faculty/principle of sympathy (empathy), the principle of gravitation of the social world

In his *TMS*, Smith's main goal is to describe the origin and evolution of moral sentiments and norms in society and the natural principles of the mind on which they are founded. States Smith:

> After the inquiry concerning the nature of virtue [addressed in part 6 of TMS], the next question of importance in Moral Philosophy, is concerning the principle of approbation, concerning *the power or faculty of the mind* which renders certain characters agreeable or disagreeable to us, makes us prefer one tenour of conduct to another, denominate the one right and the other wrong, and consider the one as the object of approbation, honour, and reward; the other as that of blame, censure, and punishment.
> (*TMS*, VII.III.intro, pp. 314–315, our italics)

The principle of sympathy is Smith's main, not to say unique, (analytic) principle of explanation for judging others' (and our own) moral behavior. In today's terminology, "sympathy" would be better called "empathy." It is an operator and a faculty of the mind with two functions: to allow for the communication of passions between men and for the regulation and harmonization of their passions. Sympathy is the equivalent in the moral or social world of Newton's principle of gravitation in the natural world. It creates order and harmony in the midst of what seems chaos, with a single, unitary principle of explanation (Dellemotte 2002; see also Otteson 2002a). Sympathy is thus like a principle of gravitation of social "bodies," reflecting RR1 in the moral sphere. For Smith, the desire to be empathetic is the founddation of people's (natural) sociability.

RR2: social interaction, with principal-agent game as building block of self-command, mutual sympathy

Meardon and Ortmann (1996a) demonstrated, building on an analysis of Adam Smith's enumeration of five classes of passions, that self-command can be modeled as an interaction ("game") whose structure is similar to endogenous quality or reputational games. Such games are arguably the simplest principal-agent games. In that particular paper, Meardon and Ortmann took the general rules of morality (and people's understanding of them) as given and laid out how people, through empathy, their understanding of blame- and praise-worthiness, and their reading of praise and blame that others afforded them, would be able to attain an equilibrium in the game of life even if self-interested.

RR3: The emergence and evolution of moral norms, driven by (lack of) propriety of conduct

Meardon and Ortmann (1996b) demonstrated how the general rules of morality (and people's understanding of them) evolve. In Smith's view, the origin and evolution of moral standards was an adaptive process akin to a repeated n-person prisoners' dilemma game. In his words, "the general maxims of morality are formed, like all other general maxims, from experience and induction" (*TMS*, VII.iii.2.6, p. 319). We do not understand what proper behavior is through a priori reasoning—deductively—we grope—and evolve our way to the prevailing standard of moral conduct by "finding in a vast variety of instances that one tenor of conduct constantly pleases in a certain manner, and that another as constantly displeases the mind" (*TMS*, VII.iii.2.7, p. 320). With time, repeated observation leads us to act and feel instantly and naturally as the impartial spectator would do by following the general rules of society.[42] As we will see below, the meta-RR plays a crucial role in this process.

The same principles of the human mind and cognitive abilities are at work when we observe the natural and the social world. However, any player who does not have these cognitive abilities in abundance—for example a child, or a person without "real constancy and firmness" is likely to behave below the moral standard at times—having the external effect of lowering the standards themselves. Smith saw the tearing of the social fabric because of a lack of reputational enforcement as a real danger, increasingly so as he grew older and was confronted with evidence that contradicted his providential view. He understood perfectly well under what conditions this danger is likely to ensue (lack of open information flows, games that do not get repeated often), and admitted hesitantly that such circumstances might call for preventive and corrective measures by the state.[43]

[42] "We have learned, however, from experience, that such a misfortune [a stranger we meet has learned the death of his father] naturally excites such a degree of sorrow, and we know that if we took time to consider his situation, fully and in all its parts, we should, without doubt, most sincerely sympathize with him…and the general rules derived from our preceding experience of what our sentiments would commonly correspond with, correct, upon this, as upon other occasions, the impropriety of our present emotions" (*TMS*, I.i.3.4, p. 18).

[43] See for example his analysis in *WN* of the social isolation of poor workers in great cities which leads them to follow the « unsocial», « rigorous» morality of small religious

That being said, it is important to understand that as a matter of principle, Smith was highly suspicious of governments' and legislators' ability to devise appropriate moral (and economic) rules and regulations. Their intervention in this domain can even be problematic. The "man of system," as Smith called him,

> seems to imagine that he can arrange the different members of a great society with as much ease as the hand arranges the different pieces upon a chess-board; he does not consider that the different pieces upon a chess-board have no other principle of motion besides that which the hand impresses upon them; but that, in the great chess-board of human society, every single piece has a principle of motion of its own, altogether different from that which the legislator might choose to impress upon it.
>
> (*TMS*, VI.ii.2.17, pp. 233–234)

And importantly, Smith continues,

> If those two principles coincide and act in the same direction, the game of human society will go on easily and harmoniously, and is very likely to be happy and successful" but "If they are opposite or different, the game will go on miserably, and the society must be at all times in the highest degree of disorder. (*ibid.*)

In sum, Smith insisted that standards of moral conduct are conventions (RR3). Government intervention was to be avoided wherever possible. Notwithstanding that, there was always the danger that reputational enforcement would not be good enough, and people might give in to moral hazard problems. Otteson (2002a, in particular his Conclusion chapter) and Fleischacker (2021, in chapter 7) have perceptive discussions of the problematic features, and open-endedness, of Smith's conceptualization of the process of the emergence and evolution of moral norms. Alas, to the extent that we are interested in the way Smith thought about this process, we can put this discussion aside for now.

sects (WN, V.i.g.12, p. 795). Against this, Smith identifies « two very easy and effectual remedies» provided by the state: encouraging the study of science and philosophy, seen as « the great antidote to the poison of enthusiasm and superstition», and increasing the « frequency and gaiety of publick diversions» (*WN*, V.i.g.14–5, p. 796).

Meta-RR: Pleasure of mutual sympathy = pleasure of the harmony of minds which restores its tranquility (disturbed by disapprobation, by the gap between people's sentiments)

Smith's meta-reasoning routine is also on display in his analysis of morality. We naturally revise our sentiments and passions, and we distance ourselves from our natural point of view in the presence of others with their own experience and moral rules as we do with our opinions, ideas, and beliefs. When we are confronted by other points of view, we gauge the "payoffs" that future interactions promise. General rules are "fixed in our mind by habitual reflection" (*TMS*, III.4.12, p. 160). The desire of sympathy, with its potential to restore the tranquility of our mind, our own psychological balance, which was perturbed by the "gap" between our own sentiments and those of our companions, is another means of prediction error minimization. What Smith underlines with his analysis of the pleasure of mutual sympathy is that observing the harmony and "concord" of our sentiments *as such* pleases us. It is the expression of the love of order in the social world.

6 Smith, Moral Philosophy, Language Formation, and Rhetoric

We have elaborated on the reasoning and meta-sreasoning routines in the domains of, respectively, language and rhetoric on the one hand, and morality on the other. We now explicate what we see as the striking parallels between Smith's moral philosophy, his theory of language formation, and rhetoric. Here we do not cover terra incognita (other than using our game-theoretic framing of the reasoning routines), see for example Otteson (2002a, 2002b, 2002c).

Bryce astutely stated,[44]

[44] The *LRBL* date from the fifteenth winter in which Adam Smith lectured on rhetoric, i.e., they were given after Smith published the *TMS*. That could confound the argument in the present article. However,

The general continuity of the lecture-course from 1748 to 1763 details apart, is established by its structure and by the set of central principles which inform all twenty nine reported lectures and which could not have been added or superimposed on the argument at some intermediate stage of its development. Basic to the whole is the division into 'an examination of the several ways of communicating our thoughts by speech' and 'an

> Smith's students must have noted the multi-faceted relationship between the ethics and rhetoric, in three broad areas. First, Smith employed many of the general principles stated in TMS in *illustrating* the different forms of communication; for example, our admiration for the great, or for hardships undergone with firmness and constancy. Smith also drew attention to the influence of environment on forms and modes of expression in a manner which would be familiar to those who had already heard his treatment of the rules of conduct. Secondly, Smith's students would note the points at which the rhetoric *elaborated* on the discussion of the role of sympathy and the nature of moral judgement and persuasion [...] Thirdly, Smith's students would perceive that the arguments developed in the lectures on rhetoric *complement* the analysis of TMS.
>
> (Bryce 1985, p. 10)

That there were strong parallels between rhetoric, language, and moral philosophy (ethics) was made clear already by Smith, whose concept of propriety is central in his analysis of both rhetoric and morality (Bevilacqua 1965; McKenna 2006).

McKenna rightly argued that generally in the literature on Smith, people note the influence of *TMS* on *LRBL*, because for Smith an effective communication is based on the appropriateness of sentiments (McKenna 2006, 77–8, 89). But the reverse is also true (and comes logically first). So, Smith's analysis of languages and rhetoric deeply informed his moral theory.

RR1: the faculties of sympathy and language and the natural desires of sympathy and persuasion

Firstly, Smith underlined in *TMS* the analogy between the approbation of sentiments and the approbation of opinions (Walraevens 2010), claiming that "To approve or disapprove...of the opinions of another is acknowledged, by every body, to mean no more than to observe their agreement with our own. But this equally the case with regard to our approbation or disapprobation of the sentiments or passions of others" (*TMS*, I.i.3.2, p. 17). We sympathize with others' sentiments as we do with their ideas and often both confound, so that the process by which an actor

attention to the principles of those literary compositions which contribute to persuasion or entertainment'. (Bryce 1985, p. 12) and a spectator tend to agree seems similar to the relationship between a speaker–writer and his listener–reader (Dascal 2006, p. 102). Life is a never-ending exercise in rhetoric, Smith claims: "The desire of being believed, the desire of persuading […] seems to be one of the strongest of all our natural desires" (TMS, VII.iv.25, p. 336). We are thus led by a natural desire to persuade others of the propriety of our passions and opinions (*LJ(B)*, 222, p. 493) because of the pleasure we take in mutual sympathy and persuasion, which restore the tranquility of our mind (meta-RR).

The analogy between moral and intellectual judgments in Smith finds another confirmation when he explains that as we cannot satisfy ourselves with being praised until we know to be praise-worthy, we crave to be believed and to be worthy of being so.[45] Being believed means being approved (or empathized with) in our ideas by real spectators. Moreover, following Smith's concept of praise-worthiness we argue that being worthy of belief has to do with the approbation of the internal and imaginary, impartial spectator.

RR2: rhetoric, morality and strategic interactions

Rhetorical interactions (relations of persuasion between a writer and his reader, a speaker and his audience), like moral interactions (relations of sympathy between agent and spectator) are marked by information asymmetries. Above we have shown that these strategic interactions are problem isomorphs that can be captured in a normal-form game widely known as one-sided prisoners' dilemma, or principal-agent game.

People start from different points of view (Smith's "natural" station), with differing levels of information, beliefs, opinions, and passions. Language and rhetoric might be strategically used to get the sympathy of others (to be approved), while the reverse is also true: we can use our sentiments and play with others' feelings to persuade them to be of our opinion (to be believed).

[45] "so we cannot always be satisfied merely with being believed, unless we are at the same time conscious that we are really worthy of belief… It is always mortifying not to be believed, and it is doubly so when we suspect that it is because we are supposed to be unworthy of belief and capable of seriously and wilfully deceiving. To tell a man that he lies, is of all affronts the most mortal" (*TMS*, VII.iv.25, p. 336).

Thus, Smith described orators in *LRBL* like actors on a drama scene, "playing" with spectators' feelings and passions. Indeed, Smith states that "The Rhetorician will not barely set forth the character of a person as it really existed but will magnify every particular that may tend to excite the Strongest emotions in us" and "He will also seem to be deeply affected with that affection which he would have us feel towards any object" (*LRBL*, ii.37–8, pp. 100–101).[46] Language is a double-edged sword. It might be used for social harmony and concord, for agreeing and sympathizing with others, but also for "leading and directing" them, i.e., for gratifying our pernicious "love of domination."

RR3: rhetoric, linguistic, and moral norms as conventions

Thirdly, Smith underlines the common origin of the rules of morality and of rhetoric.[47] Conversation and behavior follow the same "principles of common sense," or maxims, of being agreeable, and rhetoric is nothing more than the study of the propriety of linguistic action (Dascal 2006, p. 101; see also Bevilacqua 1965, pp. 12, 14 and McKenna 2006, p. 88). In social interactions, the perfect style and the proper character perfectly

[46] Or again: "The Rhetorician will not barely set forth the character of a person as it really existed but will magnify every particular that may tend to *excite the Strongest emotions in us. He will also seem to be deeply affected with that affection which he would have us feel towards any object.* He will exclaim, for example, on the amiable Character, the sweet temper and behaviour of the man towards whom he would have us to feel those affections...the orator heightens every incident and pretends at least to be deeply affected by them himself, often exclaiming on the wretched condition of those he talks of etc." (*LRBL*, ii.37–8, pp. 100–101).

[47] " ... if you'll attend to it all the Rules of Criticism and morality when traced to their foundation, turn out to be some Principles of Common Sense which every one assents to; all the business of those arts is to apply these Rules to the different subjects and shew what their conclusion is when they are so applyed. ... We have shewn how fare they have acted agreably to that Rule, which is equally applicable to conversation and behaviour as writing. For what is that makes a man agreable company, is it not, when his sentiments appear to be naturally expressed, when the passion or affection is properly conveyed and when their thoughts are so agreeable and natural that we find ourselves inclined to give our assent to them. A wise man too in conversation and behaviour will not affect a character that is unnaturall to him; ... He will only regulate his naturall temper, restrain within just bounds and lop all exuberances and bring it to that pitch which will be agreeable to those about him. But he will not affect such conduct as is unnaturall to his temper tho perhaps in the abstract they may be more to be wished" (*LRBL*, i.134, pp. 55–56).

match (McKenna 2006, pp. 92–93). Indeed, as he does about writing and speaking, Smith defends the necessity of a free, unobstructed communication of moral sentiments and opinions in conversation in order to reach an enjoyable "harmony of minds."[48]

Furthermore, languages, ideas, opinions, and moral sentiments evolve in parallel ways, as attempts of unrelated people to agree on self-enforcing norms. Rules would be formed, of course, but their formation would emerge out of the interaction between individual agents. In the same way, as two savages would assign particular sounds, names or nouns to specific objects so as to be able "to make their mutual wants intelligible to each other" *(Considerations,* p. 203), so would two unsocialized people try to figure out what acceptable forms of moral conduct are. After language had made some progress, Smith conjectured, "it was naturall to imagine that men would form some rules according to which they should regulate their language. These rules are what we call Grammar" (Smith 1985, p. 25). Likewise, after social interaction had made some progress, one could imagine that men would form some rules according to which one could live properly, agreeably, and decently in communities. Conventions about proper behavior, or self-enforcing norms, are nothing but a "social grammar" that regulates the ways people live together and evolves over time.

As a consequence, it is no surprise to see Smith making an analogy in *TMS* between the rules of justice on the one hand, and the rules of grammar on the other hand. Both are "precise, accurate and indispensable" (*TMS*, III.6.11, p. 175) for society's stability and order, and prescribe men what they ought to do in given situations. Going further, Smith adds that he who faithfully respects the rules of grammar "may be taught to act justly" (*TMS*, III.6.11, p. 176). Justice for Smith is the foundation or "pillar" of society, while beneficence is its "ornament" (*TMS*, II.ii.3.4, p. 86). Likewise, grammar is the foundation or "pillar" of language and rhetoric the "ornament" which embellishes it.

[48] "The great pleasure of conversation and society, besides, arises from a certain correspondence of sentiments and opinions, from a certain harmony of minds, which like so many musical instruments coincide and keep time with one another. But his most delightful harmony cannot be obtained unless there is a free communication of sentiments and opinions. We all desire, upon this account, to feel how each other is affected, to penetrate into each other's bosoms, and to observe the sentiments and affections which really subsist there" (*TMS*, VII.iv.28, p. 337).

Smith calls people's regard to the general rules of society their "sense of duty." This sacred respect for social norms of behavior is essential for society's order and stability because of men's natural propensity to self-deceit and partiality (*ibid.*). Along the same lines, following the social rules of language and rhetoric or persuasion is necessary for successful social interactions with our fellows and thus also preserves the stability and order of society. And again it is internalized by men from repeated experience and observation of their own and others' conduct. As Bryce (1985, pp. 18–19) justly argued,

> Just as we act under the eye of an impartial spectator within ourselves, the creation of an imaginative self-projection into an outsider whose standards and responses we reconstruct by sympathy or ability to feel as he does, so our language is enabled to communicate our thoughts and 'affections' (i.e. inclinations) by our ability to predict its effect on our hearer. This is what is meant by seeing the Rhetoric and TMS as two halves of one system.

It is as if the impartial spectator, the internal judge of our own character, internalized not only what we should feel and do in given situations (propriety of behavior), but also what is the most appropriate way to express/communicate our ideas, opinions, and sentiments (propriety of style and language) in order to be approved and sympathized with. (Of course, the already mentioned caveat that a child, or a person without "real constancy and firmness," might not live up the moral standard at all times pertains and might make necessary interventions of various kinds.)

Meta-RR: pleasure of mutual sympathy and persuasion = pleasure of the harmony of minds, the agreement restores the tranquility of the mind, we are uneasy when people differ from us in sentiments and opinions; order and coherence in the social world

As to our meta-reasoning routine, Smith underlines that we are uneasy when people do not sympathize with our sentiments and/or disagree with our opinions while, by contrast, we feel pleasure in sympathizing with and persuading others. Here we have Smith's application of his meta-reasoning routine to the social world. With their potential to restore our inner peace, the desires of persuasion and sympathy are both means of prediction error minimization in social interactions.

The desire for scientific explanation, prompted by the aesthetic love of (contemplating) the harmony of nature finds an echo in the social world where we strive for others' approbation of our sentiments (sympathy) and ideas (persuasion). In other words, we love contemplating the harmony and concord of people both in our *moral* and *intellectual* judgments, because when we reach mutual sympathy and persuasion, it restores the tranquility of our mind which was disturbed by the difference or "gap" between our own sentiments/opinions and those of other people. For Smith, order and coherence seems to be as enjoyable to reach and observe in the social world as in the natural world. The pleasure of sympathy and the pleasure of persuading are analogous, and both serve the stability and the order of society. Persuading is nothing but getting the approbation and sympathy for our opinions and ideas. Therefore, we agree with Montes (2019) when he argued that "persuasion is a foundational concept of *TMS*" and more generally of Smith's views on the (micro-) foundations of social life.

7 Smith on Economics

All three reasoning routines, as well as the meta-RR, are on display in Smith's work on economics. The Newtonian-deductive view (RR1) is on display in Smith's conceptualization of the natural desire to better our condition and the propensity to truck, barter, and exchange as the drivers of economic development and progress[49] of society. RR2 is present in the acknowledgment that economic interactions could be strategic and that interests between sellers and buyers could be in conflict and information asymmetric. Principal-agent games that already featured prominently in Smith's works on languages and morality make another appearance, and this time the reputational twist that requires repeated interactions is added. The evolutionary-inductive approach (RR3) is also on display in Smith's conceptualization of economic values or (natural) prices and of their evolution as sets of conventions similar to moral rules of behavior.

[49] Note that we use the word "progress" here in Smith's much more neutral sense of the word, as a synonym of "evolution," because clearly for Smith the (economic) progress of society can lead to serious drawbacks, and especially to the corruption of men's characters. For more details on this issue, see in particular Hanley (2009), Pack (2010, chap 8), Tegos (2013).

As to the meta-reasoning routine, it is found in the pleasure of exchanging which is a derivative of the pleasure of persuading others of our (proper) valuation of a good or service. When exchange/persuasion fails, the prediction error is addressed by adjustments in the means of persuasion (i.e., adjusting the price offered or demanded) which ultimately will bring about the pleasure of persuasion and tranquility of mind that Smith saw as the equilibrium. We elaborate briefly on this summary next.

RR1: the natural propensity to truck, barter, and exchange and the desire to better our condition are the 2 principles that explain how nations can increase their wealth

Identifying RR1 into Smith's economic thought means answering the following question: what are the few principles of human nature which explain the progress of society toward opulence? Smith's answer to this question is well-known. The human foundations of economic growth are man's natural propensity to truck, barter, and exchange (*WN*, I.ii.1, p. 25) on the one side, and the desire to better our condition (*WN*, II.iii.28, p. 341) on the other. The former is the cause of the division of labor, and the latter the cause of the accumulation of capital. Both have been given to us by the Deity to realize its ends: the propagation and happiness of the human species.

RR2: asymmetric information, strategic interactions, and reputation

RR2 is on display also in *LJ* and *WN*, presenting several cases of strategic interactions marked by asymmetric information between buyers and sellers, suppliers and demanders of goods and services. Smith did understand the issue of reputational equilibria very well (see below Smith's contrast between merchants and ambassadors). In particular, he analyzed the outcomes of repeated games in economies with goods and services of adjustable quality/effort, and the related issue of what is now known as efficiency wages. While principal-agent games feature prominently in *WN* (Ortmann 1999), social dilemma games in various forms also appear in various guises (see Ortmann and Walraevens 2021). These games, and their pervasive use throughout his oeuvre, demonstrate Smith's deep understanding of the thoroughly strategic nature of all things rhetorical, moral, and economic.

RR3: the formation and evolution of economic "norms": the principle of *gravitation* of market prices around the natural price. The natural price is a concept putting order into the apparent chaos of prices. Market prices as conventions and markets as evolutionary processes

RR3 is on display in Smith's economics with his analysis of natural prices as conventions, that is as norms resulting from the interaction of self-interested agents, regulating men's exchanges of goods and services. As we argued before, the principle of gravitation of the market price around the natural price (*WN,* I.vii) is somewhat analogous to the "Wonder, Surprise and Admiration" model of Smith's *HA*. With this economic principle of gravitation[50], Smith introduces for his readers some order and coherence into the apparent chaos of the evolution of prices (Walraevens 2014). Market prices are the result of the converging sentiments of men on the evaluation of goods and services (see the "higgling and bargaining of the market," *WN* I.v.4, p. 49) and these market prices naturally tend, in the long run, toward the equilibrium price called the natural price ("what it is worth," the "ordinary or average" price in the neighborhood…see *WN,* I.vii.1–2, p. 72). The equilibrium of the market, like the equilibrium of the mind, is stable.

Meta-RR: the pleasure to exchange is a pleasure to persuade someone, i.e., a pleasure to find an agreement on the valuation of goods and services we value

Our meta-reasoning routine can also be found in Smith's economics, in his view of economic agents as language beings and rhetoricians. Man's natural "propensity to truck, barter, and exchange" is founded, Smith claims in *LJ*, on the desire to persuade, which is a means to minimize prediction error. This typically human and social desire to persuade is a desire to be in agreement and harmony with others concerning opinions

[50] Note that Pack and Schliesser (2018) argue that Smith uses an Aristotelian rather than a Newtonian conception of gravitation in his analysis of natural and market prices.

and ideas, here about the value of goods and services, that is, in our *economic* judgments (as a subfield of *intellectual* judgments). And there is, for Smith, a specific pleasure in persuasion since we love contemplating our minds in unison. In an economic exchange, we experiment and enjoy our ability to reach an agreement and to be approved by someone else, specifically here on the price we pay or ask for a good or service.

8 Smith, Economics and Moral Philosophy

We have elaborated on the reasoning and meta-reasoning routines in the domains of, respectively, moral philosophy on the one hand and language and rhetoric on the other. We now explicate what we see as the striking parallels between Smith's moral philosophy, and his economics. Here, again, we do not cover terra incognita (other than using our game-theoretic framing of the reasoning routines.)

RR1: the natural propensity to truck, barter, and exchange and the desire to better our condition are founded on the principle and desire of sympathy—language and sympathy

Concerning RR1, it is noteworthy that the natural desire to better our condition and the propensity to truck, barter, and exchange, Smith's two principles of human nature which fuel economic growth, are both ultimately founded on the principle of sympathy (see Dellemotte 2002; Force 2003). On the former, Smith makes clear in *TMS* that people want to improve their condition to be loved, sympathized with, and admired. It is vanity, not the ease or the enjoyment of goods, that prompts men to accumulate wealth and to consume[51] (*TMS*, I.iii.2.1, p. 50). Economic progress ultimately relies on the desire of sympathy and recognition (vanity).

As we saw before, when discussing the "propensity to truck, barter, and exchange one thing for another,"Smith conjectures that it comes from man's distinctive faculty of speech and his innate desire of persuading others (*LJ(A),* vi.57, p. 352), the latter being a desire of sympathy and approbation. Sympathy and language are natural faculties bestowed on

[51] The love of systems is also quite important for explaining the accumulation of wealth and especially the behavior of capitalists, as Diatkine (2000, 2010) showed.

people by the Deity to realize his ends, the propagation and happiness of the human species.

RR2: asymmetric information, strategic interactions, and reputation in economics and morality

In economics as in morality, Smith clearly understood moral hazard problems. His model of mutual sympathy seems to be a kind of principal-agent moral hazard problem because the agent is always better informed on his situation and sentiments than the spectator. Likewise, in economic interactions, the seller is often better informed than the buyer. What then will prevent buyers from being exploited by sellers?

Part of the answer comes from Smith's moral view of economic agents. In order to get what he wants from other persons, the bargainer will be successful, in Smith's words, "if he can interest *their* self-love in his favour, and shew them that it is *for their* own advantage to do for him what he requires of them" (*WN*, i.ii.2, our italics).[52] In other words, you have to put yourself into the other's place by imagination to understand what *their* interest is (to determine his willingness to pay) if you want to satisfy yours. Moreover, reaching an agreement often requires of us to moderate our natural selfishness, to distance ourselves from our "natural station," our egoistic position (Fleischacker 2004). Sympathy, self-command, and a dose of impartiality are generally necessary to get what we want from others (Walraevens, 2010a, 2014; Paganelli 2010).

Moreover, and most importantly for economic interactions, humans are moral and social beings who deeply care about their reputation, but also about their "merit." They want to be approved by others and, often concomitantly, to be worthy of that approval. That's why they tend to make "fair" agreements.[53] Provided competition is free, the market

[52] See also *LJ*(A), vi.15, p. 347.

[53] "A free commerce on a fair consideration must appear to be advantageous on both sides. We see that it must be so betwixt individualls, unless one of them be a fool and makes a bargain plainly ruinous; but betwixt prudent men it must always be advantageous. For the very cause of the exchange must be that you need my goods more than I need them, and that I need yours more than you do yourself; and if the bargain be managed with ordinary prudence it must be profitable to both" (*LJ(A)*, vi.160, p. 390).

"Nobody ever saw a dog make a fair and deliberate exchange of one bone for another with another dog" (*WN*, I.ii.2, p. 26, our italics).

imposes a kind of moral discipline on its actors. They have to be honest, industrious, innovative, and frugal if they want to satisfy their real, long-term interest.[54] Smith goes as far as saying that "probity" is a typical virtue of merchants, and by way of extension of people of commercial societies (*LJ(B)*, 303, p. 528). To illustrate his point, he compares the situation of the merchant with that of the ambassador (*LJ(B)*, 327, p. 539). The latter's reputation is less threatened if he fools his foreign counterpart because they seldom meet (*ibid.*). But in the case of the merchant, he makes several deals a day and thus if he is suspected of deceiving his customers his reputation and thus his commerce are in danger of extinction (*LJ(B)*, 328, p. 539). "Prudence," one of Smith's four cardinal virtues in *TMS*, asks of him to keep his words and to deliver what he promised to his customers (see also *WN*, I.x.c.31, p. 146 on the "real discipline" which is exercised "over a workman" by his "customers"). In economic terms, the infinitely repeated Prisoner's Dilemma game of commerce makes cooperation a rational strategy for merchants to follow. Note how this reading of merchants in this particular setting shows Smith's astute understanding of the power of reputational enforcement in situations where that power actually can exert its influence (but see also Pack 2010 and Sagar 2021 for an analysis of situations where that power fails).

It is noteworthy that Smith understood intuitively that preaching and teaching had the same incentive structure as the acquisition of self-command or moral conduct. The process whereby an economic agent (e.g., a teacher or preacher, or citizen) comes to regard socially worthy action (e.g., giving a lecture or sermon really worth attending, or contributing voluntarily to the provision of a public good) as his self-interest, resembles closely the process whereby the moral agent comes to regard the moral injunctions of the "impartial spectator" as synonymous with his own self-command. When Smith states that "in every profession, the exertion of the greater part of those who exercise it, is always in proportion to the necessity they are under of making that exertion," he paraphrased the insight, expressed decades earlier in the *TMS*, that in every situation, the exertion to act "morally" on the greater part of those who exercise it, is always in proportion to the necessity that they

[54] For more details on this, see Berry (2013) and Walraevens (2014).

are under of making that exertion.[55] Forget about morality, forget about the provision of experience and credence goods of desirable quality if the incentive structures are not such that the exertion pays off (Meardon and Ortmann 1996a, 1996b). The incentive problem underlying the issue of the acquisition of self-command, or of standards of moral conduct, the promotion of particular manufacturing, preaching, teaching, and all other services whose quality are adjustable, are identical. (In fact, they can all be expressed game-theoretically as we have shown elsewhere.) As regards the latter point, Smith's grasp of the subtleties of reputational enforcement (information flows, whether the game is finitely played or indefinitely), is remarkable, especially in light of modern reputational theories of the firm (Holmstroem and Tirole 1989).

RR3: the formation and evolution of economic and moral "norms" as conventions

With regard to RR3, there is a striking analogy between the "moral market" (Otteson 2002a) and the economic market. Economic and moral norms, that is prices and rules of proper behavior, are conventions. In other words, they are both the result of the free interactions of self-interested and empathetic agents and provide for the stability and order of human interactions, creating order into the seeming chaos of social life.

[55] "The different situations of different ages and countries are apt, in the same manner, to give different characters to the generality of those who live in them, and their sentiments concerning the particular degree of each quality, that is either blamable or praise-worthy, vary, according to that degree which is usual in their own country, and in their own times" (*TMS*, V.2.7, p. 204).

"Among civilized nations, the virtues which are founded upon humanity, are more cultivated than those which are founded upon self denial and the command of the passions. Among rude and barbarous nations, it is quite otherwise, the virtues of self-denial are more cultivated than those of humanity. The general security and happiness which prevail in ages of civility and politeness, afford little exercise to the contempt of danger, to patience in enduring labour, hunger and pain...The abstinence from pleasure becomes less ***necessary***, and the mind is more at liberty to unbend itself, and to indulge its natural inclinations in all those particular respects" (*TMS*, V.2.8, p. 204–205).

Among savages and barbarians it is quite otherwise. Every savage undergoes a sort of Spartan discipline, and ***by the necessity of his situation*** is inured to every sort of hardship. He is in continual danger...His circumstances not only ***habituate him*** to every sort of distress, but teach him to give way to none of the passions which that distress is apt to excite (*TMS*, V.2.9, p. 209).

Therefore, Smith's moral philosophy and economic theory are consistent. In his economic theory, he attempts to free the economy from restrictive laws and from politics. In his moral philosophy, he attempts to free people from the notion that there is a priori moral principles necessarily dictated to us by an external authority. In the economic sphere, men must be able to express as freely as possible their talents and faculties, and to use their capital and exchange goods as they wish. Likewise, in the moral sphere, men must be able to express and exchange as freely as possible their feelings, sentiments, and passions.

Gold, silver, etc., are not the standard of the wealth of a nation, rather, consumable commodities are ultimately best produced if the conferral of privileges and imposition of restraints are minimized. Likewise, if there is such a thing as an objective standard of moral conduct, it may be implicit in the plan of Providence, but surely not in the rules and regulations that a state may impose. Moral norms are not given to us by reason or dictated by God; they are the product of people's interactions. In economic life too, natural prices are the objective standards for the valuation of goods revealed by the free interactions of buyers and sellers in the market and represent a kind of standard of propriety for economic judgments and choices because they are usually approved. There is a market for morality, as there is a market for goods (Otteson 2002a, 2002b, 2002c), and these two markets are consistent.

Meta-RR

The desire of sympathy and persuasion both act as prediction error minimizers, and usually combine in economic exchanges. The process of mutual sympathy is a bargaining game on the intensity of a passion, with the resulting "propriety point" as a kind of "moral price" of social interactions. Moreover, when we reach an agreement, be that on the exchange of a good or a passion, we feel the pleasures of sympathy and persuasion which are, as we noticed, analogous. And most importantly for our purpose, both are derivatives of man's seminal love for order, coherence, and harmony, our meta-reasoning routine. In both cases, the mind restores its tranquility after having been disturbed by a disagreeable gap between men's sentiments or opinions.

9 Smith on Economics, Language, and Rhetoric

We have elaborated on the reasoning and meta-reasoning routines in the domains of languages and rhetoric on the one hand, and economics on the other. We now explicate what we see as the striking parallels between Smith's economics and his theory of language formation and rhetoric.

RR1: the desire to persuade, language and cooperation

Smith's rhetorical and economic theories are also consistent (Walraevens 2010b; Ortmann and Walraevens 2018 and chapter 2) and exhibit our RR1. His analysis of the origin of the division of labor in the *LJ* is illuminating here[56]:

> If we should enquire into the principle in the human mind on which this disposition of trucking is founded, it is clearly the naturall inclination every one has to persuade. The offering of a shilling, which to us appears to have so plain and simple a meaning, is in reality offering an argument to persuade one to do so and so as it is for his interest. Men always endeavour to persuade others to be of their opinion even when the matter is of no consequence to them. [...] You are uneasy whenever one differs from you, and you endeavour to persuade him to be of your mind; or if you do not it is a certain degree of self command, and to this every one is breeding thro their whole lives. In this manner they acquire a certain dexterity and address in managing their affairs, or in other words in managing of men; and this is altogether the practise of every man in the most ordinary affairs. This being the constant employment or trade of every man, in the same manner as the artisans invent simple methods of doing their work, so will each one here endeavour to do this work in the simplest manner.
>
> (*LJ (A)*, vi.57, p. 352)

So, economic transactions are founded on the "desire of persuading, of leading and directing other people," which "seems to be one of the strongest of all our natural desires. It is, perhaps, the instinct upon which is founded the faculty of speech, the characteristical faculty of human nature" (*TMS*, VII.iv.25, p. 336). Language was given to people by the Author of Nature to get the indispensable cooperation of others for satisfying their needs. Following this logic, people who exchange goods may

[56] See also Pack (1991, p. 132) on this point.

be conceived as rhetoricians, and the exchange as a bargaining process. Consequently, it is no surprise to see Smith claiming that the development of commerce leads to a progress of language (*LRBL*, ii.115, p. 136).

We approve of others' opinions in the same way as we approve of their moral sentiments, as we showed earlier. So, persuasion, language, and exchange are inseparable. People possess an innate desire to persuade and spend their whole life to exercise their power of persuasion. In the eighteenth century, the word "commerce" had a broader sense than today and meant social exchange in general. It was not restricted, as it is now, to economic relationships. Using this extended sense of the word, we can say that throughout his works Smith describes humans as "commercial animal" or "exchanging animal," an *homo mercator* (Walraevens 2010).

Smith describes and analyzes how people exchange words, ideas, and opinions in his *LRBL* and *Considerations*, how they exchange passions and sentiments in *TMS*, and how they exchange goods and services in the *WN*.

RR2: asymmetric information and strategic interactions between writers and readers, buyers and sellers

As we noted before, there is a parallel between the rhetorician and the seller/buyer: in economic exchange (s)he tries to persuade you that it is in *your* interest to accept/approve his/her offer/valuation of the good by "turn[ing] it to your advantage or *make it appear to be so*" (*LJ*(A), vi.45, p. 347).

Smith's analysis of the mercantile system opens the door for a different analysis of the consistency of Smith's economic and rhetorical theory and more precisely of their application of RR2. Indeed, we argue that this consistency is also to be found on another level, more precisely in Smith's use of his own rhetorical principles in the composition of his economic masterpiece.

Along these lines, we proposed in Ortmann and Walraevens (2018) a re-interpretation of the structure of *WN*, and of the importance of Book V. Smith understood quite clearly that writing a book on political economy promoting the free commerce of goods and services, the "system of natural liberty," would be a very strategic enterprise (see also Pack, 1991, chap 6). While Smith had, through *TMS*, acquired a reputation as an academic, he was about to attack the Commercial and Mercantile System of Great Britain—at that point well established and without competitor—and its beneficiaries, who could be presumed to form a significant part of his readership. Surely they would have an unfavorable opinion of that which he was about to prove and of its plan of reform of the British Empire to answer the "American Question," and so Smith mustered whatever rhetorical strategies he could.

In Ortmann and Walraevens (2018), we hence argued that the structure of *WN* has to be understood in rhetorical terms. The situation was tailored to the application of the Socratick method.[57] Recall that

> in this method we keep as far as from the main point to be proved as possible, bringing on the audience by slow and imperceptible degrees to the thing to be proved, and by gaining their consent to some things whose tendency they can't discover, we force them at last either to deny what they had before agreed to, or to grant the Validity of the Conclusion.
>
> (Smith 1985, p. 146)

The Socratick method was for Smith "the smoothest and most engaging manner" and better fitted to address potentially unfavorable audiences (*ibid.)*. Using the Socratick method, Smith hence—in Books I and II—argued methodically the superiority of a laissez-faire system. He showed how here too a system could be driven by self-interested actors whose interaction would nevertheless produce desirable outcomes. All the while he stayed away from some complications of the system as provision of public goods, externalities, etc. In Book IV ("Of Systems of political Oeconomy"), after having laid a foundation that the readers could not refute lest they "deny what they had before agreed to," Smith took on the enemy openly and explicitly.

Book V, though often neglected, is the key because it is there that Smith addresses the reality of his surroundings. That is where he dealt with real institutions, institutions for that matter that he was quite familiar with. That's where he dealt with the incentive compatibility of institutional arrangements (Ortmann and Meardon 1995; Ortmann 1997; Ortmann 1999). Specifically, after having introduced early in *WN*, the notion of efficiency wage and hence the principal-agent problem, in

[57] See also Pack (1991, chap 6) for the idea that Smith applied the Socratick method in *WN*.

Book V Smith makes it into a central element of his analysis of joint-stock companies, and educational and ecclesiastical institutions (Ortmann and Meardon 1995; Ortmann 1999; he also addresses numerous public good provision and externality problems (Ortmann and Meardon 1995b; Ortmann and Walraevens 2018). Moreover and most importantly, it is in Book V and in the final pages of the *WN* that the reader told the (political) danger of the mercantile system: it leads to increasing public debt and thus threatens the sovereignty and survival of the British Empire (see also Diatkine 2021). Relying on Fleischacker's (2004; see also 2021) view of the *WN* as both "tract and treatise," we claim that Book V, as much as it is a treatise on just and optimal taxation and spending is also a tract on the polemical issue of that time in Great Britain: the future of the American colonies and the fate of the British Empire (Ortmann and Walraevens 2018, Ortmann et al. 2019).

RR3: norms of persuasion and economic norms

Identifying RR3 in this context is straightforward. At the individual level, the more people interact, the better they can learn persuasion techniques to get the approbation of others on their evaluations of goods. Norms of persuasion have the same origin (the observation and memorization of successful social interactions) and purpose for individuals (getting the approbation of others) than moral norms of behavior. In the economic sphere, norms of persuasion are the prices which are generally approved on the market. Smith defined the natural price as the "common" or "average" price in the neighborhood. This, we learn from our experience and observation of (economic) transactions, as we do with social rules of behavior. Persuasion rules, like natural prices and moral norms, are not dictated to us by reason. They are conventions resulting from the multiple exchanges of self-interested agents looking for the approbation of others. In other words, money is, like language, a convention that men use to facilitate their commerce (*WN*, I.iv), a means of communication and persuasion (*LJ(A),* vi.57, p. 352). As Smith states, "it is not for its own sake that people desire money but for the sake of what they can purchase with it" (*WN*, IV.1.18, p. 439). Money is first and foremost the "great wheel of circulation" of goods (*WN*, II.ii.14, p. 289), as language is that of words and ideas, and both are conventions facilitating commerce in its broad sense.

Smith makes similar proposals in economics and in rhetoric (not to mention morality). Again, in his economic theory, he attempts to free the economy from restrictive laws and from politics; in his rhetorical theory, he attempts to free his students from rote learning of rhetorical figures, i.e., to free language from (rhetorical) devices.

Smith defends the "natural liberty" of the commerce of goods and opinions, not to mention sentiments. Such a model, by placing words/genres within a social and communicative framework, resembles an exchange economy which attempts to shift from idiosyncratic wares to more easily exchanged—codified—ones. Idiosyncratic rhetoric and idiosyncratic wares, each expressive of some level of uniqueness, must be subordinated to a general logic of similarity and exchangeability. Thus, both words and things must be made subject to a larger economy of value, determined by pragmatic usefulness and by sympathy between people.

A similar model applies in Smith's theory regarding religious sects. Smith found their proliferation to be a benefit, since further competition of sects would lead to a greater activity and interest in church leaders for the welfare of their members. Here, Smith shifts from understanding religion on its own terms within the context of debates of the seventeenth century where Anglicans and Dissenters fought out the question of religious authority in reference to spiritual value, toward an economic model of the value of competition in any social organization. Indeed, Smith reads religion as he would read any other institutions, setting aside questions of the doctrinal purity of any sect's theology and emphasizing the positive consequences of competition. The value of religion is less in its declared intentions and its supposed institutional purpose than in its actual, practical effect on people's manners and the stability of society. Thus religion, like rhetoric, is subordinated to a larger domain of competition, practical value, and social usefulness; its end is no longer religious but social.

A similar model applies also to educational institutions.

We note that Dow (2009) identified the pervasiveness of religious issues and the nature of the education system as being among the key factors driving that the Enlightenment and the concerns of political economy in Scotland.

In all these cases, Smith goes beyond previous conceptions of value. Economic value is not based on coin, on bullion, on gold, but rather on labor—on the productive power of society itself. Similarly, the value of rhetoric lies not in the beauty of language, the allusions, the intrinsic worth of literary genre, etc., but rather in the skill with which one can use any figure or genre to communicate, and if necessary, to persuade. Rhetoric should thus be plain, direct, forceful, easily understood. Words, opinions, and ideas, like passions and goods must be visible, easily known and understood (the characteristics of goods, the causes of passions, the arguments behind opinions) for facilitating their exchange and approbation. In this way, Smith conceives of the entire field of social, linguistic, and economic relations in terms of pragmatic, transparent modes of exchange.

Meta-RR

Smith's meta-reasoning routine is found here in the pleasure of exchanging per se, which is a derivative of the social pleasure of persuading others of our (proper) valuation of a good or service through language and money. In other words, when we reach an agreement and exchange, we feel a specific pleasure of contemplating the harmony of minds. When exchange/persuasion fails, the prediction error is addressed by adjustments in the means of persuasion (i.e., adjusting of the price offered or demanded) that would ultimately bring about the pleasure of persuasion and the tranquility of mind that Smith saw as the equilibrium.

10 Conclusion: Smith's Reasoning Routines and the Principles of Human Nature

Our approach does not explain Smith's complete oeuvre. We do, however, believe that it sheds new light on the man and his work. Specifically, our analysis of Smith's reasoning routines highlights his sophisticated understanding of strategic interaction in all things rhetorical, moral, and economic (i.e., what we identified as his second "reasoning routine"). For Smith, Man is a naturally sociable creature, a "commercial animal" that takes pleasure in exchanging ideas, sentiments, and goods. He looks after the approbation of his opinions, conduct, and valuation of goods by his fellow animals. The unity of Smith's conception of Man is not based on selfishness (although Smith overall left little doubt that selfishness is a major driver of people's motivations) but rather on sociability which is founded on the desire to be approved, praised, and loved by others for our opinions, sentiments, and valuations of goods. In other words, it is based on the desire to be, and often to be worthy of being, in agreement and harmony with others. This is the love of order and harmony of the *HA*, our meta-reasoning routine which finds an echo into the social world.

While Smith started out to understand how people reasoned, and while he tried to explain the social world in parallel to the physical world in the same Newtonian, deductive way (reasoning routine 1), he realized the considerable parallels between the origin and evolution of languages and moral sentiments, all being seen as conventions that emerge in the repeated interplay between human actors (reasoning routine 3). He also noticed that the communication between individuals, while by nature interactive, could be informationally asymmetric, a notion now routinely captured in the term principal-agent game (Kreps 1990).

Most importantly, Smith emphasized the importance of a free, open, transparent communication of people's ideas and sentiments. The principles underlying this exchange had to be based on a proper understanding of the faculties of the mind. As indicated in the prefix to our introduction:

> [Smith] dedicated [most] of his time to the delivery of a system of rhetoric and belles lettres. The best method of explaining and illustrating the various powers of the human mind, ... arises from the examination of the several ways of communicating our thoughts by speech, and from an attention to the principles of those literary compositions which contribute to persuasion or entertainment.
>
> (Stewart 1795, pp. 274–275)

Consequently, we argue that Smith's interest in all things rhetorical, moral, and economic was derivative of his ultimate interest in the principles of human nature and the modus operandi of the human mind, as reflected by the ways people reasoned and thought about the natural and the social world.

Creating a new science of man and society based on experimental philosophy, that is on the observation of people's behavior through space and time (hence Smith's interest for history), required investigation and identification of the principles of human nature, as Smith's friend David Hume had claimed in the opening lines of his *Treatise of Human Nature*, a book Smith read while he was in Oxford.

In this sense, Smith can be considered a cognitive and social psychologist *avant la lettre*; he made a substantial contribution to the Scots' project of a new science of human nature. Following Newton, Smith wanted to understand the hidden drivers of the social fabric, to unveil the secrets of the "Great Architect" of nature. Philosophy, after all, was the "science which pretends to lay open the concealed connections that unite the various appearances of nature" (*HA*, III.3, p. 50). For Smith, the study of the *history* of astronomy, and of other sciences like ancient physics, logics and metaphysics, is first and foremost meant to be used as an illustration of the principles of the human mind which lead and direct philosophical inquiries, as the titles of these essays clearly indicate (*HA*, intro, p. 33).[58] Consequently, the philosopher investigates society's constituent parts (the individuals) and their principles of motion (the principles of human nature) implemented by the architect or creator of the social machine into people's mind to understand its purpose.

Along these lines, Smith's interest in the origin and development of languages in *Considerations* should be seen as his attempt to analyze the invisible powers of the mind and its "striving towards the 'metaphysical', towards conceptualization" (Bryce 1985, pp. 24–25). Indeed, Smith's story begins with humans' use of simple and concrete forms of language (nouns and verbs) and the evolution toward increasingly abstract and complex forms (from nouns to adjectives, prepositions, and substantives and inside nouns the introduction of gender and plurals until the invention of numbers). The invention process (and knowledge in general for Smith) is founded on humans' use of reason (or understanding) and experience. The imagination creates chains of intelligibility for grasping the outside world. "Observation" and "experience" create an "association of ideas" between things that memory revives when similar experiences are encountered (*Considerations*, § 1–2, pp. 203–205), as Smith also underlines in his neglected essay *Of the External Senses* (§ 61). The cognitive process is then easier and faster. People's capacities for "comparison," "generalization," and "abstraction" permit him to use inductive reasoning (*Considerations*, § 4, p. 205; § 6–7, pp. 206–7; § 12, pp. 209–210). We argued that this process of comparison, generalization, and abstraction, that was driven by the Wonder–Surprise–Admiration triad, foreshadowed emerging theories about the "Bayesian brain" (Editorial 2017; Clark

[58] Indeed, the respective essays on the history of astronomy, the history of ancient physics, and the history of ancient logics and metaphysics are all titled: "The Principles which lead and direct Philosophical Enquiries; illustrated by the History of..." (Smith 1982, pp. 31, 106, 118).

2016, 2017; Hohwy 2013, 2017) in which minimization of "prediction errors" is of the essence.

Likewise, people adopt (moral) customs of behavior in such an evolutionary, prediction-error minimizing manner, and people also adopt and use customs of reasoning. This analogy allows us to see the internalization of moral customs as necessary and automatic connections in the mind of specific events or behavior observed with repeated approbation. Both types of customs or habits emerge as natural processes from the memorization of similar experiences (*TMS*, III.iv.7, p. 159) and both are used routinely (*TMS*, I.i.3.9, p. 18–19). In other words, similar cognitive processes and motivations (i.e., restoring the equilibrium and tranquility of the mind, putting order and harmony) are at work, for Smith, when people try to understand the natural world and the social world. The desire for and pleasure of order and harmony, the love of systems, an aesthetic principle, is thus the ultimate, unifying principle of Smith's view of man, and of his system of thought. It was Smith's early and long-lasting preoccupation with the way the human mind works, alone and in social interaction, which led to his thoroughly modern views of the nature and causes of morality and the wealth of nations.

We have argued that *The History of Astronomy* was the "the juvenile work" that was formative in Smith's development of his first reasoning routine, the "Newtonian-deductive view" of the world. We have also argued that his *Considerations Concerning the First Formation of Language* was another early work that was formative both in the development of Smith's second reasoning routine—his deep understanding of social interactions—and in the development of Smith's third reasoning routine, his understanding of the evolutionary progress of languages, moral sentiments, and other conventions. We have pointed out that especially as regards the latter, Smith theorized by way of conjectural history. Finally, we have argued that a meta-routine that Smith himself called the Wonder–Surprise–Admiration mechanism (and that we have shown to be closely related to modern neuroscience's conceptualization of the prediction error minimization of our models of the world), informed Smith's thinking throughout.

In sum, we provide a new general interpretation of Smith's system of thought, showing its profound coherence through the identification and conjectural history of three reasoning routines and a meta-reasoning routine in his works on rhetoric and language, morality and economics. These reasoning routines identify a hitherto poorly understood deep structure of Smith's work, explaining its main characteristics and its development from Smith's early research on the principles of the human mind which allow humans to understand the natural and social world alike, and to exchange with others their ideas and sentiments about it.

Acknowledgements This manuscript builds on previous work of the first author with S. J. Meardon. An early draft of the manuscript was presented at the 1997 ASSA meetings (New Orleans), the 1997 ESHET meetings (Marseille), and the 1998 HES meetings (Montreal). Life's circumstances, and the pressures of academic hiring and promotion processes (which rarely look kindly on HoT contributions), had the project simmer on the back-burner until 2010 when the first author read an article on the language of exchange by the second author and proposed a collaboration. The present version is a substantially revised version of earlier drafts.

References

Alcouffe A, Massot-Bordenave P (2020) Adam Smith in Toulouse and Occitania: The Unknown Years. Palgrave Macmillan, New York City

Allison GT (1969) Conceptual Models and the Cuban Missile Crisis. Am Polit Sci Rev 63(3):689–718

Anderson G, Shugart II W, Tollison R (1985) Adam Smith in the Customhouse. J Political Econ 93(4):740–759

Berry C (2001) Social Theory of the Scottish Enlightenment. Edinburgh University Press, Edinburgh

——— (2013) The Idea of Commercial Society in the Scottish Enlightenment. Edinburgh University Press, Edinburgh

Berry C, Paganelli MP, Smith C (eds) (2013) The Oxford Handbook of Adam Smith. Oxford University Press, Oxford

Bevilacqua V (1965) Adam Smith's Lectures on Rhetoric and Belles Lettres. Stud Scott Lit 3(1):41–60

Binmore K (1994) Playing Fair. Game Theory and the Social Contract, vol 1. MIT Press, Cambridge MA

——— (1997) Just Playing. Game Theory and the Social Contract, vol 2. MIT Press, Cambridge MA

Biziou M (2003) Adam Smith et l'origine du libéralisme. PUF, Paris

Breban L (2014) Smith on Happiness: Towards a Gravitational Theory. Eur J Hist Econ Thought 21(3):359–391

Brown V (1994) Adam Smith's Discourse: Canonicity, Commerce and Conscience. Routledge, New York

Bryce JC (1985 [1983]) Introduction to *Lectures on Rhetoric and Belles Lettres*. In: Smith (1985) pp 1–37

Buchan J (2016) The Biography of Adam Smith. In: Hanley R (ed) Adam Smith. His Life, Thought, and Legacy. Princeton University Press, Princeton, pp 3–16

Clark A (2016) Surfing Uncertainty: Prediction, Action, and the Embodied Mind. Oxford University Press, Oxford

——— (2017) Busting Out: Predictive Brains, Embodied Minds, and the Puzzle of the Evidentiary Veil. Noûs 51(4):727–753

Cohen MD, Bacdayn P (1994) Organizational routines stored as procedural memory: evidence from a laboratory study. Organ Sci 5(4):479–625

Cohen et al (1995) Routines and other recurrent practices. Working paper, Santa Fe Institute

Collings D, Ortmann A (1997) Review essay: Vivienne Brown (1994), Adam Smith's Discourse: Canonicity, Commerce and Conscience. In: Biddle J, Samuels W (eds) Research in the History of Economic Thought and Methodology, vol 15. JAI Press, Stamford, pp 329–336

Considerations—Smith 1985

Corr—Smith 1987

Cosmides L (1989) The logic of exchange: Has natural selection shaped how humans reason? Studies with the Wason selection task. Cognition 31(3):187–276

Cosmides L, Tooby J (1996) Are humans good intuitive statisticians after all? Rethinking some conclusions from the literature on judgment under uncertainty. Cognition 58(1):1–73

Dascal M (2006) Adam Smith's Theory of Language. In: Haakonssen K (ed) The Cambridge Companion to Adam Smith. Cambridge University Press, Cambridge, pp 79–111

Dellemotte J (2002) Gravitation et sympathie. L'essai smithien d'application du modèle newtonien à la sphère sociale. Cahiers d'économie politique 42:49–74

Dellemotte J, Walraevens B (2015) Adam Smith on the Subordination of Wage-Earners in the Commercial Society. Eur J Hist Econ 22(4):692–727

Diatkine D (2000) L'utilité et l'amour des systèmes dans la *Théorie des sentiments Moraux*. Revue Philosophique 190(4):489–505

——— (2010) Vanity and the Love of Systems in Theory of Moral Sentiments. Eur J Hist Econ Th 17(3):383–404

——— (2021) Adam Smith and the Wealth of Nations. The Discovery of Capitalism and its Limits. Palgrave Macmillan, Cham

Diemer A, Guillemin H (2011) Political Economy in the Mirror of Physics: Isaac Newton and Adam Smith, Revue d'histoire des sciences 64:5–26

Dow SC (1987) The Scottish Political Economy Tradition. Scott J Polit Econ 34(4):335–348

——— (2009) Knowledge, Communication and the Scottish Enlightenment. Rev Phil Econ 10(2):3–23

Editorial (2017) Introduction—Cognitive penetration and predictive coding. Pushing the debate forward with the recent achievements of cognitive science. Conscious Cogn 47:1–5

Elster J (1985) Weakness of the Will and the Free-Rider Problem. Econ Philos 1:231–265

Engstroem J, Baergman J, Nilsson D, Seppelt B, Markkula G, Piccini GB, Victor T (2018) Great expectations: A predictive processing account of automobile driving. Theor Issues Ergon Sci 19(2):156–194

EPS, See Smith (1982 [1980])

Evensky J (1989) The Evolution of Adam Smith's Views on Political Economy. Hist Polit Econ 21(1):123–145

——— (1993) Adam Smith on the Human Foundation of a Successful Liberal Society. Hist Polit Econ 25(3):395–412

——— (2005) Adam Smith's Moral Philosophy: A Historical and Contemporary Perspective on Markets, Law, Ethics and Culture. Cambridge University Press, Cambridge

Fleischacker S (2002) Adam Smith's Reception among the American Founders, 1776–1790. William Mary Q 59(4): 897–924

——— (2004) On Adam Smith's *Wealth of Nations*. A Philosophical Companion. Princeton University Press, Princeton

——— (2021) Adam Smith. Routledge, London & New York

Force P (2003) Self-Interest before Adam Smith. A Genealogy of Economic Science. Cambridge University Press, Cambridge

Gigerenzer G, Hug K (1992) Domain-specific reasoning: Social contracts, cheating, and perspective change. Cognition 43(2):127–171

Goldberg E (2005) The Wisdom Paradox. How Your Mind Can Grow Stronger as Your Brain Grows Older. Gotham Books, New York City

——— (2010) The New Executive Brain: Frontal Lobes in a Complex World. Oxford University Press, Oxford

Graham G (2016) Adam Smith and Religion. In: Hanley R (ed) Adam Smith. His Life, Thought, and Legacy. Princeton University Press, Princeton, pp 305–320

Gray A (1931) The Development of Economic Doctrine. Longmans, Green, & Company, London.

HA, see Smith (1982 [1980])

Haakonssen K (ed) (2006) The Cambridge Companion to Adam Smith. Cambridge University Press, Cambridge.

Hanley R (2006) From Geneva to Glasgow: Rousseau and Adam Smith on the Theater and Commercial Society. Stud Eighteenth Century Cult 35:177–202

——— (2009) Adam Smith and the Character of Virtue. Cambridge University Press, Cambridge.

——— (ed) (2016) Adam Smith. His Life, Thought and Legacy. Princeton University Press, Princeton

Heinzelman K (1991) Economics, Rhetoric, and the Scene of Instruction. Stanford Fr Rev 15(3):349–371

Hetherington NS (1983) Isaac Newton's Influence on Adam Smith's Natural Laws in Economics. J Hist Ideas 44(3):497–505

Hill L (2020) Adam Smith as Political Problem Solver: The 'Project of an Empire' and the American War of Independence. The Adam Smith Rev 12:183–202

Hohwy J (2013) The Predictive Mind. Oxford University Press, Oxford

——— (2017) Priors in perception: Top-down modulation, Bayesian perceptual learning rate, and prediction error minimization. Conscious Cogn 47:75–85

Holmstroem BR, Tirole J (1989) The Theory of the Firm. In: Schmalensee R, Willig RD (eds) Handbook of Industrial Organization, vol. 1. Elsevier, New York, pp 61–133

Kalyvas A, Katznelson I (2001) The Rhetoric of the Market: Adam Smith on Recognition, Speech, and Exchange. Rev Polit 63(3):549–580

Kennedy G (2013) Adam Smith on Religion. In: Berry CJ, Paganelli MP, Smith C (eds) The Oxford Handbook of Adam Smith. Oxford University Press, Oxford, pp 464–484

——— (2017) An Authentic Account of Adam Smith. Palgrave Macmillan, London

Klein B, Leffler K (1981) The Role of Market Forces in Assuring Contractual Performance. J Polit Econ 89(4): 615–641

Kreps DM (1990) Game Theory and Economic Modelling. Oxford University Press, Oxford

Leser E (1881) Untersuchungen zur Geschichte der Nationaloekonomie. Gustav Fischer, Jena

Lindgren JR (1967) Adam Smith's Theory of Inquiry. J Polit Econ 77:897–915

Liu G, Weingast B (2021). Deriving 'General Principles' in Adam Smith: The ubiquity of equilibrium and comparative-statics analysis. Adam Smith Rev 12:134–165

LRBL—Smith 1985

March J, Simon H (1993) Organizations, 2nd edn. Blackwell, Cambridge MA

Margolis H (1982) Patterns, Thinking, and Cognition. The University of Chicago Press, Chicago

Marshall D (1984) Adam Smith and the Theatricality of Moral Sentiments. Crit Inq 10(4):592–613

McKenna S (2006) Adam Smith. The Rhetoric of Propriety. State University of New York Press, New York

Meardon SJ, Ortmann A (1996a) Self-Command in Adam Smith's *Theory of Moral Sentiments*. A game-theoretic reinterpretation. Ration Soc 8(1):57–80

——— (1996b) Yes, Adam Smith was an Economist (A Very Modern One Indeed). Reply to Brown. Ration Soc 8(3):348–352

Meek R (1976) Social Science and the Ignoble Savage. Cambridge University Press, Cambridge

Meek R, Skinner A (1973) The Development of Adam Smith's Ideas on the Division of Labour. Econ J 83 (332):1094–1116

Montes L (2004) Adam Smith in context: A Critical Reassesment of Some Central Components of His Thought. Palgrave Macmillan, London

——— (2008) Newton's real influence on Adam Smith and its context, Camb J Econ 32(4):555–576

——— (2013) Newtonianism and Smith. In: Berry CJ, Paganelli MP, Smith C (eds) The Oxford Handbook of Adam Smith. Oxford University Press, Oxford, p 36–53

——— (2019) Adam Smith's foundational idea of sympathetic persuasion, Camb J Econ 43(1):1–15

Ortmann A (1997) How to Survive in Postindustrial Environments: Adam Smith's Advice for Today's Colleges and Universities. *J Higher Educ* 68(5):483–501

——— (1999) The Nature and Causes of Corporate Negligence, Sham Lectures, and Ecclesiastical Indolence: Adam Smith on Joint-stock Companies, Teachers and Preachers. Hist Polit Econ 31(2):297–315

——— (2008) Prospecting Neuroeconomics. Econ Philos 24(3): 431–448

——— (2021) Was He, or Was He not? And Why Would it Matter? On Adam Smith Possibly Having Been Afflicted by Autism (Asperger's Syndrome). Available via SSRN. https://papers.ssrn.com/sol3/papers.cfm?abstract_id=3753764. Accessed 20 January 2022

Ortmann A, Colander DC (1997) A Simple Principal-Agent Experiment for the Classroom. Econ Inq 35:443–450

Ortmann A, Meardon SJ (1995) A game-theoretic re-evaluation of Adam Smith's Theory of Moral Sentiments and Wealth of Nations. In: Rima IH (ed) The Classical Tradition in Economic Thought. Perspectives on the History of Economic Thought Vol. XI. Edward Elgar, Brookfield, pp 43–61

——— (1995a) Adam Smith on the Origin and Evolution of Moral Sentiments. Working Paper, Bowdoin College

——— (1995b) A Game-Theoretic Re-evaluation of Adam Smith's *Wealth of Nations*. Working Paper, Bowdoin College

Ortmann A, Meardon SJ, Walraevens B (2022) Smith on the proper role of government, game-theoretically. Working paper. Available via SSRN. https://papers.ssrn.com/sol3/papers.cfm?abstract_id=4011744. Accessed 27 January 2022

Ortmann A, Walraevens B (2018) Adam Smith's Rhetorical Strategy against the Mercantile System. Working paper. Available via SSRN. https://papers.ssrn.com/sol3/papers.cfm?abstract_id=3300236. Accessed 21 January 2022

——— (2021) Adam Smith's Reasoning Routines and the Deep Structure of his Oeuvre. Working Paper. Available via SSRN. https://papers.ssrn.com/sol3/papers.cfm?abstract_id=3992914

Ortmann A, Walraevens B, Baranowski D (2019). Schumpeter's Assessment of Adam Smith and *The Wealth of Nations*: Why He Got It Wrong. J Hist Econ Thought 41(4):531–551

Otteson J (2002a) Adam Smith's Marketplace of Life. Cambridge University Press, Cambridge

——— (2002b) Adam Smith's First Market: The Development of Language. Hist Philos Q 19(1):65–86

——— (2002c) Adam Smith's Marketplace of Morals. Archiv fur Geschichte der Philosophie 84:190–211

Pack S (1991) Capitalism as a Moral System. Adam Smith's Critique of the Free Market Economy. Edward Elgar, Aldershot

——— (1995) Theological (and Hence Economic) Implications of Adam Smith's "Principles which Lead and Direct Philosophical Enquiries". Hist Polit Econ 27(2):289–307

——— (2010) Aristotle, Adam Smith and Karl Marx. On Some Fundamental Issues of 21st Century Political Economy. Edward Elgar, Cheltenham & Northampton

Pack S, Schliesser E (2018) Adam Smith, natural movement and physics. Camb J Econ 42(2):505–521

Paganelli MP (2010) The Moralizing Role of Distance in Adam Smith: The Theory of Moral Sentiments as Possible Praise of Commerce. Hist Polit Econ 42(3):425–441

——— (2020) The Routledge Guidebook to Smith's Wealth of Nations. Routledge, London and New York

Pauchant T (2017) Adam Smith's four stages theory of socio-cultural evolution: new insights from his 1749 lecture. Adam Smith Rev 9:49–74

Pentland BT, Rueter HH (1994) Organizational Routines as Grammars of Action. Adm Sci Q 39(3): 484–510

Phillipson N (2010) Adam Smith: An Enlightened Life. Yale University Press, New Haven

——— (2013) Adam Smith: A Biographer's Reflections. In: Berry CJ, Paganelli MP, Smith C (eds) The Oxford Handbook of Adam Smith. Oxford University Press, Oxford, p 23–35

——— (2016) Smith and the Scottish Enlightenment. In Hanley R (ed) (2016) Adam Smith. His Life, Thought and Legacy. Princeton University Press, Princeton, pp 105–119

Phillipson N, Nohara S, Smith C (2019) Adam Smith's library. Recent work on his books and marginalia. Adam Smith Rev 11:355–377

Rae J (1895) Life of Adam Smith. Macmillan, London. Available via Econlib. http://www.econlib.org/library/YPDBooks/Rae/raeLSCover.html. Accessed 28 January 2022

Rasmussen D (2017) The Infidel and the Professor. David Hume, Adam Smith and the Friendship that shaped Modern Thought. Princeton University Press, Princeton

Redman D (1993), Adam Smith and Isaac Newton. Scott J Political Econ 40(2):210–230

Rima I (ed) (1995) The Classical Tradition in Economic Thought. Perspectives on the History of Economic Thought XI. Edward Elgar, Brookfield, VT

Sagar P (2021) Adam Smith and the conspiracy of the merchants. Glob Intellect Hist 6(4):463–483

Schliesser E (2005) Some Principles of Adam Smith's Newtonian Methods in the Wealth of Nations. In: Samuels, WJ, Biddle, JE, Emmett, RB (eds) Research in the History of Economic Thought and Methodology 23:33–74

——— (2017) Adam Smith: Systematic Philosopher and Public Thinker. Oxford University Press, Oxford

Schumpeter JA (1954) History of Economic Analysis. Oxford University Press, New York

Sirak AT (2010) Adam Smith's solution to the paradox of tragedy. Adam Smith Rev 5:213–230

Skinner A, Wilson T (eds) (1975) Essays on Adam Smith. Clarendon Press, Oxford

Skinner A (1986) 'Introduction' to The Wealth of Nations: Books I-III. Penguin Classics, New York

Smith A (In our reference to Smith's works, we follow what has emerged as standard convention (abbreviations such as CL, Corr, EPS, HA, and so on). We refer to the Liberty version of the Glasgow edition of Smith's oeuvre. Typically, the Liberty version were available a few years later, so we also indicated the original publication date of the corresponding Glasgow edition)

——— (*CL*), Considerations concerning the First formation of Languages, p 201–226 in *LRBL*

——— (*Corr*), Correspondence of Adam Smith. Mossner E, Ross I (eds) (1987) Liberty Classics, Indianapolis (Glasgow edition: 1977)

——— (*EPS*), Essays on Philosophical Subjects. Wightman W, Bryce J, Ross I (eds) (1982). Liberty Classics, Indianapolis, pp 269–351 (Corresponding Glasgow edition: 1980)

——— (*HA*), The Principles which lead and direct Philosophical Enquiries illustrated by the History of Astronomy, pp 33–105 in *EPS*

——— (*LJ*), Lectures on Jurisprudence. Meek RL, Raphael DD, Stein PG (eds) (1982a). Liberty Classics, Indianapolis (Corresponding Glasgow edition: 1978)

——— (*LRBL*), Lectures on Rhetoric and Belles Lettres. Bryce JC, Skinner AS (eds) (1985) Liberty Classics, Indianapolis (Corresponding Glasgow edition: 1983)

——— (*TMS*), The Theory of Moral Sentiments. Raphael DD, Macfie AL (eds) (1982b). Liberty Classics, Indianapolis (Corresponding Glasgow edition: 1976)

——— (*WN*), An Inquiry into the Nature and Causes of the Wealth of Nations. Campbell RH, Skinner AS (eds) (1981). Liberty Classics, Indianapolis (Corresponding Glasgow edition: 1976)

Smith C (2016) The Essays on Philosophical Subjects. In: Hanley R (ed) Adam Smith. His Life, Thought and Legacy. Princeton University Press, Princeton, p 89–104

Spector C (2003) Le concept de mercantilisme. Revue de métaphysique et de morale 39(3):289–309

Stewart D (1982) [1795] Account of the Life and Writings of Adam Smith, LL.D. In: Smith A (*EPS*) Essays on Philosophical Subjects. Wightman W, Bryce J, Ross I (eds). Liberty Classics, Indianapolis, p 269–351

Tegos S (2013) Adam Smith: Theorist of Corruption. In: Berry C, Paganelli MP and Smith C (eds) The Oxford Handbook of Adam Smith. Oxford University Press, Oxford, p 353–371

Teichgraeber R (1986) Free Trade and Moral Philosophy: Rethinking the Sources of Adam Smith's *Wealth of Nations*. Duke University Press, Durham, NC

Tirole J (1988) The Theory of Industrial Organization. MIT Press, Cambridge

——— (1994) The Internal Organization of Government. Oxf Econ Pap 46:1–29

TMS—Smith (1982b [1976])

Walraevens B (2010a) Adam Smith's economics and the Lectures on Rhetoric and Belles Lettres: the language of commerce. Hist Econ Ideas 18(1):11–32

——— (2010b) Croissance et Progrès chez Adam Smith, Thèse de Doctorat en Sciences Economiques, Université Paris 1 Panthéon Sorbonne

——— (2014) Vertus et Justice du Marché chez Adam Smith. Revue Economique 65(2):419–438

Weick KE (1979) Cognitive Processes in Organizations. Research in Organizational Behavior 1:41–74

Weingast B (2018) How Adam Smith Negotiated His Release From His Obligation to become a Minister: A Game-Theoretic Account. Working Paper, p 1–9

WN—Smith (1981 [1976])

West EG (1996) Adam Smith into the Twenty-First Century. Edward Elgar, Cheltenham
Wightman WPD (1982) Introduction to *EPS*. In: Smith (1980) pp 5–30
Young JT (1997) Economics as a Moral Science: The Political Economy of Adam Smith. Edward Elgar, Cheltenham

CHAPTER 8

Conclusion

> To say anything new on Adam Smith is not easy; but to say anything of importance or profit, which has not been said before, is well-nigh impossible.
>
> —Price (1893, p. 293)

> Students in need of some grounding in these modern concepts (e.g., the principal/agent problem, moral hazard, ..., the theories of screening and sorting, rent seeking, ..., the theories of public goods and externalities ...) may indeed find an introduction to them, through the eyes of Adam Smith, to be a good preparation for the current textbook treatment.
>
> —West (1990, p. 1)

> Had Smith had more confidence in his own thoughts on rhetoric, and his lectures published earlier, then perhaps his own use of rhetoric, and its connection with his moral philosophy, would have led to a different interpretation of his economics.
>
> —Dow (2009, p. 18)

> Many of the difficulties in Smith's views and arguments arise from the fact that he was dealing with questions that remain difficult for us today. ... We can learn from Adam Smith today, but to do so we need to distinguish carefully between his local and universal teachings.
>
> —Fleischacker (2004, pp. xvi, xvii)

A. Ortmann and B. Walraevens, *Adam Smith's System*, Palgrave Studies in the History of Economic Thought,
https://doi.org/10.1007/978-3-030-99704-5_8

In the introduction to this book, we noted that over the last couple of decades Smith's oeuvre, its published parts as well as those parts not published during his lifetime, has seen a considerable re-appreciation. This re-appreciation was turbo-charged by the Glasgow edition of Smith's complete works (and correspondence) and its popularization by the Liberty Fund at the end of the 1970s and early 1980s. Apart from triggering a renewed interest in Smith's *Theory of Moral Sentiments*, the publication of Smith's oeuvre also brought renewed attention, and did so across the social sciences, to other parts of Smith's work such as the *Lectures on Rhetoric and Belles Lettres*.

Smith was commissioned in 1748 to deliver public lectures for fee-paying attendees from the general public and universities on the topic. Smith's reputation grew with each lecture series and helped him secure professorships in Logic in 1751 and moral philosophy in 1752 at the University of Glasgow. Even after he was appointed professor of moral philosophy, he continued teaching rhetoric in private lectures for students of his university for years (Bryce 1985).

In the introduction to this book, we argued that four things were remarkable about these lectures:

> Smith's focus on simplicity and clarity ("perspicuity") as important means of communication and persuasion and his aversion to the excessive use of figures of speech which he saw as barriers to the free communication of ideas and thought, foreshadowing his later and well-known critique of restrictions to the liberty of commerce.
> Smith's astute understanding that communication and persuasion might take place in situations of what economists nowadays call asymmetric information, i.e., involving writer (speaker) and readers (listeners) that have conflicting interests. We identified this facet of his thinking as Smith's second reasoning routine in Chapter 7.
> Smith's equally astute understanding that languages, social norms, and prices are conventions which evolve over time as the result of repeated interactions of motivated agents. There are strong and unmistakable parallels in Smith's conceptualization of the evolution of languages and moral sentiments and it was no coincidence, that—starting with the third edition—Smith added his essay on the origin and evolution of languages to his *TMS*. We identified this facet of his thinking as Smith's third reasoning routine in Chapter 7.

> Smith's use of "theoretical or conjectural history" (Stewart 1795 in Smith 1982, pp. 292–293), or historical theorizing, which allowed him to fill gaps where facts were not available in his analysis of the origin and evolution of language, and by extension of moral sentiments, of law, of price discovery in markets, and of government.

The fact that the strategic interaction between writer (speaker) and readers (listeners) might be afflicted by conflicting interests and that communication and persuasion might take place in a situation of asymmetric information suggests that it can be framed game-theoretically. In fact, it is a very natural thing to do. It is, after all, just a principal-agent game of sorts.

Likewise, that languages, social norms, and prices are conventions which evolve over time as the result of repeated interactions of motivated agents suggests that this repeated strategic interaction can be captured game-theoretically. Again, it is a very natural thing to do, as the relation between eductive and evolutive game theory is well-established. In particular, it is well understood that any such evolutionary process can be derived under mild conditions on the dynamics from the normal-form representation of the principal-agent game (Friedman 1991).

The advantage of bringing game theory to Smith's work is two-fold.

Firstly, it allows us to bring a well-established, precise language (e.g., players' actions, payoffs, information conditions, etc.) and an impressive conceptual apparatus (e.g., the distinction of the equilibrium outcomes of finitely and indefinitely repeated stage games, something that routinely confounds Smith scholars because they do not understand the observational equivalence of behavior resulting from indefinitely repeated actions such as the game of life, and pro-social preferences) to the subject matter. This turns out to be important when, to give just one of many possible examples, one wants to properly conceptualize the acquisition of self-command which is now recognized as a necessary step to recover the connection between Smith's political economy and moral philosophy (Montes 2016, p. 152), i.e., the connection between *The Wealth of Nations* (*WN*) and the *TMS*.

Secondly, game-theoretic framing allows us—contra scholars such as Schumpeter (see also Ortmann et al. 2019) and Cannan (see Paganelli 2020, in particular Chapter 12)—to show that Smith was an excellent economic theorist and not merely a "synthesizer". When West (1990, p. 1) wrote, rather astutely, that

> Students in need of some grounding in these modern concepts (e.g., "the principal/agent problem, moral hazard, ..., the theories of screening and sorting, rent seeking, ..., the theories of public goods and externalities ...") may indeed find an introduction to them, through the eyes of Adam Smith, to be a good preparation for the current textbook treatment.

He identified, without ever using the language of game theory or being precise about the implications of its conceptual apparatus, why Smith was indeed a very modern economic theorist. As we saw in Chapter 7, our game-theoretic framing allows us to ultimately distill the deep structure of Smith's work that would otherwise be difficult to extract.

It also allows us to identify Smith's universal take-home messages and arguments of which many remain controversial (Paganelli 2020, Chapter 12; Fleischacker 2004, 2021). Using the language of game theory gives us the opportunity to strip away context ("the local teachings" in Fleischacker's words, Fleischacker 2004, 2021) and focus on the incentive structure that the interacting players face, to identify what one might want to call problem isomorphs, i.e. structurally identical incentive problems which otherwise may be read as different problems because of the context in which they are shrouded.

For example, in some of our work (see Chapters 3 and 4) we have demonstrated that the very speaker–listener stage game is isomorph to the game that Man Today and Man Tomorrow play in the *TMS* and that the buyers and sellers of goods of adjustable quality play in the *WN*. This formalizes some of the intuition of previous writers (namely West 1990, Chapter 5) and adds considerably to the analytical depth that we can provide, as well as to our understanding of the relation of the various parts that constitute Smith's oeuvre.

In other words, Smith, in our reading, offered a very perceptive and sophisticated analysis of strategic interactions, last but not least in Book V of his *WN*, a book which, in our view, is falsely neglected by many (Ortmann & Walraevens 2018 [2014]; and Chapter 2 in this book), and often misread even by outstanding connoisseurs such as West (1976; see Tribe 1999, fn. 30) as being inconsistent with Smith's analysis in Book I of the *WN*. Smith provided in Book V of his *WN*, in our view, a thoroughly modern analysis of the incentive-compatible industrial organization of government and joint-stock companies, educational, and ecclesiastical institutions but also of the very difficult problems of public good provision and externalities and what role the state should be playing in addressing them (Chapter 4 and 5). In contrast, in Books I—II Smith laid out a system unencumbered by those potential market failures (see also Pack 1991, p. 114). By doing so he tried indeed (and we believe he succeeded in it) to demonstrate, as proposed also by Buchanan (see also Paganelli 2020, Chapter 12) that "a system of natural liberty" which emerged from fundamentally normative criteria of justice, could also meet with efficiency criteria.

Contra Paganelli and Cannan, we hence do not come to the conclusion that "The book is not just old. It is dated" (Paganelli 2020, p. 252). We do agree with the reasons that Paganelli enumerates on pp. 253–256 to rationalize why *WN* "is considered a classic and part of the great books that shaped Western thought" (p. 253). We care about, if not all the answers Smith gave, about the inquiries, or questions, that he asked. We agree with Fleischacker (2004, see the 4th epigraph to this conclusion) that many of the difficulties in Smith's views and arguments arise from the fact that he was dealing with questions that still remain difficult for us today. We also agree that we can learn from Adam Smith today and suggest that using the game-theoretic framing of various facets of Smith's oeuvre facilitates substantially the identification of his local and universal teachings.

We do disagree with Dow's suggestion (Dow 2009, see 3rd epigraph to this conclusion) that Smith lacked confidence in his own thoughts on rhetoric; in fact, it is a key argument of ours, highlighted also by the game-theoretic framing of the principal-agent games involving writer (speaker) and readers (listeners) that lie at the heart of one of the reasoning routines that we identified, that he was very confident in his rhetorical insights and applied them in full, last but not least in the structure of the *WN* (see Chapter 2) and also in the specific propositions that he chose to support (e.g., Hill's astute observation that Smith's defense of a [political] union between Great-Britain and the North American colonies in Book V of the WN was not his first [ideal] preference among the availabe options but rather a second-best, more acceptable [persuasive?] solution knowing the interests and prejudices of people and politicians on both sides of the Atlantic). Montes (2019, p. 7) has likewise argued that sympathetic persuasion is Adam Smith's foundational idea and that it, "through speech and language, plays a crucial role that extends beyond morality into economics".

We agree with Dow's suggestion that had Smith published his lectures during his lifetime, then perhaps his own use of rhetoric, and its connection with his moral philosophy, would have led to a different interpretation of his economics much earlier. Path dependency is a thing.

We are not the first to try to assess Smith's system or his system of social science. Otteson (2002a, 2002b, 2002c) made a case for a "market model" that pervades Smith's work and whose central structural components he identifies as 1. Motivating Desire, 2. Rules Developed, 3. Currency, and 4. Resulting "Unintended System of Order". He proceeds to extract these components from *TMS, WN* and *LRBL* (e.g., Otteson 2002a, pp. 286–287; 2002b, p. 80; 2002c, pp. 296–297). As a fifth feature of his model Otteson identified the mechanisms that facilitate the emergence of judgments in *TMS* (the impartial spectator) and *WN* (the price system). He argues there is no clear analogue to this in Smith's work on languages. Liu and Weingast (2021) have recently identified another interesting exemplar of what they call "Smith's social scientific *methodology*" (p. 134) and discuss the work of other scholars (including Otteson) who have followed a similar strategy rather than focus on the substantive content of his work. They argue, and illustrate in detail with two examples, that Smith used extensively notions of equilibrium and comparative-statistics analysis (these days well-known to every graduate student in economics) throughout his work. Their first illustration is using Smith's explanation of the rise and fall of feudalism in Europe while their second illustration is Smith's explanation of how moral behavior emerges and can be maintained. The second one is of particular interest given our earlier work (e.g., Chapter 3 and related) and the reasoning routines that we have identified in Chapter 7 in particular.

Inspired by his lectures on rhetoric and by game theory, we have provided a new interpretation of Smith's system of thought, showing its coherence through the identification of three reasoning routines and a meta-reasoning routine throughout his work on languages and rhetoric, moral sentiments, and self-command, and the nature and causes of the wealth of nations. The identification of these reasoning routines allowed us to uncover a hitherto poorly understood deep structure of Smith's work, and to explain its main characteristics. We also traced, in the very Smithian tradition of conjectural history, how these routines emerged in Smith's early research on the principles of the human mind, Smith's original interest arguably having been cognitive and social psychology.

By looking at Smith's oeuvre through the conceptual lenses of rhetoric and game theory, and by identifying sets of "reasoning routines" that show up in Smith's oeuvre from the very beginning, we show that there is considerable consistency across his body of (unpublished and published) work. The three reasoning routines and the meta-reasoning routine that we identify throughout his works allow us to provide a new and more comprehensive view of Smith as a (very) systematic philosopher (*passe* Young 1997; Otteson 2002a; Schliesser 2017; Liu & Weingast 2021; but contra Fleischacker 2021, see in particular p. 17), which might have the additional effect to put to sleep for good *Das Adam Smith problem* (if indeed anyone has still sleepless nights over it, which Smith cognoscenti don't seem to have had for decades).

Lastly, regarding Price's claim (see the 1st epigraph to this conclusion), we note that his book was written several decades before the Glasgow edition of Smith's oeuvre and its popularization by the Liberty Fund. We believe that the availability of the *LRBL* was one of the key drivers of this re-appreciation, and a key reason of Schumpeter's and other greats' misapprehension of Smith, and of his economic work in particular.

Thus we hope that the reader of our work, like Gavin Kennedy did,[1] agrees that there is plenty to say about Smith which has not been said before, and that there are important lessons to draw from his works

[1] We take pride in the fact that Gavin Kennedy, in his assessment of an early draft of Ortmann et al. (2019) which is informed by Chapter 2 in this book, wrote:

> ANOTHER OUTSTANDING PAPER EXPOSING SCHUMPETER'S DIATRIBE AGAINST ADAM SMITH'S WEALTH OF NATIONS
>
> ...
>
> This paper is a most interesting assessment of Schumpeter's well known critique of Adam Smith's Wealth of Nations and very personal criticism of Adam Smith. The authors are to be congratulated on their thorough assessment of Schumpeter's assessment, which also informs readers of the distinctive role of Smith's analysis of Rhetoric, for which he is less famous—even grossly neglected— *Lectures on Rhetoric and Belles Lettres* (1762-3)—....
>
> ... Ortmann, Baranowski, and Walraevens demonstrate how Smith's passion for rhetoric as a teaching method was applied throughout *Wealth of Nations* and remembering that his focus was on persuading government ministers (politicians) and significant others by the perspicuity of his arguments about the dangers of mercantile policies associated with foreign trade—such as the Navigation Acts—that led to European wars, colonial rivalries and the inhibition of foreign trade. ...I strongly advise readers to follow the link and read some truly original scholarship about Adam Smith.
>
> (http://adamsmithslostlegacy.blogspot.fr/2016/08/another-outstanding-paper-exposing.html as retrieved 20 January 2022)

for renewing and bettering our understanding of man (alone and in his interactions in society), especially in economics, as Vernon Smith, Bart Wilson, and Deirdre McCloskey recently acknowledged, making Smith the prominent foil of their Humanomics project.[2]

References

Bryce JC (1985 [1983]) Introduction to *Lectures on Rhetoric and Belles Lettres*. In: Smith (1985 [1983]) Lectures on Rhetoric and Belles Lettres (Includes Considerations Concerning the First Formation of Original and Compounded Languages) Bryce JC (ed). Oxford University Press, Oxford, pp 1–37

Dow S (2009) Knowledge, Communication and the Scottish Enlightenment. Revue de philosophie économique 10(2):1–23

Fleischacker S (2004) On Adam Smith's Wealth of Nations. Princeton University Press, Princeton

——— (2016) Adam Smith and the Left. In: Hanley R (ed), Adam Smith, His Life, Thought, and Legacy. Princeton University Press, Princeton, pp 478–493

——— (2021) Adam Smith. Routledge, London and New York

Friedman D (1991) Evolutionary Games in Economics. Econometrica 59(3):637–666

Liu G, Weingast B (2021) Deriving 'General Principles': Adam Smith's Pervasive Use of Equilibrium and Comparative-Statics Analysis. Adam Smith Rev 12:134–165

McCloskey DN (2021) Bettering Humanomics: A New, and Old, Approach to Economic Science. University of Chicago Press, Chicago

Montes L (2016) Adam Smith: Self-Interest and the Virtues. In: Hanley R (ed) Adam Smith, His Life, Thought, and Legacy. Princeton University Press, Princeton, pp 138–156

——— (2019) Adam Smith's Foundational Idea of Sympathetic Persuasion. Camb J Econ 43(1):1–15

Ortmann A, Walraevens B (2018 [2014]) Adam Smith's Rhetorical Strategy in The Wealth of Nations Against the Commercial System of Great Britain. Available via SSRN. https://papers.ssrn.com/sol3/papers.cfm?abstract_id=3300236. Posted 18 December 2018

Ortmann A, Walraevens B, Baranowski D (2019) Schumpeter's Assessment of Adam Smith and the *Wealth of Nations*: Why He Got It Wrong. J Hist Econ Thought 41(4):531–551

[2] See Smith and Wilson (2019) and McCloskey (2021).

Otteson JR (2002a) Adam Smith's Marketplace of Life. Cambridge University Press, Cambridge
——— (2002b) Adam Smith's First Market: The Development of Language. Hist Philos Q 19(1):65–86
——— (2002c) Adam Smith's Marketplace of Morals. Archiv fur Geschichte der Philosophie 84(1):190–211
Pack S (1991) Capitalism as a Moral System: Adam Smith's Critique of the Free Market Economy. Edward Elgard, Aldershot UK
Paganelli MP (2020) The Routledge Guide to Adam Smith's Wealth of Nations. Routledge, London and New York
Price LL (1893) Adam Smith and his Relation to Recent Economics. Econ J 3:239–254
Schliesser E (2017) Adam Smith: Systematic Philosopher and Public Thinker. Oxford University Press, Oxford
Smith A (1982) Essays on Philosophical Subjects. Wightman W, Bryce J, Ross I (eds). Liberty Classics, Indianapolis
Smith VL, Wilson B (2019) Humanomics: Moral Sentiments and the Wealth of Nations for the Twenty-First Century. Cambridge University Press, Cambridge
Tribe K (1999) Adam Smith: Critical Theorist? J Econ Lit 37(2):609–632
West EG (1976) Adam Smith. The Man and His Works. Liberty Press, Indianapolis
——— (1990) Adam Smith and Modern Economics. From Market Behavior to Public Choice, Edward Elgar, Aldershot
Young JT (1997) Economics as a Moral Science: The Political Economy of Adam Smith. Edward Elgar, Cheltenham

Correction to: Adam Smith's System

Correction to:
A. Ortmann and B. Walraevens, *Adam Smith's System*,
Palgrave Studies in the History of Economic Thought,
https://doi.org/10.1007/978-3-030-99704-5

The original version of the website listed inadvertently the wrong author names for Chapters 3 and 5, which now has been corrected.

The updated version of these chapters can be found at
https://doi.org/10.1007/978-3-030-99704-5_3
https://doi.org/10.1007/978-3-030-99704-5_5

A. Ortmann and B. Walraevens, *Adam Smith's System*, Palgrave Studies in the History of Economic Thought,
https://doi.org/10.1007/978-3-030-99704-5_9

Name Index

A. Ortmann and B. Walraevens, *Adam Smith's System*, Palgrave Studies in the History of Economic Thought,
https://doi.org/10.1007/978-3-030-99704-5

Subject Index

A. Ortmann and B. Walraevens, *Adam Smith's System*, Palgrave Studies in the History of Economic Thought,
https://doi.org/10.1007/978-3-030-99704-5

The manufacturer's authorised representative in the EU is Springer Nature Customer Service Centre GmbH, Europaplatz 3, 69115 Heidelberg, Germany. If you have any concerns regarding our products, please contact ProductSafety@springernature.com

Printed and bound by CPI Group (UK) Ltd, Croydon, CR0 4YY
30/09/2026
02225327-0006